T0063293

RECLAIM BLISS OF MATERNITY

RECLAIM BLISS OF MATERNITY

SARITA REDDY

PARTRIDGE

To order additional copies of this book, contact
Partridge India
000 800 10062 62
orders.india@partridgepublishing.com

www.partridgepublishing.com/india

CONTENTS

I am dedicating this book to my mother who has been my anchor in my entire life and has endured pain for my well being . Her kind heart is unmeasurable and how she cared for me in my sickness is beyond perfection. I thank God a million times to have her in my life. She is a blessing to me from God.

Maternity Suicides are on high-rise in India and all over the world because of Wheel of Power and Control.

DOMESTIC VIOLENCE WHEN CHILDREN ARE INVOLVED CREATES A HELL ON EARTH AND A TRAP CAUGHT IN LOOP OF INFINITY.

Bigotry, Abuse, Prejudice can destroy a woman and can fail her Productive career and destroy her marital bliss on an epic scale.

Crime can hide under the carpet, but evidence will nail its conspiracy ---

The world is gullible today we are living in a fake world. There is hidden Psychopathology behind every cruel intention of perpetrators of crime. Co Parenting brings out Happy Children, Narscisstic Parenting creates Scapegoats.

COMPANIONSHIP, COMPASSION, IS HAPPY MOTHERHOOD.

"Bad Mothers" are just labels given by the abusers to target the Innocent Woman, enslave her with a divorce threat to endanger her Angel's Childhood.

Parenting becomes a challenge when the Abusers use mind games, weave violence and create social stigma.

Mom's out there in chaos and crisis, fighting a silent battle behind closed doors. God is watching your perservance, endurance, sacrifices; he is feeling every pain of abuse against you.

He is shedding tears when you cry in silence and brave violence and smile in limelight, to avoid outcast in the world, which is, show cast.

When he says "Fairy now it is enough". He will change his colours and show his different shades to send his messengers to save your life and your offspring.

Outsmart abuse, prepare a safety backup plan. When help is out there, and do not feel shame. Abusers should feel the guilt, shame and they should be outcast.

You are a fallen soldier, who needs to heal her wounds and build a castle with the bricks thrown to attack you.

Marriage is one important chapter in life, but Life is like an Encyclopaedia. Do not react to the racing thoughts of suicide. Your angels will be left alone in the world.

Stand up for yourself, you deserve respect. You can rewrite your life and rebuild your self-esteem.

Moreover, relive with dignity and in a safe zone with no death or divorce threats. True Friendship and Brotherhood with Empathy will never ever fail you.

Hypocrites shouting antislogans against governance of India. Read this Epic saga of grief sorrow and pain of an Indian daughter. She was saved by the Invincible Protocols made by the Present Government of India.

DNA India and "Visa on Arrival" is for Indian offsprings without valid visa to cross a broken bridge, when their mom is bed sick and can no longer meet the angel's needs, as abuse took a big toll on her BMI and Mortality too.

Please NRI victims out there – Every Indian mom in Crisis write or text to DNA India, India will never say we cannot help you.

Air India – will stop until you board, and show utmost empathy like a daughter. They will know that you are abused and silenced.

They will outsmart your abuser. She needs some time to heal in India.

You are in the safe hands of India when you are on board in Air India. Just do not compromise on your life. Because Life is a gift from god and you, is a soldier of god saving your marital knot and your child's childhood?

Dreams will come true if you have enough nerve to face the roller coaster ride in the Journey called life.

You can stand on your feet and wear your shoes hold your angels and say, "YOU ARE NOT A SCAPEGOAT".

I am a Survivor, now I don't shed any more tears of blood in despair and I am once again ready for the battle but with a armour of empowerment and added credentials to my Resume and Profile.

A Pious woman can brave pain beyond human threshold because god makes her invincible to save her kids, with Flawless Character, Courage, Competency.

A girl child is boon not a bane, she is the butterfly who learns to fly when her fairy mom navigates her and guides her in the new world, which is new to the innocent child.

A pious mom is never ever a bad mother, she is like a fairy from god to protect her child, like god saves the world, and can swallow any venom beyond her measure, to save the integrity of her family and her Angel's future that colours the house with vibrant shades.

Men are from Mars Women are from Venus but Marriage is about trust and Companionship not a hidden Conspiracy and Control.

When Women with Venom Provoke men with AggresChauvinism. Violence takes an ugly shape.

Wheel of power control follows a Viscous Cycle of Abuse. It Makes Marital Crisis an epic saga of, suffering and roller coaster ride of pain, grief and sorrow.

CHAPTER 1

BIRTH OF THE BABY SHIVANI

This is the story of an Indian Daughter who suffered pain beyond human threshold. She endured injustice, as Mother India saving Kashmir. Yet did not leave hope faith and will power. She does not know the word Quit. She was never taught that word in her School. She took life like a Sport. She knew and followed it every day to reach her goal.

The story is about a Pious, well educated and well raised only Girl child and fragile like Goddess Sita but with no immortal powers and born in Adversity of Medical Infertility and Pride of Two reputed families.

A saviour child rescued by a young Medico Dr. RamaKrishna– now a Well-Reputed Infertility Specialist – in the heart of Warangal. He is Crusader of every woman "Fighting a Battle of Infertility".

A fragile Baby girl was born on 15ᵗʰ of august1982on 35ᵗʰ year of Indian Independence, at 2:30 am on a rainy day after a series of miscarriages. To an innocent and beautiful Telugu Indian woman Rajeshwari and Young Entrepreneur Mr Girish in a Hospital located close to the Mighty Goddess "SHAKTHI "Temple in the Heart of Warangal, India. All family members had their fingers crossed as the Survivor child was not crying and opening her eyes, yet the Pulse rate was good.

The baby's grand mom just closed her eyes for a moment and said a prayer OH Mighty! Goddess of Eternal Power and Invincible strength

This little baby is the Charm of my Daughter and now apple of our eyes.

She is a Symbol of Motherhood of my daughter who is been fighting the battle of Infertility.

We had enough of rumours and enough of woes.

You have the Power to heal anyone please show it now and heal this baby apple.

My son a Medico so he is going to place her in A medical incubator, but I am placing this doll in your Incubator.

The Baby was given name Baby <u>Shivani</u> by her Maternal Uncle a Medico.

He wrapped the baby in a warm towel and placed her in an incubator, as she was not yet opening her eyes, even after three hours of her time of birth.

The baby is in the incubator under the supervision of a famous Female Gynaecologist and Obstetrician who was a Professor of Kakatiya Medical College, Warangal. Like an answer to all prayers, the little baby opens her eyes. After 8 long hours of her birth she started crying.

There was joy there was happiness it was like a moment of bliss and laughter like a "Miracle in Medical Adversity".

The baby's maternal grandpa Mr Bhagwan goes around the city to bring new clothes for the Apple of their eye.

There are no shops opened to buy a beautiful baby suit for the Saviour child, Shivani. Yet, the grandpa doesn't lose hope, he keeps searching on all the streets in heavy rain, and at last a "Winter Clothes "shop was opened from the rear door. Quickly ran the baby's grandpa gave the shopkeeper more than the market price of the Sweater, selected a Light pink nicely woven little sweater for the newborn "Saviour Child". Shivani.

The little baby Shivani was under weight and she had less haemoglobin in her body and was not gaining any weight.

The baby had to be fed and bathed with utmost care, as she was very fragile for about six months. Shivani weighed very less weight than her Body Mass Index. Her Maternal grandparents were nurturing, enjoying and rejoicing her childhood and the young couple were very happy. The baby's maternal uncle was working as a Medical intern in a Government Hospital, he had to pass his Post Graduation and select his Specialization.

Dr. Rama kri shna makes a promise to him

"I am going to challenge stereotypes and will be a Crusader to women and will never ever leave WARANGAL to make a lavish living abroad. My knowledge is only dedicated to heal my People.

Every evening he visits the baby with biscuits and new toys. Shivani come my baby Niece my "Golden child." See what your uncle brought for you,

The baby Shivani started Blabbering and was been treated nothing less than a Princess, all her kith and kin used to play with her and say Shivani has big eyes and lovely lips with a sharp insight.

It's now time of your Cradle Ceremony Said both her Paternal and Maternal grandparents and also know that you are over six months old, let's see what are you fond of in the Holy Presence of Goddess Shakti.

They all placed a Pen, Knife, Money and the Hindu Holy Scripture Bhagavad Gita, The little Shivani Crawled and Picked Pen and touched the Holy Scripture "Bhagawad Gita".

The Baby's Paternal and maternal family rejoiced this mighty ceremony and loved her choice Pen. Very soon after this moment of bliss, her Maternal Grandpa said our Shivani would become A Doctor Healing others in pain. The Little baby was fed "Rice Pudding". Tiny little Shivani turned "One Year". She was growing as chubby and beautiful toddler with big eyes and always a smile on the face and playing with colourful toys.

Birthday Ceremony of Shivani was a Big Feast for both the Grandparents and was celebrated with affluence and bliss.

There were flowers and colour papers used to decorate the table. Both Families decked the little baby with gold chains and beautiful outfits.

Soon after Shivani's One-year birthday ceremony, her Maternal Uncle gets married.

Shivani was very fond of pens and colour papers and used to always be along with her Medico Maternal Uncle Dr. Ramakrishna

With the memories of Medical Adversity and the tensed situation, his only younger sister had to endure worse pain to bring Shivani to life and make her a healthy child.

The young medico decides to take up the challenge of Gynaecology and Obstetricsthough all his peers said it is a Female Medico's specialization.

He then Studied "Infertility" with great endeavour and dedication with support of his ever courageous and pious mom Mrs Lakshmi

CHAPTER 2

CHILDHOOD AND SIBLING OF BABY SHIVANI

Shivani was growing to be a beautiful and happy pappy baby and when she was 2 and half years old she started her KinderGarten.

Shivani had a new addition to her family – A little baby boy was born and the family was enjoying the birth of the baby boy. Shivani's dad enters into a Construction business and the family moves from a small rented house to their own home.

Shivani was very fond of her little brother and when everybody was thinking, of a nice name for her baby brother, shivani said why you people do not name him Sharath.

All kith and kin were surprised by Shivani's insight at a very tender age and her Creative intelligence. Her Maternal uncle was very fond of Shivani.

Shivani finished her kinder garten and wrote an entrance exam to be selected at the SCHOOL Sisters of Truth and Charity. Shivani is selected and starts her Year One at age of five. Many teachers for her assertive tone and creative intellect will adore her.

Her teachers used to say Shivani is creative and very good with leadership skills. She becomes a teacher's pet.

Life keeps moving on good note in the family until a direful event happens. Shivani's brother SHARATH meets a fire accident. He falls on hot boiling water, playing in and around kitchen.

The little adorable baby boy a toddler is hospitalized. Shivani couldn't control her tears as the burns were very horrific to the little one and she thinks her baby brother will not be healthy anymore to play and rejoice her childhood with him.

Shivani goes to School everyday with her teacher Mrs Suguna who believes in Jesus and visits the School Church every day.

She asks the teacher, will god listen to her prayer and heal her brother quickly.

The teacher says, "Yes My child he is everywhere. All you have to do is close your eyes, say a silent prayer, and make a wish.

Little shivani says a holy prayer with golden words – Oh! Mighty God I am a Hindu girl yet I know that you have no colour and you listen to every child's woes and worries. Heal my only Brother I cannot see his wounds and pain anymore.

Like an answer to the little shivani's prayers. Sharath responds to surgical treatment and is healed quickly.

A few days later after a week of rest and medications, the little Sharath becomes a healthy child once again. But Shivani's brother Sharath is very intelligent, logistic yet very naughty too. Come on Sissy always you are with pen, paper and books. However, Shivani says I am happy with colours and scribbling something with pen brother.

He says, let us experiment something new with this nail, Shivani says no bro you will be in trouble this is Electricity.

'He puts a nail in the Plug hole and He tries to drill it. Then he suddenly screams on the top of his voice.

The children's mom who goes for a shower finds out that Sharath is wounded; she is fumed up and smacks Shivani, as Sharath bec omes very fragile after the Fire Accident.

Shivani thinks its o k, my baby brother is safe that is important so what Mom smacks me in rage. She holds tears in her eyes but smiles at her mom.

The little champion sharath comes to shivani and says Sissy; I am sorry why you did not tell mom that I did it. Why were you silent and don't you feel bad about it? Shivani says my bro I like you so much like my little doll. It's ok even if mom smacks me, come on let's play a word game, I warned you plug holes are dangerous, my teacher told. Shivani follows every word what her teachers tell in the school.

Shivani loves to play with words, whereas Sharath loves to experiment new things and is very good with numbers.

The children play their favourite game, hide and seek whenever they visit their grandparents in the nearby village, close to the City, Warangal.

In the year 1985, on 17th of august, the children's' maternal Uncle Dr Rama Krishna will be blessed by a baby boy, Vishal, and he is first child of Dr. Rama Krishna. Vishal is very cute, chubby and adorable boy, Shivani and Sharath enjoy playing with their first cousin Vishal.

Happiness multiplies in maternal home of shivani, as there were more additions in the family, with the second baby boy addition to Dr. Ramakrishnain the year 1988 on 5th of September, who they name the baby as – Radha

Krishna – because he shares the same birthday of Dr. Sarvepalli Radha Krishanan, where India celebrates as Teachers day.

Dr Rama Krishna gets affected by Severe jaundice which was transmitted to him while operating a Patient with High complications in her delivery, he saved the woman and the child.

However, got affected by jaundice with a small cut on his hand during surgery.

The illness was getting very severe as it started off with mild fever and the hard working doctor did not give much attention to his illness, finally he collapsed in the Hospital and is hospitalised.

The family takes him to every doctor in Warangal but no doctor could give the right medicine for the illness, finally the doctor becomes very emotional he says to his sister's husband "I am unable to tolerate the stomach cramps and having racing thoughts that my life is going to end with this illness".

Please Brother In-law; I am giving you the responsibility of my two sons who you have to raise along with shivani and sharath. I am sorry for this Adversity. Girish is a Bridges and Roads Contractor, He is not only brother in-law of Dr Ramakrishna but also his immediate senior at the CKM college of Warangal.

He says, no buddy don't loose hope we have already dealt a hell lot of medical issues with Shivani's birth. Your expertise in medicine gave hope, and brought happiness in many homes.

I will make every stone unturned in Hyderabad and bring the best doctors to heal you.

Common pack your bags the car is waiting, you are a famous doctor. Crusader of many women and kids in their battle of Infertility and gyaniec issues. You are blessed with long life and Success ahead.

Trust our family's goddess Shakti, this tough time will pass away as like a wave in an ocean.

Just do not close your eyes and listen to what I say, "If a man has will power and been kind to everyone, his morals and ethics will save him and his family".

Look at your little baby boy "Radha Krishna", how cute and adorable he is, this illness will not kill you, we are all there for you.

He says to Shivani and Sharath, Vishal children common make our brave doctor smile.

There was silence, and baby shivani was almost crying every hour. As she was the only girl child and her maternal uncle's pet even after he has his own kids, Shivani is her uncle's favourite child.

She comes close to him and says "Mama don't cry I know a special healing God at my School, he will heal anyone. He listened to my prayer when sharath was sick. He is my friend and he is very good but he is not at our home. I have to go to school as his name is Jesus and he is only at our school church.

Her uncle hugs shivani tightly and says, "My bravo golden child, you are very creative and your insight is very sharp. He then says to her "God has no colour and no religion he is one".

Shivani's words make her uncle get will power, he hugs all the children and wipes his tears and says Brother in-law come on let us go to Hyderabad.

That is the spirit of our brave doctor, this is just an illness and it is not a disease.

Girish, his wife Rajeshwari go along with the doctor, leaving theirkids with the bravo "Lakshmi" and the young mom who lost her mother with cancer has tears in eyes holding Baby Radha Krishna and Vishal.

Mrs Lakshmi is a very kindhearted woman. She treats her daughter -in-law equal to her own daughter and even more as the young mom lost her own mother when Vishal was born affected by cancer.

Mr Bhagwan makes every effort to arrange enough funds for the surgery and for the expensive treatment atHyderabad. The doctors at Hyderabad monitor Dr Rama Krishna find out the real reason behind the Jaundice. He got it from a newborn child while operating a Critical maternity case. They give him the right medicine for his Jaundice. Shivani goes to school few days later, she goes to her favourite church.

She shares the sad story to her friends too. In her lunch break the little year two girls goes to the church and says a holy prayer.

The church is at the rear door of the school at "**SISTERS OF TRUTH AND CHARITY**".

Oh, my god Jesus, I know you are here and listening to me. You healed my brother who was suffering with burns, now I have come to make a very holy wish than any day until this day.

My Dr Mama is the one who made me alive and he loves me more than he loves anyone. I am his Golden child he says, but he is my God Father.

Heal him quickly I want to learn so many new things from him and tell him stories too.

My mama says shivani can we play word game together; he is my best friend too.

You are very kind Jesus, you will heal I know I am writing a small prayer and placing here at your feet. The little girl's handwriting is same like her Dr Uncle; every teacher likes her writing.

Shivani writes "Heal my Mama; I will put all my pocket money in the Charity box.

Within a month, Dr Ramakrishna becomes normal. He is discharged from the NIMS hospital in Hyderabad.

As promised Shivani says, "Jesus thank you very much, you are my best healing friend.

Here I am going to put Rs 500 in this Charity box, which I collected for my three birthdays.

Charity was a part of the school curriculum and the school-nurtured creativity in kids.

Mr Bhagwan is a bilingual expertise, who could speak very good English, Teluguand Urdu.

He is a rich landlord with high intellect, morality. He was serving the people as the Leader of the Village, guiding them with good irrigation and cultivation process. With high productivity. He made fisheries farms, poultry farms and even brought turtles

Moreover, he brings tortoises too, to show his grandchildren and to all the children of the village about the aquatic species.

To encourage girl child'seducation, he used to sponsor the education of every girl child who scored merit in her year10 exams. He is a man of substance and high elegance, he was encouraging the students of every caste, religion and economic status to go to school.

Mrs Lakshmi is very logistic and good at managing the household and the workers at the fields, she is like the genius mathematician Shakuntala Devi but she never went to school.

She can calculate simple, compound interest without penand paper yet does not even know the number system.

In the year 1990, Girish father who is also a rich landlord and only son. A owner to a property of almost 40 acres of land, was been negatively influenced by some of his followers in the village.

He was selling very Valuable lands to pay off the debts in his Rice Merchandise business, to collect money to for his youngest daughter Ramya.

Girish feels very sad and he tries to negotiate with his dad about paying off the debts, but his dad who is under venomous influence of the people who want chaos in the family so that they can get the ownership of the fertile valuable lands less than the market price, add more fuel to the fire.

Rajeshwari a very good homemaker and better half of Girish gives a sensible advice to Girish saying, "We will bear all the costs of Ramya's wedding, so that this chaos in the family will end on a good note. Finally, Girish says dad you just chill, these people are trying to fool you around, so that the land gets into their hands of ownership.

Don't even worry about Ramya's wedding she is the only responsibility you have now, we will carry on with the wedding proposals and select a noble guy for her, you just relax and retire now from your business.

Girish searched a noble person who is a younger brother of a NRI return Medico. Who holds a good position in a Multispecialty Hospital?

He arranged an "A well-organized wedding" for his sister with all his hard earned savings, which he got with his Construction carrer. Things settle down for a while between Girish and his dad. Once again, a year later in the year 1992, there was a trigger in the chaos.

His dad once again gets into the words of his own wife's brothers and makes a decision to sell them the property Close to the Aerodrum at a less cost, to clear off his remaining debts. The Place today is now called as Mamnoor Airport. All his cousins Keshav and Raghunath also have a good amount of land near the area. The good will followers of Girish share the news to him, as he is also a leader of a National party of Warangal, who actively participates in the state and National Politics of India.

He gives an assertive shut up call to his dad. Now he can relax for good from the entire responsibility of ancestral properties and he will pay off all the remaining debts.

He says to his Dad today it's a piece of land but tomorrow after the bifurcation of the state Andhra Pradesh, our family will be in the records of history of Telangana as there will be a Domestic Airport constructed here.

His dad gets addicted to alcohol and does not listen to Girish, and block his way towards the Novel "SYPHON Irrigation" Process he imports from Punjab, to meet the irrigation needs of all the agricultural lands of his village from the nearby lake, which has surplus amount of water,

Girish approaches other elders in his bloodline and reveals that his dad is doing with his ignorance.

His Dad's cousins support Girish and neutralize the issue, and give him the permission totakes up Irrigation Project at his village.

The family chaos affects Shivani and sharath as all their privileges will be reduced, as funds will be shifted to the village.

Yet, Rajeshwari and Girish tell them that Wealth can be earned anyday with endeavour, but Reputation of the family is very important.

The kids think about chaos in a sportive way and start enjoying their vacations in the village. They start visiting the fields and playing in the green woods and the orchards. Meanwhile, Girish gets an excellent opportunity in the National Party to take up the responsibility as Film Censor Board member during the regime of Chandra Shekhar government.

Girish rejoices with the offer and announces it among the kith and kin. The appointment letter states to come to New Delhi and go through a nominal interview process, within a week.

Girish shares the news with his Ex M.P grandfather who is sibling of his paternal grand mother and books his train tickets to Delhi.

His mom, who is very fond of her daughter Prakya, shares the news with her as Girish objects the sale of very precious lands to her siblings.

To his ill fate Girish who is very fond of his sisters and parents falls in the evil eye of his brother in-law –Satish, who has scorn in his mind to destroythe family unity and take control of all their ancestral property.

They make a drama of family chaos and ring Girish saying Prakya is very depressed and is attempting suicide at his home.

Girish visits the village and tries to resolve the domestic issue. He tries to liaise with both wife and husband and tries to counsel them with the advice of other elders. He falls into their trap and postpones his tickets to New Delhi.

The counselling process takes almost two weeks and his sister returns home with her husband. Girish plans his trip to New Delhi after all the family chaos in the the month of May 1994, he takes blessings from his parents and in-laws and with lot of hopes and dreams; he boards the train on 30th may. He reaches New Delhi a day later, but hears a news that Chandra Shekhar government has been dissolved and the interview letter in hand has no value now as the government is about to be governed by New Portfolio of Congress Party.

Girish feels like all his dreams are shattered and gets depressed, rings his wife and shares the news with her. Rajeshwari who is a well-read woman and a very humble, kind-hearted supports her husband and counsels him like a true friend.

It's all matter of destiny, do not get depressed, you are a good leader, a great husband, and a wonderful father. Her words make a positive impact on Girish and he returns home.

He brings Shivani her favourite books and pens, and to sharath, he brings a Cricket bat, as sharath becomes a very good cricket player in his school.

Shivani will be selected as the Class pupil leader. With her leadership skills, assertive tone and bilingual expertise with good grades.

Sharath scores well in maths and science but he never concentrates on languages unlike Shivani who starts writing acrostic poems in the school.

When shivani is in Year9, her (Regional Mother Tongue) Telugu teacher takes a good note about this Creative Bilingual expertise of the beautiful girl Shivani. She says "My dear Shivani, can you recite this poem and translate it in English. Shivani reads the poem asks her teacher the summary of the poem.

She takes two days' time from her teacher, goes home and brings good notes of translation in English of the famous poem.

"Education without ethics has no essence.

Ethics morals and a good character make a person pious and wise.

Character of a person is the real treasure in him and not wealth and gems.

The Class 8 student with her acostic style surprises the schoolteachers. In addition, great translation expertise. Shivani scores very good marks and she holds a great rapport with all her friends.

On the other hand, Dr Rama Krishna opens his own Infertility clinic and decides to register the medical shop on his only Niece Shivani.

Time machine moves on and the bond keeps increasing between the two families, until women with venom, Dr Rama Krishna's wife Sister loses her Husband to a ill-fated death. She takes monetary help from her Sister and keepsvisiting her regularly than ever before Like a Idle mind is a Devil's workshop, the widow with a jealous eye on her own sister and her affluence, starts creating differences in the family.

To deviate Dr. RamaKrishna from his ever loving niece Shivani she sends her daughter to stay in his home for the holidays.

The lady becomes a back stabber to Dr Rama Krishna's wife polluting her mind against his only sister and his Parents. Shivani though very young understands the negative vibes and stops visiting her Maternal Uncle's home as he becomes very busy and plans to Construct a **"SUPER SPECIALITY HOSPITAL".** But all his partners, young aspiring medicos with different specializations meet a road accident and the Project turns as a Mirage with their death.

Girish brings the Permission with his Political grounds at the Central department to even build a Medical college along with the Hospital from the Indian Medical Association. However, the Mishap of the road accident makes everyone in the state of bereavement.

The Beautiful Dream of First Super speciality Hospital in the heart of Warangal remains as an Incomplete Project.

Dr. Rama Krishna goes into a deep thinking process and the death of his best friends, who dreamt with him about this Project day and night and planned big with good investment capital, are no more alive.

His inner consciousness always spoke to him. We wanted to make Medical services available to all the Villages around this Great town Warangal.

God wills this Project ever be possible without my Best friends who lost their lives in a road mishap.

Few years later, some of the distant relatives of Dr. Rama Krishna and brothers of his wife, and one more cousin of Mr Girish come forward to invest in the Project in the year 1999.

Girish meets a very conninving business Partner Ranadheer, who aims big to deceive Girish with his gullibility?

He asks him to invest in his Construction Company and to lend him some money within his near relatives, who are rich and successful.

Girish being the only Contractor among the far distant relatives wins credibility of all his relations. Unaware of what Mr Ranadheer is grinding against him; he lends him money from the famous advocate of the High Court, Mr Narayana.

Ranadheer, who is famous with cheating, deceives Girish and tells him that the Project has incurred loss and he cannot pay debts to anyone.

Girish suffers a major loss of all his twelve years of earnings. He finds very difficult to accumulate funds to pay high fees to Shivani and Sharath who grow up together.

Shivani understands the financial crisis, decides to give up on taking Science as her choice, and switches to Mathematics. However, writing becomes her hobby and she keeps writing articles on Indian Soldiers – with her article name "Heroes of India". One of Girish friends who is a famous journalist comes across Shivani's Diary.

He suggests Girish and his wife Shivani is a born writer, let her study Journalism. I am taking this with me and ask my friend who is an Editor in an English newspaper to publish this.

To everyone's surprise, the article written by Shivani is published. The journalist friend comes with the newspaper with the Published Article and says to Shivani "Shivani you are deep thinker, you have a sharp insight".

Study Journalism you can rank up to the highest position in this field. Shivani gets perplexed, she says uncle it is just my hobby. I have decided to become a Engineer and study about the Machines used in the field of Medicine. Shivani's mom tells the journalist friend, we all know how dangerous those Reporting and Journalism jobs are for young girls. Goons will destroy my only girl child who is a saviour child to me.

Mr. Bhagwan always wanted shivani to become a doctor. But Shivani comes to an understanding of reality about the Caste system in India. Her family crisis in business.

The Payment option for Study of Medicine would cost very high. Sharath also needs money to pursue his further education.

Sharath also has a goal of becoming a doctor, like their Maternal Uncle Dr. Rama Krishna. He often used to tell Shivani, Sissy you are a girl, doesn't matter you pursue higher studies or not, one day you will have to get married. Once you are married, it's all your husband's wish whether he allows you to go to work or not. So take a chill pill, and do not be a daydreamer.

Shivani does not get offended by her brother's words and remembers the lines. Which she writes on the request from her teachers. She knows her skills and her dedication towards education.

"Dedication, Motivation and Endeavour" this is what needed, which field you have chosen to study doesn't make any difference.

Mr Bhagwan used to call her, Dr. Shivani – My Princess with healing power. Mr Bhagwan becomes sick and suffers lung problems.

Shivani feels very bad for her grandpa and his dreams for her future. She gets very scared to see him hospitalized.

With a low voice, Shivani says Grandpa I am sorry I am not interested in Science.

I likemathematics, I want to settle down soon as a Engineer, not continue my study for ages like Mama (maternal uncle).

Mr. Bhagwan gets shocked, he says do not even speak to me Shivani. Do whatever you want to do, and do not visit me even in the hospital too.

With tears in her eyes, yet confidence in her heart, shivani comes home.

Few days later Shivani's maternal uncle who becomes a successful and busy doctor sends his assistant to Bring Shivani for a meeting and to sign some papers related to medical shops registered on Shivani's name.

He says "Shivani my golden child what happened you look so dull "? Don't you want to tell your best mama why my Princess is so sad? Shivani replies nothing mama, just feeling bit low, and tensed a bit as college is going to start in few days.

Shivani is outspoken and she speaks to the point in her assertive tone, as she has been a Leader for years in the school. Her Dr. Mama says ok if you don't want to tell me what is the real reason behind this dull face. Don't tell me there is nothing you are upset about, because I know when you are calm its like a storm inside you.

Now close your eyes and see what Mama ordered for all of you kids from Delhi, when I went to attend a Conference at AIIMS. Her uncle deep inside wants Shivani to Nail Civil Services Examination. Because shivani is very good at logistics and linguistics, a rare combo of intellect and courage, says his fellow doctors.

Shivani opens the Gift box and she finds it is a "World book of Encyclopaedia", with eleven books in it. Shivani smiles and hugs her uncle. She says can I borrow one book Mama, rest is for the brothers.

Amazed by shivani's maturity, her uncle says one day "You will make the family Proud". You can have all of them Princess.

None of your brothers can write like you, you are so creative my child. All my fellow doctors say "Your Niece is very creative".

Shivani asks her uncle "Will Grandpa recover, he is very upset with me". Her uncle says do not worry, nobody can be angry with you for a long time. You are our Princess. You are very precious to us.

Shivani leaves the place and within a two weeks' time she joins her Intermediate college, with her school friends.

They have fun and they study well, they become a group of those backbenchers who are not bookworms. They watch movies after the college; have Study groups in the weekends.

They are like Birds of the same nest, who flock together and want to be together. Among all of Shivani's friends, she is close to Radhika, Haritha, and Nazia. The entire curriculum won'tbe taught by the Teachers of the college.

Therefore, the students have to take tuitions to study the syllabus, to get good scores in exams. Shivani asks her mom to buy a two-wheeler for her, so that she can go to tuitions. And enjoys the ride too, . Sharath who always pulls shivani's legs says Sissy this is a two wheeler not a rocket, slow down, you are strong but I am fragile.

The College Faculty announces the dates for the board of Intermediate and the Entrance exam for Admission into Engineering and medicine.

One evening around 6:00 pm, Shivani eats her snacks and starts to her Chemistry Tuition.

A spoiled brat who is drunk, violates the traffic rules and strikes Shivani's two wheeler, Shivani falls down and gets deeply hurt, with brusies and she gets wounded with bleeding knees, and her bike gets broken.

All people gather and keep screaming at the Drunk Brat who is riding the Bike with no sense of Traffic rules. Some men who know Shivani's Uncle and her Dad say, "SHE IS ONLY GIRL CHILD "of two Reputed Families. We will not spare you. The person says "I AM TRULY SORRY", Please forgive me, to all the people and Shivani too. Shivani says Uncle "LEAVE HIM". He learnt his lesson. He is also a Student; his career will be ruined with POLICE COMPLAINT.

Very soon, Shivani's best friends come to the spot and say, "LEAVE HER ALONE "Stop this DRAMA. Don't you all see our Friend is Bleeding and her Dad is out of town, UNCLE IS IN SURGERY. They are also coming soon. However, we have come to take her to HOSPITAL.

LEAVE US ALONE. You had enough of drama. Please go back to your homes.

They Park Shivani has broken bike in a Government Office Building.

Shivani keeps slowly loosing her Conscious, yet her Friends wake her up and say friend we are just 10 mins away from the "ROHINI HOSPITAL".

Do not close your eyes, we love when you talk, please say something.

Within Minutes, they arrive at the Hospital. Shivani's uncle as soon as his Surgery is finished comes to see her. Doctors at Rohini Admit her as its not a Critical Accident case and she is Niece of famous Gayenic surgeon "Dr. Rama Krishna".

The nurse cleans all the wounds and doctors do all tests. The Orthopaedic Surgeon confirms, its sad Shivani has a Fractured Knee. It will take more than two months for her to walk again.

As they have their exams in three months, Shivani and her friends get very disappointed. However, they all say Buddy we are there for you.

You need notcome to Tuitions; you relax and heal your wounds first. We will bring all notes to you, you can study at home.

Shivani who was very good with acostic poems wrote in her diary.

I am facing a tough situation in life I have to do a lot
of endeavour
Yet I know the only thing needed is dedication
My friends are here to help with the missed lessons.
They are not only my friends they are the sisters who I
adore always ever and ever.

Shivani attends all her exams in a Wheel Chair. Her friends' help to get inside the classroom, the college faculty get surprised by her courage, and her dedication towards education.

They say Shivani; we know that a girl like you will one day be an inspiration to many.

Within two months, Shivani is healed and the exam results are published in the newspaper.

Shivani scores seventy five percent in the total exams, and her friends score better than her.

They all celebrate Shivani getting back on her feet and the success of the exam on Shivani's birthday.

We have made it now buddy let's all sing and rejoice

Nothing is impossible if we are all together and help each other.

Shivani and Radhika get admission into the same engineering college.

A College that follows Principles of Swami Vivekananda, and the Chairman of the College is an Ex- Member of Parliament, elected twice from Warangal, who belonged to B.J.P.

Shivani and Radhika enjoy their Orientation classes and they like ambience too.

Girls grow up faster, and time flies with them, when they dress up for parties, all have their eyes drolling on them.

Such adorable girls where Shivani and her friends. Shivani participates in all Symposiums all people in the college give much respect to Shivani for her assertive tone and for her impeccable attitude.

She always says, "My Warangal is the best", there is a hidden magic here. Looking at Shivani's extrovert and good public speaking ability, Dr Rama Krishna says to Shivani, Princess now that you are about to complete your Engineering I want you to enter into Civil Services. I believe you fit very well in that arena as you love working for People and you have a sharp insight. Shivani nods her head, but then she thinks, "I hear a lot of ragging cases in Delhi biased by region".

Let me travel a path, which is easy without ragging (bullying) and other stuff.

Shivani Completing Engineering and Marriage Proposals

Shivani and her friends finish their Final exams of Engineering and think "What Next".

They enjoy their farewell party and even celebrate the Festival of Colours, Holi with bliss and joy and forget they are grownups too.

Shivani attends a Marriage of her close relative and a good family spots her. who are looking for a Prospective bride for their well-raised son who works in an MNC.

They ask shivani what are you planningahead, Shivani says I want to study "Management".

Within a week, they just send a family friend saying, "They liked Shivani and want her as a bride to their son."

Shivani's dad says that he is into financial crisis, because he is cheated by his Business Partner and in a year or so they can celebrate her wedding.

The person and his family say we do not want anything, just a simple Wedding, as our son and we liked your daughter.

Even then Shivani' dad who is a very stereotype person, and who dreams of a big fat wedding for his only girl child Shivani says, I have planned a lot for my only Daughter's wedding and it cannot be a simple event.

Shivani keeps silent buy says to her Dad the guy should be good, what is the big deal in a celebration

However, Shivani's dad says when I Plan I will plan you are only twenty-one years old.

Shivani applies for GRE and TOEFEL too as her dad's friends say there is good future by Studying masters in America.

Shivani scores good marks in both the exams and she starts to apply for the Universities. She has big dreams of becoming a good Fibre Optics and Laser Instrumentation Engineer.

Shivani scores very good in Fibre Optics and she enjoys the subject with inquisition. But, her mom says no I cannot send you without you getting married. If you want to study your masters, do it after your marriage. Shivani who obliges with her mom says, it is ok.

Among all their friends group Shivani' friend Radhika gets married soon and moves to America with her husband.

Shivani 's dad who gets some amount of the Good will from the Construction Business, collects money and plans for Shivani's wedding. When shivani turns twenty-two, a marriage Proposal comes to Shivani from a person called Sudhir who is working in a reputed firm in Sydney.

Girish, gets this proposal from one of his new business partners, who is benefitted by Girish. Girish gets the guy's pics to shivani and asks her opinion. Shivani says its ok, I don't mind, you will definitely look for a prospective groom for me and if he has a decent job and good morals that is enough for me, for a good quality life.

Girish gets another letter to house, where a guy who interviewed Shivani in a Job Interview at Hyderabad wants to marry her. Girish says Shivani you have many proposals, this guy is very fair and good looking, he says he wants to marry you.

Shivani says to her dad, Dad the guy may be good – looking or whatsoever, but his job was to interview me and look at me as a aspiring candidate for a job, is he hunting for brides there with his HR manager.

Moreover, how can you judge a person who just saw you in an interview?

Something goeswrong dad you are going to say, "YOUR CHOICE I WON'T HELP because, I know you very well you are very strict. Girish always was proud of Shivani, but he was strict too, he used to give her any privileges but always used to say, "You should have attitude as a Soldier".

Shivani and some of her friends in her Peer group used to say you are right buddy, your dad is like a Tiger, and he raised you like a soldier. Within a month Shivani 'Dad says there is a rich family who wants to get their son married to you.

However, when he comes to see Shivani, he looks very open minded, but Shivani notices that guy was a bit intimidating Shivani's Economical status when compared to his Lavish lifestyle.

The guy says I want to marry you, We are so well off we don't need anything, I just want you in my life. Do you know to cook? Do you drive?

Oh! My mistake our family friend was saying your dad incurred loss in business and he had to sell his car. The last question he asks Shivani makes her so angry and doubtful.

Shivani you are good looking, and very good at studies, don't you have any boy friends at your college. I am a bit open minded person just asking you? Shivani says no I have male peers and most of them are my dad's friends, I don't have any Boy Friends, I never had any crush on anyone.

I do not look at any person in the college with that intuition. My Dad is very strict, and I just feel that living up to the expectations of your family is the best a girl can do. I do not say nobody has these days. But my upraisal is, my dad everyday says Remember Shivani "THE FAMILY'S REPUTATION IS IN YOUR HANDS".

Shivani's dad who always protects shivanifrom other guys eyes even makes her to complete her Engineering Project alone.

Nope, no need of you having boys in your team, I know what all these people will try to do

The guy again says Common shivani we can be open minded, you can tell me if you have any, it's very common in America.

Shivani gets fumed up inside, but says to herself, this person looks like a spoiled rich brat with good computer knowledge.

Shivani says to the guy "I think my Mom is calling me", Girish who is very stereotype and thinks only about status, and other aspects says Shivani these people are very nice.

The person says ok to marriage, he gave his number to you to speak to him. The person looks a bit older than they told us says Shivani.

Dad this person keeps on saying "I have everything we are very rich, we don't need any Dowry. He is intimidating us, that's not good, these rich brats will always think they did a big favour marrying middle class family girls.

Dad something is wrong with the person he earns so well, and even a Project Manger at Verizon, Boston. However, why did he wait until 30 years to get married?

Moreover, look at him, his dressing style looks like he came for jogging in the ground, and he uses Shoes inside the house. He is just an NRI not American.

In addition, says SWAMI VEVEKANANDA POSTERS, in your room, DO GIRLS EVEN FOLLOW HIS PRINICPLES?

What is this stupid Question Dad "Following Principles of a Legend" do you need to be only a guy. I do not want to marry him he is very older than me and he is very Western in his behaviour.

Girish says don't be in a rush, they are into Construction Business since ages. All software engineers look old as they work in odd hours too.

No responsibilities on this person's shoulder, the person liked you at a glance.

Shivani gets angry and says I am not a doll to be presented to these people do not ever let me do this again. I am feeling very intimidating.

Yes, I am a girl that does not mean I should present myself like a doll and they keep asking "SILLY QUESTIONS".

After a week later Girish's good will friend Nageshwar says there is a good match for shivani from a simple, educated family. I know shivani is very pious and is very assertive, she is very choosy too. Her sharp insight is very good.

This guy Sudhir is childhood friend of Ravi and he was also his roommate before he went to Australia. What she said about the rich brats is true, they don't respect the girl and think they are doing a big favour by marrying them.

This guy is a very close friend of my Business Partner Kushalov's nephew Ravi, he has only one younger sister who is a dentist married to a Business man in Dublin, Ireland.

Mother is a government schoolteacher and father is a retired auditor in a Co-Operative. Girish looks at the Guys pictures says Shivani what do you think about this one.

He is working in Sydney, Australia and completed his masters too.

Shivani says he is a son of a Teacher may be he will be well mannered as all my teachers are very good. He has a decent income, so it is enough for a good quality life. I can also study further if this goes well and can earn too.

Shivani's dad says to his friend Nageshwar let us meet his parents first, as the person is in Sydney.

They decide one day to go and meet Sudhir's parents; they react in a very positive way. Your daughter is very good looking; we are tired searching a bride for our son.

Looking at the positive response, Shivani's dad says she is the only girl child in our family.

However, my daughter is like a flower and she never ever has brought any complaints from school or college, she is the doll of our families.

Moreover, chosing a good person for our pious daughter is like chosing a Ram for my Sita. I can truly say I am giving the honour of my home to you.

Mrs Sunandha is very good at articulating her speech says. We are also happy that your daughter who is just twenty two years old, with big ambitions and goals has accepted to meet our son.

On the way back home, Girish says may be this match will be an ideal match to the Sita of my home. In the middle of their journey, they meet Mr Srinivas, he asks Girish bro why you came to Nalgonda. Girish knows Mr Srinivas, as he is an Engineer in Irrigation department where Girish is into Civil Constructions.

Girish gives him details that they have come to meet family of the guy Sudhir. He works in Sydney as a Mechanical Engineer, who is a Prospective groom for Shivani.

Mr Srinivas says What a coincidence he is my own Sister's only son. You are not a stanger to us, come; let me introduce you as my friend to them.

Mr Srinivas and Girish, Nageshwar go back to Mr Sudhakar's home, Mr Srinivas gives a very good introduction of Mr Girish, how active he is into national politics, and how credible heis.

How ethical and honest he is, and says your daughter must be the charm of your house. Girish says yes bro Shivani is impeccable there are somany rich guys'proposals but she says "Dad rich people don't know any hardships", theyhardly havevalues in life. If the person is fair and tall, even if they like her, she says No Dad this person will daunt me all my life that I'm dusky. She is very choosy, and my only girl child.

Mr Srinivas finds Mr Girish words very interesting about Shivani. Mr Girish comes home and our daughter Shivani' match is almost settled only the guy has to come from Sydney to meet her. But shivani it's up to you think about status too.

Girish who is always about status thinks these people have a very small house, how can they manage with the wedding?

They do not have any lands too, both are government employees. Only good thing is the person has no family burdens ahead. Yet, I am still open with many options Shivani is my only daughter in the family. Moreover, the impeccable reputation of my doll and her charm is enough.

Girish does not show much interest in this match. When Sudhir comes to India. Girish flies to Delhi for a National meeting of his Party.

Sudhir and Shivani get Engaged

Sudhir waits three days to meet Shivani, as Mr Girish is in New Delhi. Shivani's senior gives her a Referral to attend an interview in a startup on Electronics and Semiconductors. Girish tells Shivani you don't even need to meet the guy, you just attend your interview, if they come to meet us in Hyderabad you just meet casually.

Shivani says Dad I will not present myself again like a doll, what I am so I am.

Shivani's Dad says ok let us keep the options open, I do not want you to get confused. Sudhir comes to meet Shivani and her Parents at Shivani's Uncle's home in Hyderabad.

His Mom Mrs Sunandha and his Dad Mr Sudhakar accompanies them with Mr Srinivas and his family, Sudhir only speaks to Shivani's uncle and smiles at Shivani.

He answers to questions of Shivani's uncle who is a manager in Finance Firm. Sudhir's mom asks her details. What did you do after engineering, whatare your job aspirations.

Shivani's uncle asks her if Sudhir can speak anything in personal to Shivani. However, sudhir says no, I am comfortable and happy to know about Shivani through my maternal uncle and my friend. Sudhir's uncle says we are being very frank when Sudhir's sister Bindu got married they gave good gifts, there is a flat they gave her, and also lot of gold and even cash too. What about you Girish bro ask Mr Srinivas.

Shivani's dad says I can sum up to twenty-five lakhs and all wedding jewellery.

There is a plot very next to my home, which Shivani's maternal uncle always says it's my gift to shivani as a blessing from my late dad Mr Bhagwan. They have sweets and ice-cream and leave the place.

Shivani says mom there is a nice collection of trendy watches here in "My Home Tycoon "close to uncle's home. I want one; shivani's mom says I do not know what to do with this child at heart girl.

But how many watches you want Shivani??, you don't buy an expensive one, Mom trendy, dresses should be trendy, shoes trendy and watches, hand bags, jewellery you won't even ask. You do not like to attend weddings. She just says, "I wont No to marry this guy if you give me money to buy my favourite watch.

Shivani's mom says I don't know when will you grow old, you speak like a teenager only.

Sit and watch your own channels and say to sharath why don't you go with mom and dad to the weddingsWhat do you always write in your dairy.

Shivani says, mom writing is one thing, which I cannot tell what I write because you and sharath say nobody earns on writing. Ok, leave about your hobby, Did you like this person. He looks decent, and fits to your criteria neither he is very rich neither nor fair and handsome.

Are you ok with this guy at least, they are not very rich and you are a teacher's pet at school and his mom is a social teacher. Shivani thinks if I comment on this guy alsoI think my dad is going to stop talking to me.

Shivani 's cousin and shivani think, looks something fishy here the guy doesn't even utter a single word and keeps on staring at people. Girish says to shivani its your wish, but one thing I can say these people are not strangers to us.

Ravi knows Sudhir from his childhood and they are good friends. He is nephew of my old friend Mr Srinivas too.

Shivani thinks about the anger of her dad, and she decides that if I don't abide by his words, he will not even bother about me in his entire life. Shivani's dad is a very stereotype person. To him thinks status, reputationis more important than anything in life.

Sudhir rings his friend Ravi and says he wants to get married to Shivani. Shivani's dad says now there is a positive response from the guy itself where you said that this guy is being controlled by his mom.

Shivani asks her dad, can I speak to the person on the phone regarding his interests in life. Shivani's dad says I will ask Ravi to give Sudhir a call and then find out if he can ring you.

Sudhir rings to Shivani and speaks in a very sober way, he says I am so very happy that you have agreed to marry me.

Shivani aks Sudhir Do you drink?? he says casually, Do you smoke?? He says no.

What is that you are expecting from me as a bride to be, in your life. Sudhir says you won't be only my wife, you will be integral part of my life. You are also good looking and good at studies; you are well raised and have high values. What else do I need in my life? He speaks to Shivani in a very sober and respectful tone. He says hope you will not reject my proposal.

Shivani asks him you work 24/7 in your firm, what do you do, Sudhir says I am a Mechanical engineer. Shivani gets impressed by his conversation and says dad I am quite ok with him.

He looks decent, and is respectful to girls, So she says Yes, I'm ok with this guy. Girish, says you will be happy Shivani they are not strangers to us

I know his maternal uncle from a period of ten years. Shivani says ok for the wedding. Mr Girish tells them that he needs time to arrange for it.

I am about to get funds from a business partner who promised me to give all the money once her wedding is arranged. Girish asks his partner what about money. Shivani is about to get married and she is my only girl child. I have dreams of my own since her childhood about her wedding. The Partner says, "I don't have all the money right now, I have only some amount which can cover quarter of whatI owe to you.

Girish says "Ok! Arrange that atleast now. Dr. Rama Krishna comes to Shivani and say Princess do not worry, you are my only niece too. I will arrange all that your dad lost by a cheater in business who betrayed him. You are apple of my eye. Sudhir and his family come the very next day, and ask Girish that they want a quick engagement.

Girish his friends and Sharath's friends do impromptu arrangements for the Engagement ceremony.

Sudhir and Shivani get engaged on 11th may 2004 in the city of the great Kakatiya Dynasty.

Draped in a beautiful Orange sari and decked with matching gold jewellery. Shivani becomes a showstopper to all her kith and kin.

Everyone says shivani is not even dusky, look at her she is glowing like a Princess with big eyes.

Sudhir and Shivani exchange their rings and smile at each other. Sudhir looks very introvert to all and her friends say to Shivani.

The person looks very introvert but is not keeping his eyes away from you. Though shivani is outspoken when comes to personal matters she says, stop it girls. We are just engaged now do not say all these words which is embarrassing to me.

It is just a start of a new relationship with blessings from elders and god.

Stop it! Yaar just let us have fun and this ceremony is over I want to just want to wear a simple sari. Shivani changes her dress, she does not feel comfortable wearing all jewellery and the Silk sari in hot summer month of May.

Sudhir says, "Can I get some water please to Shivani! He does not even say her name,

Shivani thinks how nice is his gesture, this is what an ideal man should have.

Girish tells Sudhir's uncle bro, Shivani is just twenty two, and she is my only girl child. I need to invite many friends of mine leave no dearth, to make this wedding of my only girl child a feast.

I am expecting my money back from the creditors for Shivani's wedding. Yet, Mr Srinivas says Girish bro; My nephews is very intrested in getting married to shivani and take her along with him.

He says I do not have leaves in my work further. Do as much as possible, but we want a wedding, and not just being engaged and a wedding planned later after few months.

Girish, Dr. Rama Krishna and his friends say, if the guy is well qualified and the family is well educated why second thought. Dr. RamaKrishna says I know my Niece very well it's she doesn't want to be decked with gold.

Because she herself is a golden heart and with good intellect. Lest, she is my only niece too, I will arrange anything you wish too. We are a Family, it's the wedding of our only Princess, the apple of our eye who is as Pious and as impeccable as Sita.

Mr Girish gives assurance toDr. RamaKrishna, that he he will repay all the amount once that cheater returns me my hard earned savings for Shivani's wedding. They start the wedding preparations Mr Srinivas rings Mrs Girish.

He says "I know its very tough on you as I know the hardships of Contractors, if their bills are not sanctioned at the right time.

Yet, my sister Sunandha is asking what about atleast some cash in hand. Shivani's Dad says how much are they demanding. Its 3 lakhs in cash, one lakh for bindu and the rest 2 lakhs for my sister.

Girish says ok, Sudhir's mom rings Rajeshwari and says all girls in my family have been gifted lot of gold by their parents. We want shivani to look rich too.

Hearing this Shivani rings Sudhir and says Sudhir I know you might have spent good amount in your sister's wedding. However, I am the elder child in the family and I do not want to stress my dad with all this heavy gold ornaments.

Why do I need so much of gold, once we settle in Sydney after wedding? Who wears all this heavy stuff there?

Sudhir says it's your wish Shivani, once married does not even expect that I am going to get that for you. Shivani says I do not even expect anything of that sort from you. I want to study and stand on my feet. I am not like a Parasite or a gold digger. Shivani's assertive tone and her simplicity impress Sudhir.

Shivani comes to her dad and says don't worry too much, make the wedding as simple as possible.

I do not even need as much of jewellery as they are expecting. And if things are out of your reach I do not even want this wedding.

How long do we know them is not important, how well they can respect us and understand our economic crisis is what builds rapport in relationships.

Dr. RamaKrishna hugs Shivani and says, no shivani if you want gold as they expect, I will arrange it for you.

Shivani says mama, I don't need all this stuff when it's becoming a hassle to you.

I know how muddled up you are too, You bought a very updated Scanning machine which is of high price. Things are not easy at your side, you need to manage your family too.

Do not stress yourself I know when you get your returns back one day you will gift me anything I want. Sudhir's mom starts controlling Rajeshwari I do not want any gifts less for my bindu from your side. Shivani keeps saying to herself how can a social teacher be so rude about such silly things.

Now, we cannot do anything I guess, as dad will say you will settle down in Sydney. Sudhir looks sensible, he is not demanding anything.

Both families plan to do shopping together for the wedding. Sudhir calls Shivani, saying don't keep on roaming with your friends, in this hot sun. You will be tanned, as you are already dusky.

Shivani says do not worry I know that I am dusky. But, you are much darker shade than me, you care about yourself too. I look at the character profession, and education of the person.

To me inner beauty matters a lot than physical beauty that fades off with age.

Sudhir laughs on the phone and says you are very assertive Shivani. This is the attitude, which makes me more and more willing to make you my wife and not just a fiancée. Moreover, I will tell one thing my relationship with my parents is not very good too. I myself could not handle them and flew to Sydney.

My sister is only important to them, I am a second priority. Listening to this Shivani thinks Is this guy bluffing me?, or he is hurt deeply in childhood. He doesn't utter a word infront of his folks and now says, I am not very attached to my family Shivani says in my home, I am an apple of eye to two families. My parents have never shown any difference infact, my dad says to my bro who is quite intelligent than me.

Look at Shivani, she is hard working, why is that you are always with sports, bikes, friends.

Sudhir says, "You are lucky shivani, to have a family like yours who love you so much. And now "You are the best thing that happened to me in my life". Beauty with empathy what else is needed for me. It is the best favour my friend Ravi has helped me. You are not at all stereotype, and understand people, unlike my sister who is naive always.

Sudhir's birthday falls on the same day of their Wedding-shopping day. Sudhir says Shivani tomorrow is my birthday. Shivani asks him, what you are expecting from me then as a gift. Sudhir says nothing, I do not expect anything from you.

Shivani rings her friend and says, "Buddy I need to get a Birthday card for my Fiancée Sudhir tomorrow is his birthday.

Let us shop in Archies, they have good quality cards and gifts. Shivani and nazia her friend goes together and selects a nice card for Sudhir.

Shivani writes in the card "May our relationship blossom with friendship and compassion for each other".

Like they say if the couple becomes best friends, then clashes won't even arise between them.

You are very simple, intelligent and can read my mind, in very few days. I just want you to be one of my best friends.

Once I travel with you to your home after wedding, I will always miss my friends.

Can you ever understand my heart like them?

Nazia says Shivani do not worry the person does not sound bad. This card is good and what you wrote can make him see a mirror reflection of an impecabble attitude in you.

The next morning Girish, Rajeshwari and some kith and kin in Shivani's family start to Hyderabad for the shopping. To their ill fate, a vehicle moving before them is trapped in an accident and the traffic does not move.

Shivani forgets to charge her phone and she is very shy to ask her dad who is very strict.

Shivani do not sleep late beta, and do not talk too late with Sudhir. Therefore, shivani does not ask her dad, can you tell them that we will be late for the Shopping.

Shivani says to her mom, if Sudhir's mom is too controlling I am telling you mom I will not even will marry this person. Neither he is one of our far relation, I hardly know him. What his mom think about us.

Always this is for bindu that is for bindu. She does not even have a instinct that her son is getting married. Rajeshwari says Shivani this is not movie, this is life and stop saying I will not marry this guy.

I do not know what to do with you. You are engaged my child, and according to our Hindu tradition, engagement means you are almost that family's daughter in-law. You are always busy with your friends, do not attend any weddings, your way of life is unending childhood.

Rajeshwari prays Oh mighty God! Please give a good life to my only girl child who is a child at heart always.

The traffic slowly clears and after a long wait, they get to reach the shopping mall. Sudhir looks very furious and Sudhir's mom behaves very rude.

The actual reason behind this was that Sudhir's sister bindu, losses her money the day before, but to hide that Mrs Sunandha behaves in the most intimidating way to Rajeshwari. Rajeshwari who is a very fragile and innocent woman gets scared as Girish also leaves the place to get cash ready for the shopping from the bank.

Rajeshwari says We are sorry, we were stuck because of an accident.

Shivani looking at the furious looks of Sudhir feels that her life is going to be a roller coaster ride, he is not even listening to what we say.

Nobody is bothered, how did we reach safe when the accident happened to the vehicle just infront of ours.

After few minutes Shivani gives her card to Sudhir He does not even speak a word, but he takes it. Shivani says in a day or two I need to ask this person whether his family approvedthis marriage or not.

Sudhir does not like any of the stuff which Shivani likes and selects, he does not support her selection and says do as what my sister says.

Shivani understands the game, which bindu and his mom were playing. The very night Shivani and her family go to stay with Rajeshwari's maternal uncle High Court Advocate Narayana's home.

His wife Mrs Saraswati who is a very insightful good woman says, to Rajeshwari, these people are very demanding and commanding. Do you all think our flower like Shivani can adjust with such women?

Look at the way his mom treats Shivani, and this guy doesn't even utter a word, when we are all worried about the accident that happened to a vehicle just before yours.

Rajeshwari with tears in eyes says all our relatives came and you know Shivani's dad once he gives his word to someone he will never back off.

We have to go with this wedding as now everybody in our family also know most of their family members too.

Mrs Saraswati says Shivani beta leave about what mom and dad says what do you think will you be able to cope up with their Controlling attitude. Look at them once when I was assertive to his mom, that they didn't come late on purpose and relationships should start with understanding they also didn't have lunch.

She revealed the actual reason that her daughter bindu lost her valet, the same day. Moreover, Sudhir wanted to take shivani with him for lunch. Did that person tell you shivani?

Shivani says no grandma he didn't even tell, now I am also getting sacred thought atleast this person is good. Being puzzled by Sudhir's impulsive reaction, shivani thinks deeply what my fault is.

Sometimes things are very unpredictable, that's what life is, but when they don't understand and behave so self – centred saying you guys don't even have time sense.

That is a big word to hear from Sudhir's mom being a social teacher.

Looks like this family is entirely under her control where she is good in commanding and demanding to her brotherMr Srinivas too.

Few days later shivani rings to Sudhir he does not take her call, for more than ten times he picks up and asks, "who's this? Shivani feels very sad and she cries, if you do not want to marry me please do not nobody is forcing you.

My dad is doing every endeavour in such business crisis to meet the demands of my wedding as per your demands. Do people lie about accidents too.

Sudhir and his family think that Shivani got an instinct of stubborn attitude of Sudhir beyond his taciturn mask.

They ring Rajeshwari and say Sudhir likes Shivani so much that is why he was upset, these things are very normal between newly engaged.

He wanted a quick wedding, because he just cannot wait to get married to Shivani. Moreover, you people are with strict rules you do not send Shivani alone with Sudhir after engagement. Sudhir came from Sydney so he expects some kind of good time for him and Shivani alone.

Rajeshwari tells Girish; see these people have nothing such as privacy. I do not know what they are going to do with my only saviour girl child who is born by grace of Godess of Eternal power in the worst crisis of Medical adversity.

If we do injustice to the pious shivani in haste. I will not be able to forgive myself. I am getting an instinct that something bad is going to happen to Shivani.

Girish says don't worry he is nephew of my old friend only, this is new generation, may be that guy likes Shivani so much. We fight with people who we think are our own.

Shivani also says dad that guy is very stubborn says to me your mehendi will not be seen on your hands you are dusky.

What is that dusky complex, he is darker than I am. Look at him, is he not darker grandma, I think people these days have gone crazy with this dusky complexion.

Shivani, you think all people are like you, who only speak about swami Vivekanandasome men are just witty. Nobody forced them to marry you.

Why worry my child, and remember once I gave my word, I can't back off, you only said ok. Shivani thought my dad is such a stereotype, he will make our lives chaos, let me say ok otherwise Mom will face all the price of cancelling engagement.

The very next day Sudhir's mom calls Rajeshwari and says, Shivani and Sudhir horoscope is like Sita and Ram, what else are you thinking, don't think twice, they are just made for each other.

Rajeshwari gets another red flag this woman first behaves as though the guy only likes Shivani and next minute she says Shivani will be Sita of our home.

Sudhir rings Shivani and says I was angry but its ok I have forgiven you; do not cry tears do not suit an assertive girl like you.

I can see some hidden smile in your face, you are stopping it why Shivani why are you hiding the smile Shivani says I am afraid to get married to you.

I will abduct you and marry, you are just 23 years old what life did you see, I am 30 years old I know what life is.

Shivani smiles finally and say you are very bossy, but can read me.

Rajeshwari thinks with her Mother Instinct yes Sita and Ram are ideal couple but Sita ended up like a single mom.

Moreover, she sacrificed herself to Fire, where was a blissful marriage to her.

She takes Shivani's horoscope to the Priest at the famous Hanuman Temple, who is a Sanskrit lecturer too. Shivani is a golden child; she has an invincible power she is blessed by Goddess of Eternal power.

Yes what they are saying is quite true something is very strong here. Their horoscopes match really well this marriage will take place at any cost,

Nobody can stop this wedding, the guy has so much of admiration for Shivani like Sita was adored by all. And we were looking for a groom for Shivani nothing less than the Marital test for Sita in the holy scripture Ramayana. As she is like sita of your two reputed families.

Do not worry about the person, shivani has so much of invincible power that she can sustain any chaos and can win over all.

We all know Mr Girish, for him once he gives his word, he will never back off. He will not leave you all alone and taunt you everyday, saying your stupid intuition made him give up on his word.

He is just a People's man, he benefits many people and how many women saved their marriages and have happy kids because of Dr. Rama Krishna.

God Hanuman will always save the sita of our Colony. Just place the first wedding card in Hanuman Temple and in Shakthi temple where hivani's horoscope is registered.

With many redflags showing about the hidden pride in Mrs Sunandha and the mind games of bindu, silence of Sudhir.

Shivani says ok, otherwise dad who is very obsessed with his honesty towards his friends will never leave us at peace.

Mr Girish who is a very ignorant of the power and control by women says Shivani is not staying in India with her in-laws

Whats the matter of so much tension Sudhir says shivani will fly in few months to Sydney she already has her passport.

MARRIAGE ON CARDS – SHIVANI WEDS SUDHIR

Shivani and Sudhir on 25th may 2005, in the presence of Goddess Shakthi, the eternal power.

Sudhir keeps calling Shivani every hour and says I just cannot wait for us to spend time with each other after wedding. You will not be my wife, you will be my life.

I will never make you cry hereafter, you will just keep smiling. This is my Promise to you, You're the best thing that happened to me in my life.

Shivani though bit doubtful thinks optimistic about Sudhir as he is well read in India and as well as in Sydney. Moreover, is working in a good position in good firm in Syndey.

Shivani's maternal uncle doesn't compromise on any thing to make the only wedding of niece as a memorable event. Shivani looks gorgeous in a white and green combination sik saree and beautiful jewels on her Bridal Ceremony.

All her cousins keeps saying Sudhir is just missing to see the real beauty in the night who is glowing with smile and looks like a Princess with big eyes and dimples when she smiles.

Shivani's maternal uncle who treats shivani as his own child says, "Princess it's not good for your health to be awake at this late-night. Common go to sleep.

Shivani says to Sudhir ok time to go to sleep. I have somany pious rituals to perform to deities of Purity, Power and Piousness.

In Hindu Wedding, the very morning the bride has to perform the most crucial Prayer to the goddess of Eternal Power "Shakthi".

On 24th may 2004 at 10:10 am Shivani and Sudhir tie the Sacred knot to be together with all the seven vows in marriage.

Seven vows of Holy wedding according to Hindu Marriage

Sudhir ties the sacred knot and makes Shivani his wife. Girish and Dr. Rama Krishna shed tears of happiness seeing their only princess now being called as Mrs ShivaniSudhir.

Moreover, no more just Shivani, the little saviour child, the butterfly of their two homes and the apple of their eye, is leaving the house with all her childhood memories.

The wedding will be a big fat wedding and the who's who of the cities Warangal and Hyderabad attend the wedding.

The marriage Registration takes place at the wedding avenue. Shivani is Dad, is a good leader in the B.J.P. Marriage

Register says to Sudhir, this is the wedding gift I got for you both. Shivani is my best friend's only girl child nothing less than a Princess of two reputed families.

Therefore, we are registering your marriage here in the wedding avenue itself. May you always be toggeher in every walk of yout life and keep our Shivani smile always on her face?

Almost 2, 000 guests come to wedding and bless the couple. All medicos whoever know Dr. Rama Krishna come to wedding to bless Shivani. They all adore his niece, as she is the apple of his eye.

Shivani's great grandfather, who is an active leader in the National B.J.P attends the wedding.

He adores Shivani so much and calls her as a warrior princess; from the day one, she joins his Engineering College.

Sudhir you have got the best girl in Warangal, who is as pious as a flower and is very courageous too with good intellect. Guide her well; she will multiply your wealth and prosperity.

Suddenly Sudhir's mom keeps saying my Bindu's jewellery is missing. All people in the hall get perplexed, Sharath and his friends keep searching for it and they find the box in the same place where Sudhir's sister left her luggage.

My sister bindu always forgets her own things and makes chaos in the home says Sudhir to Shivani

Shivani leaves the venue with Sudhir and his family, she cries a lot leaving her parents and friends.

She runs back to maternal uncle, hugs him, and says I am leaving now; your Princess is starting a new journey.

Let my childhood memories be fresh in your mind, do not forget me forever I am your niece.

These people are new so are their attitudes too, I don't know marriage is a Pandora's box or a Treasure box, whatever it is I will not bring any complaints to you.

Sudhir and Shivani perform the Pious "SATYNARYANA PUJA". God who guards all the newlyweds and any small or big beginnings.

Mrs Sunandha holds a grumpy face as Rajeshwari who is worried about her butterfly Shivani forgets to bring a Silk sari for bindu and instead she gets a normal designer wear sari available in the house

The next day bindu has to leave to Dublin, so she starts packing. Sudhir and Shivani think of their Personal Quality time in a Holiday Resort. She interrupts shivani and starts giving her suggestions.

Bindu is older than Shivani but in relationship with her brother. Bindu has to respect her, as she is his wife. Yet Mrs Sunandha says shivani she is your sister-in-law and she must always be given highest priority.

Both Sudhir and Shivani do not even like her suggestions and Sudhir gives Shivani a hint with a smile saying all is planned well.

Bindu understands how much Sudhir is giving importance to Shivani and gives a hint to her mom this girl has mesmerized brother. Finish he is going to be a henpecked husband soon.

Sudhir whispers to Shivani while travelling in the vehicle back to her parents' home.

After the Holy Wedding Ritual at your parents home and the pious puja.

I am going to take you to a very nice resort, than what places my sister has suggested.

As we have spoken on phone, a secluded greenary and with nature's touch. I am sure you will definitely like it. Shivani says ok, I know that you are quite good in reading my mind.

Sudhir and Shivani spend few days in a Honeymoon resort. Sudhir suddenly gets into a silent mode when shivani says, how come you eat food without brushing your teeth. He speaks to a Female colleague of his and talks to her as though she is very close to him.

After that conversation he stops talking to Shvani, even when Shivani trys to talk to her, Shivani gets an intuition why is he speaking to that lady at the middle of the hour, and is not speaking to Shivani.

Sudhir does not speak to her for a day or more and Shivani does not even understand what is wrong with this person. When she does not eat her lunch and gets tears in her eyes, Sudhir says I got offended when you said that I am not even brushing my teeth and eating breakfast.

Shivani asks who is that lady you spoke to, what is her name he says Oh! She is a colleague, her name is Rosy Ortiz. She is quite older than me she was my senior at part timework. Shivani asks is she married, Sudhir says she is a Mexican she is into a Live -in relationship with a rich man John; they all do not have such things as marriage.

Shivani thinks may be its western culture, she does not even work with Sudhir why should I worry. But some where in her mind she thinks this lady is speaking at such a night hour, doesn't her partner object her. Sudhir says Shivani you are just 23 years old, you have not even left Warangal or stayed in a hostel in Hyderabad. You don't know the world. You are like a small pious flower. Shivani gets a clear understanding that Sudhir and his entire family are full of super egos and something is fishy too. She, just tells Sudhir, neither have I known you from my kith and kin nor from my friends. It is very hard for me to adjust with you and mood swings of yours are quite unpredictable.

We are newlywed couple now, we need to understand each other and then develop friendship.

Sudhir says ok, Shivani as you say hey don't get so sad and start thinking you are in a wild goose chase. Shivani's intuition says I'm like a fish put in a bowl. Sudhir plans to bring Shivani on Visit Visa as the Dependent visa process usually gets delayed.

He tells the same to Shivani, I want to start my life with you, you are like a flower which I want to decorate in my home forever. Shivani feels happy that atleast Sudhir is not hostile like the rest of his family, who are being so rude to her.

Sudhirs mom rings them and says it's a family heritage to visit a temple with the newly weds.

Sudhir and Shivani leave the resort and join her inalws. Sudhir's dad keeps asking Sudhir how much did you spend on your stay. This looks like an awkward and weird question to Shivani.

Yet she maintains her poise and visits the temple. Sudhir's mom starts to daunt Shivani saying,

Look at your Complexion, you don't look good at all, you have become very dusky, what's wrong with you? Sudhir doesn't utter a word when she says all this to Shivani, in a temple.

Shivani doesn't even cry as she remembers Sudhir's words, I don't care what they say, you are my better half that you should remember.

Shivani and Sudhir return to Sudhir's home, Sudhir says I have to meet my friends, don't wait for me if I am too late, have your dinner. Can you pack some of my luggage, as I don't have much time. Here are your documents needed to apply for a visit visa, as you already have a Passport, things will be easy. Do not worry toomuch, you are my choice just remember that is important.

Shivani keeps packing Sudhir's luggage and she collects Visit Visa documents. Sudhir's mom enters the room and says what are those papers you are putting in your suitcase.

Shivani says these are visa documents, Sudhir's mom says I am a school teacher, show me those, I want to see them.

Shivani gives the documents to Sudhir's mom. She is fumed up seeing those papers. What do you all younger generations think; you do not even inform elders before you take decisions,

I don't know why my son is so mad about you?? What bindu said is true before leaving.

Who will take care of the house and bindu's son, this person has lost his mind. With fumed up anger she says, "Don't touch my son's luggage. Come out of that room.

She shows the same papers to Sudhir's dad look what Sudhir is doing with this new bride's influence on his own. Mr Sudhakar also says this Sudhir is stupid, bindu is the best child.

Shivani comes out of the room and packs her luggage. She goes to Sudhir's maternal uncle's home with bindu's son, which is very opposite to Sudhir's home. Therefore, that she can ring Sudhir. Shivani rings Sudhir, but he does not answer her calls. Shivani then rings her mom and says "Mom I can't stay in this house Sudhir's parents don't like me at all. I want to come home; she is daunting me every second.

Shivani's mom says "I will speak to Dad", don't worry marriage comes with such things.

Just be patient, do not worry if she does not want to send you to Sydney on visitingvisa.

Sudhir's mom tears off the visitingvisa papers infront of Sudhir and says you didn't marry the girl of my choice and now want to take your bride without even informing us.

Sudhir does not speak a word and gets inside the room. Shivani, I was busy with my friends, so I could not take your calls.

Shivani says it is ok Sudhir I am not so very desperate to join you in Sydney if your parents do not want me to. I am not a gold digger that you need to tell your parents.

I rejected a very rich guy's proposal from Boston because I want a simple, moral, quality life with bliss and joy. Anyways I don't want to trouble you with this family drama, as you are leaving tomorrow. I can understand your situation.

I couldn't pack your luggage as your mom said not to touch your belongings.

I have packed mine as soon as you leave to Sydney from airport, I will leave to my Dad's home.

Sudhir says "I love this character of yours, which adds more to your beauty straight to the point I will miss you.

I will try to get you to Sydney soon as I want you at my home. Shivani thinks all night, he is leaving now, the other visa takes more than six months, his parents will nail me and dad is so ignorant with his rules to understand their game. Shivani you are the honour and pride of this house be careful I don't want any complaints from anyone.

He behaves as though he is from a king's dynasty, anyways dad cannot change, for him reputation comes first then family.

HOSTILITY AT IN-LAWS PLACE

Sudhir leaves to Sydney, Shivani says bye to him, she is more worried about staying with Sudhir's parents who daunt herevery day.

Sudhir gives shivani his contact number in Sydney. Also says I will ring you as soon as I reach there. After he reaches Sydney he rings Shivani and says to her I have to attend a Training session, . Shivani says its ok carry on with your study and training.

He says fill the forms and I have asked Ravi to give the visa fees to your dad, he will arrange for your visa fees. Shivani informs her dad, that Sudhir has given Ravi visa fees amount.

Mr Girish rings Sudhir 's friend Ravi and says do you have the visa fees amount Sudhir has sent you for Shivani.

Ravi says uncle "He sent me the amount, his mom rang me and shouted at me and now the money is not with me". The very next day he rings and says, I don't have the money Shivani my mom took it. Shivani becomes assertive

Why can't you tell it to me. Sudhir im getting tired now your mom will make me walk on eggshells. Suddenly he disconnects the call and does not ring Shivani for the next week.

Shivani gets scared, and his mom rings and says to Mrs Rajeshwari finish all the visa process, and then send Shivani to our home. Shivani rings Sudhir and in a weird way he says"

Ask your mom to say that we are not able to afford to pay visa fess", can you please arrange the amount which Sudhir sent.

Mrs Rajeshwari a woman of self-esteem and humility, listens to Sudhir and gets a clear idea, that Shivani's life is going to be a roller coaster ride. Mr Girish says I am going to ask this person and his uncle what is this game.

MrsSunandha says my son is asking whether they have any idea of sending Shivani to Sydney or want to keep her at their own home. Mrs Rajeshwari says its ok, we will arrange the amount, we have only one girl child.

The next day Sudhir says Shivani now your family got their conscious that a girl's wedding is not a joke. Shivani loses all admiration for Sudhir and thinks she is cheated too. However, he says we are better; there are some who take the bride on visiting visa, impregnate and send her back to India and desert forever.

Shivani gets butterflies in her stomach, its better I didn't go with this guy, Shivani says Sudhir, you people are very powerful and I am vulnerable, but let me clear this to you.

I do not want any kids until we share a good rapport and study further or get a job.

Sudhir says, Shivani I was just kidding you know my Mom right, she shouts at anyone, and everyone has to listen to her.

Shivani says I do not even know you what will I know about your mom and dad. All I know is I have to nod my head otherwise I will be a deserted bride. Sudhir says now pack your bags go to my home, they have a marriage in my sister's marital home.

My mom wants you there, Shivani says Sudhir I am having severe stomach pain, I had sunstroke and cannot go. Suddenly, Sudhir disconnects the call and then he keeps ringing Shivani all night Will you go or shall I start drinking, smoking all night.

Shivani' s mom tells her Dad you have pushed Shivani into a well, look how they are making her dance, she had a sunstroke, they want her to go to an unknown place.

Shivani says dad I am unable to understand this person.

Shivani's dad says we will attend the wedding on your behalf. You just take care of your health.

Shivani thinks all night, will I be able to live with this person?, what is his attitude. Why does he suddenly change his behaviour?

As days, pass by one after the other in the calendar

Mrs Sunandha makes Shivani's life miserable asking her to come to their place and daunting her, you are dusky. I do not know how the kids of Sudhir would be, as none of you are fair.

What gifts did your Dad give we thought you people are rich, but your Dad is not coming out of his financial crisis. I was so angry when Sudhir was adamant about marrying you.

For the first time Shivani says, I am only twenty-three years old I had no hurry to marry your son. It is my Dad's choice, didn't you all attend the wedding. Why are you daunting me so much? What is my fault?

She cries all night and does not eat her dinner. Nobody even bothers too. Infact Mrs Sunandha beats the baby sitter badly when she is assertive to her, to threaten Shivani.

She packs her bags and catches the next bus and leaves her in-laws place to come to Warangal, saying I'm having an exam; I need to complete a course.

She rings Sudhir asap and says if your parents don't want this marriage to continue, call off now its better, we haven't even consumated our wedding as we stayed together only for a week.

Sudhir says Shivani calm down are you kidding, what calling off wedding, don't you know how much eager I'm waiting for you. I'm sending you the Visiting Visa papers. However, you need to collect it from my Mom, go after a week and she will get them. Shivani says I just can't understand you, we already filed the Dependent Visa papers and now you are saying you will send Visit visa.

I just cannot understand you and your parents. I do not know what is going to happen with me. You have made my life a tennis ball.

After ten days Shivani goes to Mrs Sunandha's home, with full rage Mrs Sunandha shouts at Shivani, You have asked Sudhir to send Visiting Papers, why can't you stay long here with us, I need your help with bindu'sson.

Shivani keeps quiet, Mr Girish rings Mr Sudhakar, it's been almost six months Sudhir left, I will only pay the money, can you give the papers to Shivani. Suddenly Mrs

Sunandha changes her tone, oh! Why not, we all want the new couple to live together.

CHILD LABOUR AT SUNANDHA'S HOME

Mrs Sunandha gives very tough time to the eight-year-old baby sitter. Shivani starts feeling very bad about the eight-year-old girl who is being exploited with Child labour.

Shivani teaches Alphabets to the girl and Mrs Sunandha doesn't give her proper food and threatens her saying there is an old man in the colony, who wants to marry you, if you steal any sweets in the fridge, I will get you married off to him.

Poor Girl that Baby sitter Sujatha, asks Shivani, will I get into trouble as this Teacher says.

Shivani says don't worry I will bring you the sweets you want, don't steal, nobody will marry you off at such childhood age. You are working at their home they are not your family.

One day Mrs Sunandha finds that an amount of Rs 200 is missing from her purse. She starts beating Sujatha who took the money tell me now.

Sujatha says I didn't steal it, but she does not believe at all. Moreover, suddenly with her aggressive impulsive attitude she says, did Shivani take it, who took it I want to know.

With this word Shivani is fumed she rings her Dad and says what rubbish is going on Dad; I will never come again to this house.

My in-laws have crossed all their limits, what do they think of me. You give me Rs 2000 every time I come, I just cannot stand here a second, send Sharath I 'm coming home.

Mr Sudhakar says We are sorry, Sudhir's mom just slipped her tongue, she is ashamed to say sorry to you. Mr Girish says Shivani those words are not to you, calm down is not fumed up.

Mrs Sunandha says I just said that word because the girl will tell the truth. Why are you making a big scene out of it? Shivani maintains her poise she understands that Mrs Sunandha takes Shivani for granted because her Visa papers are with her.

After a while, Mrs Sunandha finds money on the table below the newspaper, Shivani observes it. When Sudhir calls, she says why your mom beats that poor girl without searching the papers properly.

Sudhir says you don't worry about such things she won't listen to anyone, don't you see the aggressive women in the movies, she is of that sort nobody should go against her. Leave about that we are not going to stay with her.

Hey! I have good news for you, you have the Dependent Visa, and we can stay forever in Sydney together.

Dependent Visa approved to Shivani

Shivani says to her in-laws Sudhir said I have got the Visa, now I do not need the Visiting Visa Papers. Shivani looks at her in-laws both of them show grumpy faces.

Sudhir rings her the very next day and says Go and take blessings from my Paternal grandmother, she likes you and me so much.

Sudhir's paternal grandmother likes Shivani she says I thought Sudhir has nothing left in the house.

God had given my grandson a golden heart wife, be happy and your upraisal is from one of the best family, you are just like Sita in attitude.

Everything is given to bindu and it's bindu who is the most important child to them. Sudhir is just a scapegoat he sends money by sacrificing his own comforts. He arranged everything for bindu's wedding. The car he only bought, I never told you as your in-laws were there.

He had an abusive Childhood, both parents used to beat him so much. Moreover, infact his dad beat him before going to Sydney that he is good for nothing.

He stayed away from the house with his friends, even never visited anyone. Do not be sad if he loses his temper, sometimes may be his abusive childhood memories reflects on his mind.

I have seen both of your maternal and paternal families truly that day they arranged your wedding like Goddess Sita Wedding, and you are pious like Sita.

Shivani says do not worry grandma I do not want anything from Sudhir. I will study or get a job, but will not ask him anything. Why should I trouble him, I did not marry him for any money.

Do not tell all this I told you. I like your mom so much, she is so kind and well mannered, and your dad is very honest. God bless you both; I know you will keep Sudhir always happy.

Mrs Sunandha says know enough of your family visits, ask Your Dad to arrange the ticket money.

Shivani does not feel bad with her words, because the day to escape from her daunting has come.

Mrs Sunandha's house cleaner while sweeping the floor finds a Paper and asks Shivani to see what is it.

Shivani looks at that Paper, she finds it is from a travel agent in Hyderabad. Mrs Sunandha and Mr Sudhakar got their tickets confirmed to Visit Dublin.

Shivani thinks, all is well planned, they planned to Dublin and she is shouting at me asthough im going to Paradise. Mrs Sunandha keeps on daunting why do you need expensive Indian dresses when you are going to Sydney. I don't know why this Sudhir is about a good status quo, to a dusky girl like you, where her dad is in deep financial crisis.

Ask your Dad to stop having get together, visiting New Delhi political parties meetings and with friends and collect that money to fund all your expenses.

Shivani doesn't say a word, she just packs her luggage, and travels back to Hyderabad. After reaching Hyderabad, at her Uncles home, Shivani meets her Parents and say to them how much egocentric these people are. They have already booked their tickets to Dublin, but they are so grumpy about my Visa confirmation to Sydney.

Shivani's dad says don't worry about them, lets go to the Travel agency and book your ticket. Shivani and her parents, book her ticket.

Sudhir rings Shivani and says, you got to meet my maternal uncle, who is your dad's friend too. Do give a treat to my cousin's daughter, shop with my paternal aunt, who lives in Jubliee Hills Hyderabad.

Shivani says its ok I will go, don't worry, Shivani's uncle drops her at Mr Srinivas home, where Shivani meets his Cousin's Daughter, Suprabha at Mr Srinivas home.

The girl seems very sarcastic saying; Hmm looks like you are on Cloud nine going to my Uncle's home forever. Shivani gets fumed up with her words, yet maintains her poise, thinking it is their kind of upraisal. Anyways you got to give me a treat, now that you are going to my uncle's home.

Shivani says ok, the girl who is in her second year of engineering Suprabha, says common lets go to a restaurant and you need to pay the bill.

Shivani says never mind, order as many items as you want I will only pay the bill. She observes that the girl keeps talking only about boys and she speaks about love affairs, telling her all the stories.

Shivani doesn't seem interested at all. Suprabhasays it's fun making guys fall in your trap, pay your bills and then dump them. She asks, did you all do this kind of stuff in your college days as you have completed your Engineering.

Shivani says to Suprabha. I never did such kind of things, and I don't believe in exploiting anyone.

I maintain the same kind of rapport with my girl friends and male peers. Friendship is same to me despite any gender, this is what we were taught at our college and school.

I advise you as your Sudhir's niece, don't do such things, it may sound fun making guys fall in your trap, but the consequences will be bad. Suprabha does not bother, and meanwhile Shivani gets a call from her best friend Haritha who came from America.

Haritha says Buddy I am in India. Let us meet, at my home. Shivani says to Haritha, we can meet two days later, as I got to shop with Sudhir's paternal aunt. Yet, I will meet you, as I am going to Sydney two weeks later that is on 11th march.

Shivani finds to her surprise that Sudhir's mom who said I have got nothing to do with you, lands up at Sudhir's paternal aunt's home. She keeps daunting shivani, you thought I won't come here, and you can spend as much as you want as Sudhir is paying the bill. Good way you have trapped my son. Shivani gets fumed up, yet in a low voice says, Ticket is confirmed dad paid the amount too. Its on 11 th march at 10:30 pm Malaysian Airlines

Mrs Sunandha keeps on daunting Shivani saying, I have taken all the control of the money, you got to select according to my choice.

Shivani doesn't speak a word, she just rings her mom and says why should I buy all these dresses, when, I like to be dressed according to my choice.

Why can't dad pay these bills too, it's hardly one fourth of the ticket price. Hearing this Mrs Sunandha gets alert and says "Hey Shivani why are you complaining on me, what's the big deal doesn't a mother in-law have this much right on her Son's wife. Shivani doesn't say a word, and she says ok to every choice of theirs, she doesn't even bother what they are selecting.

Because even Sudhir's paternal aunt says, you are dusky may be this color doesn't suit you.

Sudhir rings Shivani, and says my mom has come to buy some stuff for my sister, so I told her to buy few of them for you too. For all of it I'm paying the bills.

After all the shopping Shivani meets her friends, and her family, and then collects her ticket, shops as per Sudhir's choice, yet gives all the stuff to Mrs Sunandha and says, you have the control of all, please take all this, and I am not greedy about the dresses or any small piece of Jewellery too. Moreover, goes back to Warangal with her parents.

On 9th march, Mr Girish arranges a farewell to his only daughter Shivani, he invites all their kith and kin and Mr Srinivas as well as her in-laws too.

Shivani buys some stuff to bindu even without asking Sudhir, she gets a Silver Ganesha and beautiful archies card "Happy House Warming". She gives it to Mrs Sunandha, now that you are going to Dublin give it to sister – in-law bindu.

Bon Voyage to Shivani by Friends and Family

On 11th march 2006, Shivani and her family, visit the Shakthi temple and Shivani offers her prayers to the goddess of "Eternal Power".

Shivani's maternal and paternal families bless Shivani and her new life in SYDNEY. Sudhir rings Shivani and for the first time Shivani's mom speaks to Sudhir, Shivani is my only girl child, we have raised her with much love and care, as she is the apple of eye of two familes.

She is a child at heart girl; you are almost seven years older than she is. She has not left us anytime, not even stayed in a hostel. Please do not be tough on her; she is the apple of my eye.

Sudhir says, you all don't need to worry, I know how innocent and pious Shivani is, I will take good care of her, she is my legally wedded wife, who is my choice.

Shivani's maternal uncle Dr. RamaKrishnaand his mom, Shivani's maternal grandma comes to the airport, she becomes emotional and hugs Shivani.

Mrs Sunandha comes to the airport and screams on the top of her voice. Don't you all want to send your Shivani to her husband's place, why you all are making big deal?

Shivani doesn't say a word neither her family, Mrs Sunandha asks Shivani to come to her in Private place, she says do not trap my son and extort money. Moreover, its better you plan for a child in a week, I told Sudhir the same and Sudhir will never cross my word.

Shivani's dad who has a friend Rahman, in the customs department, gets feasibility to accompany Shivani till the Departure Gate,

Shivani's experience on the flight is novel, she finds its exciting, though bit perplexed about her new life with Sudhir's unpredictable behaviour and also about how aggressive Mrs Sunandha is and how she controls everyone in the house.

CHAPTER 3

MARITAL LIFE IN CITY OF BEAUTIFUL BEACHES - SYDNEY

Shivani reaches the City of Beaches --- SYDNEY on 11th of March 2006 at 12:00 pm where she boards the flight on 11th at 12:00 am.

She finds the City dazzling with lights and it looks amazing to her, as she has never been abroad. From the Window of the Aircraft while its landing in the Sydney Airport, the beautiful Harbour Bridge and the Opera House looks amazing. Shivani's so thrilled and she feels she has come to one of the beautiful cities in the World.

The customs officers check her luggage – And there she gets stuck, because when they scan the luggage, the camphor crystals look different to them. They get Perplexed about those white crystals, Shivani gets frightened too, as these were not what she packed.

Who packed them she doesn't know, then she recollects at the neck of the moment. Sudhir's mom gives her a Packet, and asks her to put inside the suitcase.

She is terribly fumed up with Sudhir's mom yet, she maintains her poise, and thinks, I am finally out of that Treacherous den.

After a While, the Customs Officer asks Shivani to touch them, she explains to them in a precise manner. These are used in offering Prayer to a Hindu God. You light them and the Fragrance creates a Pious Ambience.

They are not any prohibited goods, and if you want me to give all of them to you, I can do. Please give me my Passport, the Hindu God's portraits and the Wedding jewellery my Parents gave me.

I am married to an Australian citizen from an Indian Origin. I am a new Indian bride to Sydney. I can give you my Husband's number too. You can talk to him.

Looking at her confidence, they just say we apologize for all the inconvenience caused Mrs Shivani. Here is your passport there is your luggage. Welcome to Sydney and Australia.

Sudhir waits at the Exit gate, Shivani gets there, and looking at him, she is very scared as well as excited too.

He says to her what happened to you Shivani, you have lost lot of weight. Sudhir rings his mom and says she reached safe, and I know what you said, don't repeat it again and again.

Shivani hears these words of Sudhir and she gets reminded of Mrs Sunandha's words. plan kids in a week. She suddenly gets startled. What is that you are saying to your mom, Sudhir says nothing important?

Shivani and Sudhir reach their home, and Sudhir says did you like it. Shivani says yes I do, it is a nice place. I like the house. It is good and how long have you been here before I came.

Sudhir says I have just moved a week before, you came. Moving is a big thing and I had to buy all the stuff new, he says. Shivani says you have done a lot of hardwork. I am truly impressed.

Hey, Rosy helped me you know, Rosy Ortiz, the one I spoke that day in the resort, she is the one who helped me.

Three days later, when Sudhir is in the shower, Sudhir's mobile is ringing; Shivani picks the phone and finds it is a woman who is calling.

When Shivani says Hello, the woman disconnects the call. Shivani gets an intuition, that may be someone is involved with Sudhir, that is why his behaviour becomes unpredictable.

Shivani questions Sudhir who is the lady on the phone and she says, I am having a strong intuition that you are having an extramarital affair here in my absence. Now book my ticket to India, don't even come close to me. Its Rosy were you living with before I came to Sydney.

Sudhir gets worried and rings his friend Ravi, saying Shivani is doubting me, please tell her how loyal I am you know me from my childhood.

Ravi says to Shivani, Sudhir married you against his parent's choice, he likes you so much, and how can he be disloyal to you.

Moreover, Rosy Ortiz is very older than Sudhir she has her own life partner, how can he maintain an illicit relationship with such a woman she is a Mexican. It is all because you are in lot of fatigue, you are feeling like that.

Shivani believes Ravi, as he is the one who introduced Sudhir to Shivani. In addition, Ravi is nephew of Mr Kushalov, and Shivani has utmost respect for all of her dad's friends.

Also Shivani gets reminded of her dad's words, you are the pride of this house, be careful. I do not want any complaints from your marital home.

So shivani keeps quiet, and believes ravi and sudhir, too also she thinks, how can a older woman than him as well as she has a Partner john, how can she be his illict partner.

Sudhir takes Shivani to his friends home, she meets all his friends, and likes all of them, though they have their own circle of groups and no room for one more sign on their faces.

Shivani feels alone, and Mrs Sunandha starts daunting her, what did you all do about what I said, just plan a child, that is what bindu did.

Shivani sometimes gets annoyed with her, but doesn't say a word, as Sudhir might turn against her.

Shivani sends e-mails to her core friends in US, Haritha, Nazia and Radhika, I feel sometimes happiness is no more with me, my in-laws bullied me so much, I feel I have lost my confidence. I get an intuition that something is fishy here.

Nazia says to her Shivani we are miles apartbut a call away too, we are connected don't you worry, We will always be in contact with you, and don't think too much about that older Mexican woman, Rosy Ortiz, she has her own partner.

Shivani says ok, nazia I won't suspect him, and I will be happy. Sudhir says I have planned a week trip with another young couple, my friends, who came with you Shivani from India? She is also new to the city.

You know how much a flawless character, loyalty and honesty matters to me. That is all what I expect from you Sudhir too.

Sudhir, Shivani and his friends who are a new couple visit Coffs Harbour. Shivani finds the place, very interesting, and she loves the ambience too. Shivani seems happy too, for the week they spend at Coffs Harbour.

ROSY ORTIZ INTRODUCED AS A OLD COLLAGUE

Shivani and Sudhir become almost like friends and Sudhir starts to admire Shivani's innocence.

Rosy Ortiz comes to visit Shivani and says your skin is dusky; you have some pimples, too.

I am almost 15 years older than you are, but look at the way I look, that is the beauty of a Fair skin.

Shivani who gets tired of this "Fair Complexion "thing from Sudhir's mom, Says to Rosy, Sudhir is not complaining about the suntan and the Pigmentation.

Shivani becomes very assertive and gives a shut up call saying. Marriage brings lot of hormonal changes and south Indians are mostly dusky, we live in a hot climate.

Pigmentation is not a disease. Do not ever talk about my complexion I know I'mdusky, but I'mnot ashamed of it as my husband is darker than I am.

Rosy says you have taken my words seriously, don't bother too much, take it easy. I will ring Sudhir and let us go and have old colleagues get together.

After a week, Sudhir starts complaining, Shivani you have some Pimples. You need to do something about it, let us try some creams here.

Shivani though offended says it is ok Sudhir I will try those creams. Mrs Sunandha who reaches Dublin as she already planned ever before Shivani's visa was confirmed, keeps ringing Shivani and asking her, to show the flat.

Shivani gets annoyed yet she shows it with her webcam.

Bindu keeps feeling very jealous, saying Sudhir bro does everything for Shivani. I did not even have half of what she has. Shivani says to her you have your own home within three years of your marriage, how many can afford a own house in Dublin.

Mrs Sunandha picks the phone and says what do you think about yourself how dare you say to bindu that she is more lucky than you are. Don't you have any manners?

Shivani says I did not mean anything of that sort. Now say sorry to her otherwise I will tell the matter to Sudhir and he will show you the real game. I Already told you Sudhir is very short tempered and also very stubborn. With no interest in her statements, Shivani says, "I'm sorry I didn't mean to hurt you.

Mrs Sunandha keeps saying to Shivani go with Rosy, keep searching a job. Shivani tries to apply a job in Electronics companies. However, she cannot even get through as they ask experience.

She has no experience, as she is a young graduate. She got married less than a year, she completed her graduation.

Sudhir says just go and apply more and more you will find some where one or the other, but Shivani gets tired of Mrs Sunandha's constant daunts, yet could not express it to anyone.

She constantly keeps boasting that her daughter bindu has achieved a lot.

Shivani who has cousins in India, U.S in much higher positions, like medicos and Software engineers than bindu finds her not even her competitor because she is a graduate of Dental Science and not even on merit and the college licence has been cancelled by AIIMS after she graduated.

Shivani is an Electronics Graduate, who scored the best in Fibre Optics and Bio-Medical Instrumentation. She finished her Project in Bio Medical Instrumentation, on Pacemakers.

Shivani always remembers about her maternal grandpa. How much his soul might be weeping seeing Shivani getting daunted by a social teacher whose daughter is a dental graduate?

I think I should have listened to grandpa I would have dared to study Medicine, as Science seems very interesting to me even in Engineering.

I scored the best in Bio -Medical Instrumentaion. Sudhir says hey I have my annual leave now, you can try your job more and more harder, my mom won't leave you alone until you find a job.

Shivani says can we go to Gold Coast I love to see Surfers Paradise. She pleads him a lot, Sudhir says ok, let us go. Shivani feels very happy and packs their bags to the Sunshine Coast.

Sudhir and Shivani book their one-week trip to the City of Sunshine Coast—

The blue waters and the sea coast line looks beautiful to her

A girl inside her comes out and she plays with water and collects the shells

The rides make her fuzzy and they enjoy the day trip to
the Island on the cruise

They enjoy the sun and the rain and sunshine coast
brings them closer.

Shivani and Sudhir return from their holiday and Sudhir
who gets enchanted by her says I have 15 days more left.

Tell me which place, you want to visit. Shivani says
Newzealand that is the place of hot water springs.

I want to visit the place, do you have enough money to
go there. It is my only wish. Sudhir says let me see if I can
plan.

Mrs Sunandha rings to Sudhir and says why do not you
people plan to Dublin. Your sister bought a house, and you
guys can visit too.

Sudhir says ok, but Shivani gets butterflies in her
stomach, again with her daunting, oh! my god I can't do
it she says.

Sudhir says you speak to my mom, Shivani says its very
expensive to visit Dublin, we just started our new life, we
can't visit now.

Mrs Sunandha with a high tone says what is this drama
you are doing, why can't you guys come, what's the big deal
in it.

How come you know about Sudhir and his savings, he
is my son, better always be on your feet. Give the phone to
Sudhir, Shivani does not speak a word, she gives the phone
to Sudhir.

Sudhir says we have to go, and I am applying visa for
you, I don't need one as I am a Auz Citizen. It will be a
family gets together.

Shivani doesn't know how to react, but she still agree to go to Dublin and gets a visa in a week

Experience of Prejudice in Dublin.

Sudhir and Shivani make their travel arrangements, and they book their flight to Dublin, through the Gulf Air. They have a 17 hour stop over at Bahrain, so Sudhir plans a visit to his cousin' s place, at Bahrain. Shivani and Sudhir reach their home and visit the place. Shivani likes their hospitality.

After the stopover they board the flight to Dublin. Shivani gets butterflies in her stomach, as she knows Mrs Sunandha is going to make her life miserable there in Dublin.

They land in Dublin at night, Shivani finds herself very uncomfortable as she knows how bad her In-laws behave with her. Mrs Sunandha keeps waiting and starts daunting Shivani, how lucky you are, you got to travel round the globe. My daughter made everything on her own. Shivani feels very bad, but she maintains her poise.

Mrs Sunandha says now you have people have to move all the things to their new home. Shivani feels dizzy and has jetlag too.

Sudhir says let Shivani rest for a while she is just 23 years old, she is having stomach cramps too.

Mrs Sunandha says you are talking as though she is a teenager. Shivani does not speak a word and says I am ok Sudhir do not worry. Within a day, they plan a tour to visit all the places.

The heavy cold winds, and the rainy weather makes Shivani catch cold and fever. Yet, she goes with them though neither the city appelas to her nor the weather.

Mrs Sunandha keeps saying to Shivani bindu is very thin, why you do not become like her. She is working, they had a kid ever before their first marriage anniversary, what about you guys, and don't you have any plans.

Shivani gets fumed up when Mrs Sunandha asks somany personal intimate questions to Shivani and doesn't speak a word.

Sudhir says to Shivani when all of them are together, look at bindu she knows how to dress, how could you pack some of these Indian outfits.

Shivani feels intimidated and she gets tears in her eyes, Sudhir doesn't notice, yet she finds herself alone and they keep talking to each other ignoring shivani.

Shivani catches cold and fever, she finds difficult to wake up early.

Sudhir and his family keep talking about Shivani and her family, saying MrGirish is just a showoff person, he didn't even celebrate the wedding properly.

Shivani comes into the hall and says to Mrs Sunandha if she can help her in the kitchen. Mrs Sunandha says you are a princess, how can you work here, you wake up at 7 : 00 am in the morning at your sis in-laws place, I don't know why my son married a girl like you.

Shivani goes to the room and closes the door and starts crying in silence. Sudhir who always comes after her whenever she is crying, doesn't bother at all and is all happy with his family.

Shivani says to Sudhir, can I ring my parents, my brother has a visa interview at U.S counselate today. I just want to wish him best of luck.

Mrs Sunandha says, why do you need to speak to your family, we will ring your dad and find out, don't make a scene here.

Go and eat the left over breakfast we all had ours. Shivani tries to give a sign to Sudhir but he doesn't care about it.

After two days Shivani says to Sudhir, can I ring today, will you give me a chance. Sudhir says, ok I will try to ask bindu.

Shivani speaks to her dad and he tells that Sharath's visa interview is a success, he is flying to America soon. Mrs Sunandha who is always with unwanted curiosity with scorn in her mind, comes to Shivani and Sudhir, talking in private about Sharath Visa interview. Sudhir even feels happy about Sharath and congratulates Sharath.

Mrs Sunandha says that just an interview being successful doesn't make any difference, I have seen kids of my colleagues getting rejections in their passport. Shivani who knows about competency of Sharath, doesn't bother at all and feels very happy.

Because, Shivani likes Sharath a lot, and even is very close to all of his friends too.

She ties Rakhi every year to all of Sharath's friends. Shivani counts her everyday stay at Dublin.

Shivani gets offended by Mrs Sunandha's constant daunting asking her why does she need so many t-shirts to buy, when Shivani doesn't even buy half of what she used to buy during her college days.

Shivani always used to feel, why should dad get me married to this family, when they are against this marriage.

His one word changed my whole life, now I can't even say anything, but I am also a 23year old girl why doesn't they know, she made all odd remarks on me when I was in India and now she is playing a Power game with me.

I never saw a social teacher like her, where my social teacher used to adore me so much. This social teacher is digging my grave to my self-esteem and confidence.

Shivani spends all time alone or takes bindu's kid to a park, next to their home.

Sunandha keeps telling bindu, how the maid used to be assertive to Shivani when she was away.

Shivani gets fumed up and says when you talk something talk with meaning. I am going to tell Sudhir that you are comparing me with a maid. Mrs Sunandha says see how many tricks this girl has, she wants to turn Sudhir against our family and me. Moreover, sudhir says she is the best girl he has chosen.

Sudhir starts to ignore shivani slowly when she says your mom is crossing all limits. Whenever she sheds tears he starts saying why are you being so silly. Shivani thinks to make things better she needs to maintain silence as he is prejudiced now with their words.

Shivani gives the gift she bought for bindu and Mrs Sunandha a pair of gold earrings at Bahrain.

Shivani says to bindu, I know what you have is much more, but we just started our new marital life, so this is what I bought for me, for you and for mother-in-law.

Suddenly bindu shows a grumpy face instead of accepting the gift, she says shivani is intimidating me. Mrs

Sunandha fills Sudhir's ears that Shivani hurt bindu, by bringing such small earrings.

Shivani doesn't understand why she is reacting this way and goes to her room. Sudhir comes to her and says, what did you say to bindu "I just said this is the same I bought for myself and you, they are very small". What is wrong in this statement.

I just cannot understand your family; I am missing my family and also even your friends in Sydney. I just want to go to Sydney. Do not postpone the stay, at least let us get away by our 1st wedding anniversary. Sudhir says ok, don't worry I will do, but come and say sorry to bindu.

Shivani thinks sorry has no worth at all in this family. But to avoid any stupid drama she says sorry, I didn't think you will get hurt by such simple words.

I do not wear heavy jewellery so I chose the same for you as you are just 5 years older than me.

Sudhir's cousin in Bahrain takes them to a gold shop where she says to Sudhir why don't you buy Shivani some gold stuff, here people buy gold in a bulk. Shivani says she is going to buy for bindu and Mrs Sunandha as bindu bought a newhome and Sudhir is her elder brother so they need to gift them as per Hindu traditions.

Sudhir's cousin says you have got the best girl, she is not greedy at all. She is buying for herself the simplest ones and she is thinking what you did not even think of.

Sudhir says Shivani is very simple, she likes colourful trendy dresses and some fashion earings that too very simple. She is a child at heart girl. Mrs Sunandha says she is immature too, I don't know why you chose her. Sudhir doesn't say a word even when Shivani feels sad by her words.

He just says to Shivani, bindu and her husband jagan have given us road map to travel round Dublin. Let's go Shivani says ok. Mrs Sunandha and Mr Sudhakar put up grumpy faces, when they know that Sudhir is going with Shivani alone.

Shivani thinks it's the right time to ask Sudhir what makes his family so intimidating about her family and her credibility.

Sudhir doesn't answer to her questions and says you are also behaving like them. Shivani says that is not the answer Sudhir my question is why did your sister bindu invite us when your Mom hates me?.

Sudhir leaves Shivani in the Phenoix park in Dublin and goes away. Shivani who is new to the country does not know where Sudhir went and she gets perplexed, as she only knows the address of bindu and jagan.

Moreover, their phone numbers, but she has no euros with her, to ring them. She tries to search Sudhir all over the "Phenoix park".

However, she doesn't find him as the park is very big and it has many exits and entries.

Shivani tries to locate the place from where Sudhir left her and calms down, she says to herself if he doesn't come, I will ask someone here to help me.

She gets tears in her eyes though she has enough courage to face the reality. She meets a Irish lady and tries to explain her what happened, She understands Shivani's Indian English accent.

But she says, you need to have your Passport if you came on Visit all the time, otherwise you might be in trouble.

Yet, don't worry Ireland is a very friendly country and every woman is treated with respect you look very young like in teens, Indians don't look aged you hardly look 23 years old. Meanwhile Sudhir comes to Shivani, and says I was upset with you so I went out. Shivani says yes may be you went to smoke as usually.

Nicarette is what you bought to show me, so that I do not complain about your smoking and this is what you do now. Shivani says how you could leave me alone here in a different country. Sudhir I am getting scared, with you and your family.

If you don't want to stay with me all your life, please send me to India. I will not even complain tell my dad that you and your family do not like me. Sudhir says Shivani, do you think marriage is a easy thing, every married girl has to face this. Your dad will blame all of us, don't even think or say those words. Things change, after a while, anyways we are going to Sydney three days later. Above all I want you, You are my choice, you need to understand me.

There is one more family get together trip planned, we have to go to this. Shivani says Sudhir I'm feeling dizzy today I can't come with you all to the hill top and cross the bridges. I feel like throwing up, and my temperature is still not normal.

Sudhir says, whatever, I am going, stay here with my dad. He is also not coming with us. Shivani who lost her grandpa at the same age of Sudhir's dad, looks up with very much respect to Mr Sudhakar. But he doesn't even like or adore any aspect of Shivani, to him bindu is everything.

She tries to speak to him with utmost respect, but he starts his questions. Did you send any money to your parents from Sudhir and to your brother, because Sudhir never spoke to anyone like you in his lifetime. He was adamant about marrying you, though we said, they can't give as much as his mom's colleague's wife is offering.

Shivani says I don't ask Sudhir anything about his financial statements. My Dad is working through his financial crisis, we have lands. He is just cheated in business; he will get back his money.

Shivani says to herself had my dad been in this hostile environment, I think he might have felt the same. Their hostility can hurt men too; I am just a 23 years old new bride.

Dad your Princess is getting such hostile treatment which you never saw in your life. Your friend Mr Sriinvas didn't tell you, your girl is a good punching bag to Sudhir and his family.

Shivani doesn't say anything and she maintains her poise at the Family lunch, when Mrs Sunandha says, you need to get thin like bindu. Shivani gets fumed up and says, I can't and I don't need to, most of us in Sydney are chubby, And I am not obese, to change.

To this bindu says why do you take Shivani to your friends home bro, she is thinking she is too good from the odd.

To this Shivani says, why are you asking me to become thin, why can't you put on some weight. Sudhir is not thin we complementeach other well. Sudhir doesn't say a word, but the night they were about to leave bindu says Shivani is so happy to go back to Sydney. I think that place is beautiful and bro might have arranged everything well because he was so adamant about marrying her.

Shivani packs their luggage, cleans the room and says to bindu, while Mrs Sunandha is asleep, it's not that I don't like to stay here, but for some reason my health is not good here in this cold weather.

We had good time, and you all can come sometime with the little one, I miss him so much, never been so close to any kid, as I am the eldest in my family.

Next morning when they were about to leave, Mrs Sunandha says in an aggressive tone, get a job don't give me reasons that you are not having experience, I don't care, otherwise plan for a child, don't give me excuses.

I will tell your mom and she must tell you too. Shivani thinks I do not discuss such things with my mum. My mum cannot even dare to speak to me about these things, which I know better than her. My mom will know face her daunting.

She tells to herself, When Sudhir and I are ready to have kids we will plan. I am just 23 years old.

Sudhir and Shivani start at the airport, Shivani feels very light hearted, that she can go to her zone of peace and happiness, not getting targeted by her in-laws.

They reach Sydney, a day before their wedding anniversary, Sudhir asks Shivani what do you want as a gift, she says I want you to quit smoking forever.

That is all I do not need anything. I have everything I need, but your smoking makes me very uncomfortable. Sudhir says, Shivani from which planet are you. Shivani says don't try to flatter me, I know your behaviour is unpredictable.

Yet, you try to affirm that you wanted me as your choice, so Im managing somehow, anyways I'm so happy that we are reaching Sydney in a short while. Shivani and Sudhir reach Sydney and then the very next day, they celebrate their wedding anniversary with some good friends, who arrange a nice party for them.

Sudhir gets a watch and a pair of earrings to Shivani with a heart shaped locket, which he silently purchases in the Aircraft.

Shivani who loves Estelle earrings likes the gift. She opens her bag and gives a Brand new shirt and 200 $ to Sudhir, this is what Dad has given me, for our wedding anniversary. Sudhir says its ok, say thanks to your parents. Above all, of their gifts, they gave you as my life partner, that is the best I can have.

Shivani feels happy and she finds that even on their anniversary Mrs Sunandha and her family do not wish them. Shivani thinks why bother that is the true feelings they have for me.

I am an outcast to them. I am just Sudhir's wife but not family, to them. Sudhir is many other friends wish them, on their First anniversary and Shivani's friends too wish them. Sudhir speaks to nazia, as she always says Sudhir, Shivani is a innocent flower of our core friends, we are like sisters. Please take care of her she is a child at heart.

She will multiply your happiness; her heart is an open book to her closed ones. Sudhir says to nazia don't worry she is happy now, yes I can see how much she appreciates little things.

Was she always likes this, she is not greedy or fond of jewellery and does not expect from me anything. Nazia says yes she is like this since our kindergarten. We all love our friend. She never changed and she will never.

Sudhir says to Shivani lets go to the Darling Harbour, the night view is so beautiful, I'm sure you will like it.

Shivani says Sydney is beautiful, and Im in love with the city, after visiting Dublin, so much of wet weather.

They reach Darling Harbour and the spectacular view makes Shivani very happy. I just love the sea in the night.

Shivani and Sudhir have similar food taste, both love Continental food, they both like watching Hollywood movies. Their intrests are alike.

Sudhir says you are so happy today Shivani, look at you, you are glowing when you are blushing. They enjoy their dinner with much compassion and they are bonded with each other more and more.

Shivani's cousin kiran also lives in same city, yet he never gets to meet Shivani. He rings Shivani and wishes her a week after their anniversary, Shivani is very close to her cousin Kiran like a best friend and she says, get me a gift if you are coming to my home. I am cooking well; I will not starve you at my home.

The very next day, Sudhir's mom rings him and he Sudhir picks a fight with Shivani, you don't clean the house properly. What's wrong with you and when will you learn.

Shivani says, I am doing the same type of work ever since I came, why are you being so rude to me. Sudhir says your honeymoon is over, you need to think seriously about life.

Shivani says Sudhir come to the point what did your mom say on the phone, why can't you tell me the truth. Sudhir says nothing.

She doesn't like me and she can't see me happy,

I have never heard a single word good about me from her. Sudhir shouts at Shivani don't dare to speak to me like that and he slaps her on her face.

Shivani cries a lot, and she doesn't eat food at all. Sudhir comes to her after an hour and says I'm sorry, it just happened in a bad mood.

See I won't go to work, if you are continuously crying, I know how much you have been hurt. Shivani says its ok, hopefully you don't repeat it again. I never expected this from you, anyways go to work.

Kirancomes to their home and meets Sudhir. Kiran gets them a nice gift, they eat the lunch prepared by Shivani. Shivani doesn't show her sadness, compliments Sudhir's surprise gift to her, yet kiran finds that Shivani is not whole heartedly happy. Kiran rings shivani a week later and says, you are my cousin I know you since childhood what's wrong with you are not wholeheartedly happy. Shivani says it's hard to say but Sudhir slapped me, once and though he said sorry.

Kiran gets shocked Shivani, are you ok, don't encourage it again, talk to him in an assertive tone He is older than you, I saw him looks like he is a different person behind closed doors.

How your hands were shivering while you were serving food I have seen it. Yet, I'm telling you, tell him again, don't ever raise your hand against me. You are a brave girl, I can't hear such things you are very precious to your family and a charm of our kith and kin.

Shivani says kiran I'm unable to find a job and Sudhir's mom is after me all the time daunting about it. His entire family hates me, dad didn't know this, that this marriage is entirely of Sudhir's choice though its arranged by dad.

Shivani finding a job as a fresher here is not easy, why can't they understand. Tell Sudhir about the same.

Kiran then says Shivani what happened has happened, forward your resume to me, I will tailor it well and don't worry things will settle down slowly.

Shivani says don't tell mom and about this, you know mom is very sensitive, she will fall sick if she knows I'm not happy.

Kiran says ok, I won't say, but be careful and don't hesitate to ring me anytime. I'm your cousin and we are family, it's like a responsibility of a brother on me to be with you in your odd times.

The very next week Rosy comes home and says Sudhir and all of us have planned a Reunion of our past colleagues. Shivani doesn't like Rosy but she gets scared as if she is against her, then she will be in double trouble with Sudhir, as his family doesn't like her. Sudhir says get some appropriate outfits for the party Shivani, go with Rosy and shop some good stuff in the City.

Shivani says ok and Rosy takes her to QVB (Queen Victoria Building), she keeps saying see again you are having some pimple marks, doesn't Sudhir talk about it.

Shivani says why Rosywhat's a big deal about it, they will come and go my maternal uncle who is a famous medico told me.

Shivani makes her own choice, though Rosy shows her around. Shivani doesn't like the way Rosy gets dressed, she looks at the women who are dressed well in and around QVB in western outfits and chooses a outfit that resembles like theirs.

Rosy says that's expensive, Shivani says its ok Sudhir doesn't mind, I have my own money too, my dad has given me and my maternal uncle too. Shivani styles her hair well when Sudhir asks her to do, she asks Sudhir do I look good enough in new western outfits. Sudhir says you look good and stylish, you look different today.

They go to Rosy's party with his past fellow colleagues, Sudhir introduces Shivani with her educational qualification.

All of them says Sudhir you are lucky she is beautiful and her hair is so silky and dark, above all she speaks English fluently.

Sudhir likes all the compliments on his wife and he says she comes from a family of Doctors and Engineers.

Rosy says to Shivani, your hair is looking good today, Shivani says beauty is how we can present and look elegant.

Fair Complexion is just one skin tone, Rosy says you are very assertive. Shivani doesn't likes to drink wine like others, she just sips it, but gives a sign to Sudhir with her eyes, I don't like the taste.

Sudhir shows her, try coke, Shivani tries coke, she relishes all the savouries except beef and pork.

She is a die heart Hindu and hindus don't eat beef and pork if their home diety is Godess of Eternal Power, Shakthi.

Shivani finds very uncomfortable when Rosy and her friends start to crack some adult jokes. Sudhir smiles at them, but Shivani doesn't like, after they come home from the party.

She says Sudhir I don't like these adult jokes, we don't use such language in our Indian Traditions.

Why is Rosy after my pimple scars, did you ever talk to her about them, they are biological changes, what's the big deal, your mom did the same, she asked me to go through some Lasik Treatment in a Beauty clinic in Hyderabad

My doctor uncle, said don't even think about it, they use steroids, and your skin will get damaged and in the longrun you will loose your young charm that's innate in you.

Sudhir says nope I didn't tell Rosy about it, she is far older than you, may be she wants you to look scar free. The very next week Sudhir orders a big pack of ProActive, he says to Shivani use these you will be scar free and look beautiful.

Shivani doesn't much bother about those creams, but she tries, and slowly gets a change in her skin, but it even irritates her face pores, she has a burning sensation. So she stops it after a while.

PREGNANCY – SUDHIR IS VERY HAPPY – SHIVANI IS PERPLEXED

Shivani says to Sudhir, I think I'm Pregnant, I missed my menstrual cycle which is always regular. Sudhir says its good Shivani, infact it will be a great news to all of our families.

Shivani says, I don't know is it right to have a baby unplanned and also I'm perplexed as I am unable to understand you and your family.

Sudhir says it's not yet confirmed, I wish I had a baby, it might be early to you as you are twenty four now, but I'm in my thirties and my friends who are younger than me already have kids. I love kids Shivani, and a baby girl is my choice.

Ok, leave it you already booked an appointment with the doctor so they will find the reason and don't stress yourself. Let's go to the LUNA PARK, all your favourite rides are over there.

Shivani says, ok let's go and they enjoy at LUNA PARK, Shivani finds that she is feeling dizzy.

A week later they go to the Doctor and after the Blood Test, she confirms. You are Pregnant, she is going to be a mom of your child.

Sudhir rejoices like anything, he says you have no clue as what this is for me. Shivani never saw Sudhir so happy. So even though she is not ready in her mind for a baby, to make Sudhir happy she says ok let's see how it goes.

She rings her maternal uncle, and he says that a great news. I wish you have a baby girl my child.

One more little Shivani, don't get so worried and I want you to take care.

I know the pain of Infertility, seen it in your mom, you are a saviour child, so be careful. She then rings her mom and says mom it's an unplanned Pregnancy, I don't know what to do, I'm confused, but Sudhir is very happy.

Rajeshwari says don't worry Shivani, a baby is a gift from god, just be careful for the first three months of your pregnancy. And ring your maternal uncle he knows all about your health concerns since your childhood.

Shivani sends all the reports in an e-mail to her maternal uncle.

Sudhir celebrates Shivani's Pregnancy like a feast, he says whatever you want to eat, just tell me. Shivani says Do you know to cook?? I never saw you cooking.

You just say whatever I cook is ok. Can you manage if I get sick and have nausea, headaches, stomach cramps. Do you want me to go to India. Because I won't have any change of my life style in India and my maternal uncle has the latest scanning machines and he has now a World Recognition attending Webinars.

Sudhir says no, I can manage I want to see my baby growing in your little tummy I want to speak to her I can't keep you and her away, my doll is coming all the way. I want a baby girl, and she should resemble you in every way, one more little shivani.

Sudhir says lets inform my mom before she knows the news from your side of family. Shivani says you tell her, I can't do it and how can I talk about it, she is always daunting me.

Sudhir says she won't now as she wanted me to have a baby, very soon and now she won't say I'm not a ideal son.

Sudhir rings Mrs Sunandha and she speaks to Sudhir in a lovely voice and when shivani takes the call, she says Congrats, but search a job, how can my son feed both you and your baby on his own.

Shivani gets very fumed up with her words and gives the phone to Sudhir. The very next week, the doctor says there is a complication here, Shivani's Heamoglobin count is very low, this may affect the growth of the baby, and make delivery complicated too. She is not gaining any weight. Shivani then reveals to the doctor, that she is a saviour child born in the medical adversity of infertility.

The doctor says Sudhir, you need to make sure Shivani's haemoglobin is good, because she is showing signs of weakness. Something is bothering her from insidetoo, are you happy Shivani.

Shivani says doctor frankly speaking I'm not very ready for the baby as I'm married for less than two years.

My husband is not very known person to me before marriage. Yet, I know how much my husband wants this baby, his own offspring. So, I have made up my mind, to enjoy his happiness.

The doctor says Shivani you are 24 years old and by the due date, which is going to be an easter, you will be close to 25 yrs, which is a good age, so nothing to worry, except if you have violence in your marriage and also severe medical complications. Tell me if your husband is controlling you emotionally orphysically.

NAUSEA AND WEAKNESS

The doctor gives her a form to fill and she says you have to answer all these questions without hiding anything. Shivani finds the question, Did your husband ever raise his hand against you?

The question makes Shivani shiver, but she answers no, as she accepted his apology.

Yet, this low haemoglobin count should improve, otherwise the baby 's growth will be affected by this. Sudhir says to Shivani, I bought a Complete Pregnancy guide, foods to be taken, during pregnancy and after pregnancy too.

Shivani likes the book as she saw a similar copy at her maternal uncle's clinic. But she doesn't say I have seen it, as she appreciates Sudhir who bought the book on his own as a surprise.

A week later, when shivani gets bed sick with horrible nausea, shivani rings Sudhir about her condition, and he rushes to home from work and gets scared to see Shivani becoming very weak and having terrible nausea where her throat gets ruptured and stains of blood on her dress.

Shivani starts to cry, seeing the traces of blood as she thinks this nausea might get worse and without any family's help she feels terrible and just gets a thought about her maternal uncle.

Sudhir looks at her with tears in his eyes, my dear, you are a brave girl and child at heart nothing will happen to you or our baby. We will ring the emergency, don't worry, eat some biscuits, its written in the book. Shivani's nausea doesn't stop and they visit the doctor asap, there the doctor reveals that Shivani is having cravings of citrus fruits and she is not enjoying food.

Sudhir brings Pizza for a change of food and she could digest it wthout nausea. Sudhir says may be my doll like Pizza.

Mrs Sunandha who is always a money calculator worries that Shivani might get some maternity outfits and spend money.

So, she keeps ringing Shivani, ask your mom to send all your outfits, its waste of money here. Shivani rings her mom and says Mom my mother inlaw doesn't want me to spend a penny on my clothes, so why bother, send me whatever I need, through the Courier Service, I am never a burden to you.

Listening to this Shivani's mom says don't worry Shivani I have arranged even new jewellery to you and your unborn baby too. I will send all the necessary stuff.

Sudhir says can your parents get a gold bracelet to my friend's new born son, as they are sending you stuff through a friend from Warangal. Shivani says mom don't bother about me, you know I am not very fond or obsessive with jewellery but can you get a small bracelet for a new born 5 months old baby.

Without a second thought, Shivani's parents send some new stuff through her parents. Even Dr. Rama Krishna sends some nice pictures of the new born babies too.

You have no clue Shivani we are so happy don't be sad, you will have a healthy baby. Sudhir makes sure within three months Shivani eats well, he makes her eat good amount of grilled lamb and drink lots of juices.

The doctor to her surprise says you guys with your companionship have made it, Shivani your haemoglobin is now in a good ratio, your baby will be healthy.

Sudhir takes good care of Shivani but Mrs Sunandha doesn't stop her daunting, you don't have a job. Shivani says it's hard for a fresher's to find a job, moreover I have lot of pain in my knees.

Mrs Sunandha keeps daunting her more saying every woman has to go through this phase, you are not special. Your parents have spoiled you with privileges, they give you anything you want.

Shivani says to her mom, Sudhir's mom just hates me, I don't know what will be my baby's future in their hands. Mrs Rajeshwari says don't worry Shivani, a baby bonds the couple with more marital bliss. A child brings a smile on anyone's face.

THE UV SCAN SAYS MOSTLY A BABY GIRL

Shivani gets closer to five months of her pregnancy and the Gender Determination scan would be scheduled a week after.

Sudhir says I am unable to fit my roster to your scan date, but I will be there as soon as you finish, I am very eager to see the baby in your womb. Shivani thinks since she is very fond of Sharath and her brothers, she thinks if it's a boy she will raise him like a Prince, if a girl she would be a princess or a doll of the house. He rings Rosy if she is free to take Shivani to the hospital.

Rosy takes Shivani to the RPA. She says all this may look quite rich to you Indians. Shivani says no, I have seen good hospitals in India, yes these are verylarge in area and updated infrastructure, but the medical equipment are not new to me. My quality of life is same, I have all the privileges that I have here at my home. I am a privileged child of two families.

Many of my relatives are in a good positions in America, and India. I have a cousin who is a Cardio Surgeon in America.

Rosy says pregnancy has made you vulnerable now as the baby might bring differences in Sudhir and your quality private time. Shivani finds her words very fishy, she has never heard such words from anyone. And even medically it's a proven fact that a baby multiplies marital bliss.

They go to the scan and Shivani looks at the UV- image of her baby. They say she is moving like a fish in a fish pond. Looks very hyperactive. We are quite sure it's a girl. Are you happy? Shivani says I am happy, because my husband wants a girl. Sudhir comes to visit her after his work and he rejoices it's a girl, Shivani looks at Rosy, her face colour changes, suddenly, she says I am going I have some work to do.

Sudhir says just wait I am going to bring my car from the car park.

He brings a pink teddy bear and says this is for the unborn baby girl of mine. I just can't wait to see my doll, who will be myoffspring.

Shivani feels happy, her nausea slowly comes to normal, but she gets another problem its terrible pain in her legs and can't even walk for long.

The doctor doesn't understand one thing, why are you so dull, you are not happy from inside something is bothering you.

Shivani says I need to find a job, and I'm unable to find one and I get daunted by in-laws though my husband doesn't bother me much as of now, his priority is the baby.

The Doctor says Shivani you don't need to worry, you will get a job you are well qualified. The very next day, Rosy rings Shivani and says we are going to a Casino and Sudhir asked me to ring you, do you have any objection.

Shivani says I would have come but it's my b'day today and Sudhir will be home, it's better we go to a temple.

Rosy says you visit temples all the time in a year, why cant you make this day special.

Sudhir brings a Big brown teddy almost a size of a real one. Now everyday when you do your house chores, carry this one in your hands and do it. Sudhir celebrates her b'day with a delicious cake after their dinner at the Star Casino.

After a week Sudhir takes Shivani to the Immigrant English training course, there they ask Shivani to write an essay. Shivani writes about "Child labour" in India. The centre people say to Sudhir, your wife doesn't need any spoken or written classes for English, her vocabulary is very good, looks like she is been to a good school and well qualified too.

Sudhir tells the same to Mrs Sunandha, she is well qualified the institute here says, Mrs Sunandha says, maybe she is lazy and wants to laze around and extort you with motherhood.

Shivani hears these words and says Sudhir send me to my dad's home I just can't keep up with this intimidation and my maternal uncle has a upgraded clinic, so my delivery will be safe.

Sudhir says to Mrs Sunandha, Shivani wants to go to India, to her parent's home. Mrs Sunandha in a rage says already they are saying it's a baby girl, and you are not even fair, now if you don't drink fresh juices and enjoy life at your parents' home, the baby will be dusky like you. No, she can't go to India, who will bear her ticket expenses too.

Shivani thinks she never saw a social teacher so much being a self centred money calculator like her.

She even thinks twice again if I go, she will put all restrictions on me saying you have to stay in Nalgonda, that prison is worse than her daunting on the phone.

Sudhir's friend Vishal comes to visit Sudhir after his e-3 visa has been approved to America.

Vishal likes Shivani's cooking and says that since Shivani is going to have a baby soon, he can get Pure Saffron, to drink with milk for Shivani as his dad visits Rishikesh every year.

Hindus in India believe that Saffron milk can bring a fair complexion in the new born baby, when it is consumed by the Pregnant woman during her pregnancy.

It's a myth though, as Complexion or skin tone of a baby is determined by their genetic tree. Shivani knows the fact as she is a niece of a medico and is very close to him than her own dad.

She seldom speaks to her dad on the phone, because of his strict stereotype beliefs, to him his reputation and fame matters the most than anything in the world.

Shivani shares the same idea of saffron with her medico uncle. He says be least bothered about complexion, your baby doll will be beautiful as she is a offspring of a "Creative Child".

Saffron is good for health, but be sure you don't take it too much, these are all myths.

You shouldn't believe in such things, drink milk, fresh juice, eat a balanced diet and be positive.

That is the secret of a happy motherhood and a heathy baby. Shivani follows the same and also takes saffron with milk, even when she develops heat rashes on her body. Because, its Sudhir' mom who insists her to take it as she is obsessive about the complexion of the baby. Bindu being a dentist in Dublin supports her mom on her every word.

Sudhir takes Shivani to the Floraide show in Canberra and to Jervis bay, to keep her happy. Shivani thinks that may be the baby will bond them forever as Sudhir is very caring now.

Sudhir likes to travel a lot but Shivani feels the best thing for her in Sydney is to relish a Magnum icecream stick on a summer night at a Look out point which gives a spectacular view of SYDNEY CBD.

One day Shivani's taste buds change suddenly and she avoids drinking her orange juice for 2 days, and eats spicy pickle without Sudhir's knowledge as she was scared of Sudhir.

Sudhir finds out about it and stops talking to Shivani for about 3 consecutive days, he stops eating food at home and doesn't even tell Shivani when he is coming home.

Shivani tries to explain him in a much pleasing way, that she had a craving and its quite common in pregnancy.

But Sudhir doesn't even listen to her and with utmost stress Shivani faints on the floor when Sudhir comes home. Sudhir gets panicked as she looses her conscious too.

He sprinkles water on her face, even then Shivani wakes uponly after 5 minutes and says I am so afraid of you, I don't even know how to predict your mood swings and what triggers your anger.

I feel I am alone, and this baby is going to make me very vulnerable. Send me to India my maternal uncle who is a medico will take care of me well and the baby will also be safe, I want to speak to him.

Sudhir says with tears rolling in his eyes, I'm very sorry Shivani I never thought about your cravings, I'm muddled up with my family's suggestions who keep saying that spicy foods make the baby complexion dark.

Please don't go to India and now you can't travel you are close to your seventh month of pregnancy.

I promise you to keep you happy, and moreover we have already sent Visiting Papers to your parents, so don't take any impromptu decisions.

Why don't you go around with Rosy and see the city. Shivani says I'm better off without her, I don't like the way she speaks.

Sudhir says ok, leave it but few days later Sudhir rings Shivani and says Rosy is laughing at you that you are worried about your career, Shivani gets fumed up and says my friend Nazia is ringing from US. Sudhir doesn't repeat about the topic when he comes home.

Shivani is quite sensible and even brave too, agrees to Sudhir yet she feels like these are like redflags to show that once the baby is born he is going to make my life miserable.

Her intuition always says, Shivani you are stuck in this trap and now even your beautiful offspring too. Shivani rings her medico uncle and shares all her fears and also about unpredictable behaviour of Sudhir.

Dr. Rama Krishna says you are my golden child and brave, don't worry the baby will bring happiness, couples get more closer after a new baby, you saw many of them at our WISE clinic.

Sudhir takes Shivani to one of his friends home, for dinner there she meets Sudeepa. She finds her rapport with her good moreover she is few months older than Shivani and is a new bride too. Shivani thinks this is the only way she can get rid of Rosy, and also Shivani's mom daunting her to get a job even when she is getting closer to seventh month of pregnancy.

Shivani asks Sudhir if she can study along with Sudeepa at their home. Sudhir says ok, but don't share any of our personal issues with her or anyone. I'm warning you about it, and you know when you break my rules, what would be the outcome, don't complain later.

Shivani says no I won't say anything, let me go she is a computers graduate and both of us can study. Shivani meets a sweet, outspoken girl Siri at Sunitha's home.

She says to Shivani I have seen you many times, but you never noticed, we live next to your building. Shivani doesn't share any of her woes and they study as well and enjoy quality time together.

Sudeepa is so warm-hearted, and she says to Shivani tell me whatever you want to eat, I can cook for you, you are not gaining any weight and look so dull and stressed. Yet Shivani says this baby is very important to my husband, though I'mvery new to Sydney. So, my severe knee pains at night make me sleepless and I feel alone at home.

Siri says to Shivani if you have any trouble cooking, tell me I can get curries for you, don't be so stressed. Shivani finds both Sudeepa and Siri very nice warm and kind hearted.

She enjoys her time with them and feels happy just like she enjoyed with her school buddies.

Siri and Sudeepa help Shivani with Curries until her parents arrive wheever she says to them her knee pains are worse on some days.

Shivani gets a call from her brother Sharath, saying sissy I lost about 1500$ dad sent me, a roomie stole it and he vacated the room, he stole from all of us. I want to change my college now, the fees is higher and our cousin Rama in Atlanta is arranging half of it as a credit, can you arrange the remaining amount as a credit, without mom and dad knowing about it, you know dad is so strict. I don't want to hear him shouting at me, Shivani says ok, I will ask if Sudhir can help with it. Sharath says I will return the amount in less than six months as my senior has started a start up and we can work part time there as programmers.

Sudhir hears Shivani speaking to Sharath and says its ok, I will send him the money, and he can return me when he earns it back.

Shivani says thank you to Sudhir and pleads him not to tell to Mrs Sunandha about it. Sudhir sends money to Sharath.

Few weeks later Shivani's mom says that something went wrong at the medical test and she might have to go for the test again for the visa.

Your Dad got his visa, but I didn't get it, Shivani gets perplexed why didn't mom get her visa and why she has to appear for the tests again.

Meanwhile Sudhir says if your mom doesn't get her visa approved, we will ask my Mom to come to help you. Shivani who knows the aggressive nature of Mrs Sunandha rings her mom and says take good care of your health mom, Australia is very keen about minute things in Visitors health.

Sudhir says don't panick lets keep my mom as option too, Shivani says how can your mom come, bindu's son is with her. Sudhir says it's ok I will send papers to both.

Mrs Sunandha who is a money calculator, keeps calculating things, Shivani says if my mom doesn't get a visa approved, my dad will fund the tickets for your mom. So, she need not worry about the same and daunt on me on everything.

Sudhir says let me first talk to her, Mrs Sunandha as usual says bindu handled her delivery alone, can't you guys do it and its quite easy too.

Shivani gets scared and rings her mom the next day, are you ready for the test, you don't have any health issues and complications too.

Mrs Rajeshwari reappears for her chest scan and she gets passed. Within a week she says Shivani the embassy people took my passport. I am quite sure I will get the visa.

Rahul plans to Visit Sydney on Study Visa to Melbourne.

Sudhir's paternal uncle Mr Shekhar rings Sudhir that Rahul got his Visa to Study in Melbourne, and wants to come to Sydney and then go to his college as he is new to Australia. They speak to Shivani too, that she needs to guide him like a brother of her own.

Shivani says to them I will do my best to guide him and he is nothing less to my brother, I have many classmates of mine, my male peers in melbourne who are dad's friends sons. We will settle down Rahul well like his own brother and sis in-law.

MrShekhar says Shivani you are such a well-mannered girl, at such a young age you have such maturity, Rahul is hardly two years younger than you. Shivani says its ok, I will make him get serious about life without any unwanted distractions. Sudhir picks up Rahul and Shivani even with terrible pain in her knees cooks well for him and invite him home.

Rahul is very outspoken without any hypocrisy, and within his one week trip to Sydney they form a sister- brother rapport as he has no siblings too. They travel round the city and visit temple, Shivani gets very tired and her sleep gets disturbed, yet she makes sure she makes all meals for Rahul. Shivani finds that Rahul is smoking too, and she confronts Rahul saying you are hardly 22 and what is this habit. Don't get addicted to it, it will take a toll on your health.

You are a only son of your parents who are well settled, I am telling you like a sister not as your cousin's wife since your parents have told me to guide you.

Rahul says no sis- in- law I don't feel bad at all, infact I feel more happy that you are treating me as a integral part of your family. I hardly met Sudhir bro, it's only at your wedding I met him in person.

I will stop smoking and you eat well and take care our princess inside you, she will be soon coming into this world, as your daughter. I adore baby girls too, they look like dolls.

Mrs Sunandha asksSudhir to go and drop Rahul and stay for 2 days settle him down in the college. Bindu always takes help of them and stays in their home, so what's a big deal your wife can handle everything on her own.

Bindu handled her pregnancy on her own even delivery too. Sudhir says Shivani is 5 yrs younger than bindu, she has become very weak, she fell unconscious few days back.

Shivani sends a message to her cousin Praveen about her vulnerable situation without immediate family and getting closer to due date.

He says don't worry Naveen is there, I will ask him to ring you and if not you ring him. Shivani takes Naveen's number and rings him, she leaves a voice message.

The very next Shivani gets a call from her friend, classmate. Naveen is a son of her dad's friend too. He says' good to see you in Australia. I am in Melbourne and there are other few friends of our college too.

Your cousin Praveen told me you are here and gave me your number that you need a favour.

What's that Shivani? I can help you in anyway possible to me. Shivani says Naveen I'm closer to my due date and with terrible fatigue, can you manage to have my brother in-law Rahul as your new roomie. Sudhir has to come and settle him down and then fly back, you know how hard things are, as you have two sisters of your own.

Naveen says Shivani don't worry at all, we have enough space for Rahul. Sudhir needs to take care of you, at this crucial stage.

Naveen speaks to Rahul and Sudhir, he says I have no problem to have Rahul as our roomie, just take care of Shivani

He says, I came to your wedding, your lucky. She is a very nice girl and we all respect and adore her, she is flawless and with good intellect.

Shivani tells Rahul about her health condition, Rahul says it's ok. Naveen seems to be very outspoken and very frank. You don't need to worry take care of your health and our new unborn princess of the family too.

Naveen receives Rahul with a warm welcome and makes him feel comfortable as their roomie. Naveen and Rahul gel well as friends and Rahul says sis in-law your friends are very good and cooperative. I am having good time in Melbourne.

Sudhir hears a sad news that his maternal grandmother who raised him was ailing with Kidney cancer has passed away. Sudhir feels terrible grief and Shivani shares his grief and bereavement too. She consoles him that it's a freedom from her sickness, she was going through a lot of pain with Cancer in Kidneys.

Sudhir who loves the unborn baby who starts to kick the womb, speaks to her everyday even while shivani is asleep, he says your great grand mom is no more Princess, She has left the world before she could see my offspring. Shivani rings Sudhir's mom and all of her family and conveys her deep condolences.

Shivani says Sudhir don't be so sad, just have a quick shower and pray to god, so that her soul Rests in Peace. I have arranged all the Prayersof Condolence on your behalf too.

Sudhir says I like this attitude of yours, you evaluate people by their own attitude and not by family baggage, though my mom keeps daunting you, you are showing your empathy to her on her Mom's death.

Mr Girish and Mrs Rajeshwari attend all death rituals of Sudhir's grand mom and on the day of 1st month deathceremony, they say we both have got our Visa approved, to help Shivani and their unborn baby.

Mrs Sunandha who is always a money calculator, says what jewellery did you all get for the baby.

You know it's a baby girl your daughter couldn't even have a son, yet we are accepting the girl as Sudhir is so stupid to rejoice on the birth of a baby girl, he doesn't know the burdens if the girl is of dark complexion.

Are you all prepared for all the jewels and new clothes. Mrs Rajeshwari says we have purchased as per our financial capability.

Mrs Rajeshwari who is a pious and kind hearted woman offers her prayers to the Goddess of Eternal power Shakti, to bless the child with flawlessbeauty and good health and safe delivery to Shivani.

Shivani gets very close to her due date and she even gets terrible knee pains on the day when Mr and Mrs Rajeshwari start to Sydney.

Girish gets a good will from his construction project and he leaves no dearth to fund for the air tickets and also some nice jewellery pieces for Shivani and the unborn baby. He gets all the money he has converted into auz dollars.

Mrs Sunandha gives a red flag to Sudhir saying your father in-law is a spendthrift be careful you don't let him spend all money on his wish list. you already married without our choice better listen now that you are having a baby girl.

Hearing this Shivani feels very intimidated, how can she say such words to a person who had planned to buy few ounces of gold for his only girl child's offspring.

Sudhir says I don't have any dayoffs so will ask my friend Rosy to drive you to the Airport and pick your parents. Rosy rings Shivani that she is happy to help her and then says now that your parents are going to come, Sudhir might feel uncomfortable and also alone.

Shivani doesn't understand why Rosy is getting too much involved into her Personal life and what's big deal they are coming to help me.

She says, for me My baby and husband are important nothing else. I know my boundaries well. Shivani doesn't like Rosy picking her parents but as no option left she says ok.

Mrs Rajeshwari and Mr Girish arrive at the airport on 18th march 2007, and Shivani will be given 5th of April as her due date.

A day before her parents come Shivani says to Sudhir I'm so tired, can you please help me in cooking. Sudhir says cooking is one thing I can't do, and it's a matter of one day, do it it's your parents. Shivani with much pain in her joints cooks well for Sudhir and makes sure he is healthy.

When Shivani takes Rosy to pick her Parents she gets dressed in Indian outfit because she knows how strict her dad is, when her mom sees her she gets tears in her eyes, What happened to you?

Shivani you don't even look you are about to have a baby in two weeks. You didn't gain any weight. I am so worried, Rosy says your daughter is lucky to have Sudhir as her husband he is so nice and good looking.

Shivani after coming home with her parents says I don't like this lady Rosy mom though she has a partner very older than her, yet I need to put up with her as you know my in-laws they already create much differences,

If I don't be nice to this woman almost 15 years older than me, Sudhir gets angry may be because she helps in driving me around, she looks like a seductress to me, I hate her, And I'm avoiding her too, she is so proud of her fair skin and Sudhir himself sometimes says she is crazy. I have two nice friends of Sudhir's male peers wives Siri and Sudeepa. They are from Hyderabad and we gel well. Mrs Rajeshwari says even I noticed the way she speaks, don't worry once baby is born Sudhir starts ignoring his family's control over him and you and this lady too.

BABY SHOWER TO SHIVANI – A FEAST BY FRIENDS AND FAMILY

Sudhir and Shivani takes them to some visiting spots as Shivani gets very close to her Delivery.

They avoid long hours of travel and Rajeshwari finds Shivani 's knee pains are making her loose her sleep. MrGirish plans to Visit Melbourne, but Mrs Rajeshwari says she is not coming with him as She neds to take care of Shivani. Mrs Rajeshwari gets intuitive that Shivani is not happy as all pregnant women are wholeheartedly smiling. She asks what is bothering you,

Shivani says it's my in-laws daunting me over everything and Sudhir's unpredictable behaviour and Rosy supporting him, why does this lady be so much involved with my family life, just because she is helping me to drive around, she should know her boundaries.

Mrs Rajeshwari says don't worry Shivani things will change, once the baby is born both of you will become busy with the baby.

On the day of last scan of Shivani, she books a cab to take her mom to the Hospital as Sudhir plans to come from his work.

One of Sudhir's friend Sudeepa invites them after her morning walk to visit them as her mom is new to Sydney, just for a cup of tea in the morning.

Shivani inform Sudhir about it after they reach her home as she thinks he might be busy at work.

Sudhir disconnects the call and doesn't call back when Shivani comes home, and she gets ready to the hospital reaches on time.

She doesn't know why he is not answering the call, and when they were about to finish the doctors' check up, Sudhir comes to the hospital. They say the baby is very active, and will be healthy too.

Sudhir stops speaking to Shivani even when she tries to explain him and doesn't eat what Sudhir's mom has cooked. Mrs Rajeswhari doesn't even speak much, she is a very introvert person and isn't assertive. She cries in silence looking at Shivani's vulnerability saying sorry to Sudhir to make him happy.

When Mr Girish returns from Melbourne she says to him this guy's behaviour is unpredictable and his family treats shivani worse, you have no clue and don't see, she cries every day in silence in the bathroom. She just braves to smile to keep her husband happy and to make us feel everything is good.

I can see my daughter's pain who always used to smile with confidence, these people took that smile from her, don't know what will be the future of the baby.

Mr Girsh says let's change the atmosphere and celebrate Shivani's Baby Shower.

Sudhir's friends and their families become close to Shivani's parents and her warm behaviour.

The only friend who is assertive to Sudhir is his bestie jay's wife Sindhu, Shivani also can't be as assertive as she is, but she feels good that there is someone who can correct him, when he controls shivani with his eyes.

Sudhir's friend's wiveshelp to arrange a Blissful Baby Shower to Shivani. Sudhir also enjoys it, though he keeps daunting shivani when she is alone that your dad is boasting everyone about the gifts he bought.

My friend jay's in-laws have gifted him so much, what's a big deal, better tell him to stop his boasting. You know me well, how my anger gets triggered, don't repent later.

Shivani tells Sudhir thatSudhir's friends appreciate all the gifts Shivani's parents have brought for her. Mrs Sunandha and bindu feel envious that they couldn't get a visa during Bindu's baby shower and shivani is enjoying all these privileges, looking at her pictures, which they instist toomuch to send each one of them.

Mrs Sunandha and bindu then start filling Sudhir's ears saying that look at your in-laws they haven't even registered the land they promised to give to Shivani and are enjoying. They have no responsibility at all.

Shivani's mom who notices with her intuition says Shivani you have to get a job to survive with him and his family. These people are very tough, you need to stand on your feet.

AMEYA IS BORN ON A EASTER FRIDAY.

Shivani wakes up at 4.00 am on 4th April and she starts watching T.V as she starts to get pains and doesn't want to disturb Sudhir whose mood swings are unpredictable. After her parents are sleeping, wakes her mom, that I'm unable to bear this pain. I feel the baby is going to be delivered soon.

Sudhir takes Shivani to the hospital but they say that the time pulse of the Contractions is not appropriate to admit Shivani.

They come back and the contractions speed up around 7 pm on 5th april, Shivani rings the hospital and tells them, that she needs to get admitted as the contractions time pulse is very less. She is afraid that she might be in trouble, They again say she has to wait as they are very sure that she can't have a baby tonight.

But Shivani's contractions intensify and around 10 :30 pm she says she might end up worse with the baby.

The RPA people tell Shivani and her friends, that she has to move to Campsie and not RPA. As they have given her space to a complicated case.

Sudhir's friends follow him, and they reach Campsie at 2:00 am. The midwife gets a clear understanding that Shivani is going to deliver the baby very soon. She might have complications as Shivani is exhausted and is slowly loosing her conscious too

They arrange everything required and encourage her that, she is brave enough without any epidural, and asks her to cooperate with them, they find that Shivani is very weak and she gained no weight at all other than baby weight. Finally a beautiful, gorgeous baby girl will be delivered at 2: 38 am on 6th of april an easter Friday.

Shivani feels very happy to see the baby who is so beautiful and looks pink and healthy with beautiful smile just after she is placed next to her.

Sudhir feels very happy and Mr Girish and Mrs Rajeshwari rejoice too. All of their friends come and see the new baby and congratulate them.

Shivani becomes very weak after the delivery and she finds difficult to manage the baby on her own at night. They give her a shared room and nobody can stay with her all night.

Shivani feels dizzy too sometimes, She asks the midwife and the doctor that after the mandatory check ups are completed can she be discharged.

The doctors say yes you can, you need to be taken good care, the baby is healthy but you have become very weak. Three days later Shivani informs Sudhir that she has completed all the check ups for the baby and the doctor can discharge her if he agrees as he is the father of the baby. Sudhir who doesn't like Shivani taking any independent decisions without informing him, says nothing. She thinks he is also agreeing and signs all the papers.

On 8th of April 2007, Shivani vacates the room but forgets the BABY BONUS form at the hospital as she wants to relax and sleep all night. On the way home in the car she just says Sudhir I just forgot to bring the Baby Bonus forms, can you go back and get them as its only 8: 00 pm. Sudhir says you said you completed all, why didn't you that.

Mr Girish says those are government benefits you can get them anytime. Sudhir suddenly stops the car in the midddle of the road and says I'm going to drop all of you even if you utter a single word. Shivani doesn't speak a word and Mr Girish feels very intimidated as Sudhir spoke without manners. Sudhir says to Shivani now you all stay at house I'm leaving the house because you do things all on your own. Mr Girish gets into the kitchen and he cuts his finger when he tries to cut an apple as he feels hungry. He starts bleeding yet Sudhir doesn't say a word when Shivani says sorry and starts crying, can you please tell me where is the band aid box. He just drives his car and leaves the house, Shivani doesn't stop crying and rings him several times, after 10 consecutive messages he says he will come after 10 minutes. Finally he comes home at 3:00 am.

Mr Girish says to Shivani I need to ask him what is making him loose his temper can't he see how weak you have become, you have gained no weight at all. Shivani says Dad he will not say a single word if you ask him and his mom will bombard you, saying you are being mean, I am enduring this since marriage.

MOTHERHOOD OPENS THE PANDORA'S BOX OF TROUBLES –

Motherhood multiplies marital bliss according to medical science. But Negative People make it a danger zone with the vulnerability of the young mom "STORM AHEAD".

Sudhir stops speaking to all of them, even when Shivani says that her mom has cooked meals he doesn't respond and he calls his parents and sister all the time instead of spending time with the baby. When the baby cries he shouts at Shivani even when she is in the shower, saying do you have any clue that you have a baby.

Rosy comes to visits the new baby and Sudhir insults Shivani infront of Rosy when she forgets to dress the baby in the clothes his mom sent as they are too big for the tiny baby. Sudhir doesn't understand it even when Shivani explains that its very cold outside so she dressed her in a baby suit.

Rosy laughs when Sudhir shouts at her, she just maintains her poise and keeps quiet. Shivani gets so angry on Rosy she just gives a angry look to her when Sudhir doesn't observe her and is busy with the baby. Rosy enjoys Shivani's vulnerability and while leaving home she says babies make marriage vulnerable.

Mr Girish observes his hostile behaviour for a week and decides to book his tickets back to India. He says to Shivani to take care and with tears in his eyes for the first time in his life he leaves to India, Sudhir drops him at the airport when Shivani request him to do one last favour as he didn't even pick them when they came.

Shivani rings Mrs Sunandha and tells her how hostile Sudhir became to her dad and he left as he was unable to tolerate his misbehaviour.

Mrs Sunandha instead of confronting Sudhir adds more fuel to the fire saying, may be he thinks all should leave his home as the baby has come and the purpose is served, these days Couples want to handle their babies alone. Bindu did it all alone, we went only after three months after her delivery.

His dad is also the same, for them wife doesn't matter only their parents and kids. Shivani thinks it's waste of talking to his mom, she is just enjoying what she has planned in her head ever before her parents came.

Sudhir informs his mom every tiny thing about the baby and takes only suggestions from her,

Mrs Sunandha says you need to name the baby, since the baby is born on Friday, they need to pick a name which has meaning of goddess Lakshmi – Shivani who picks the name – AMEYA – and Sudhir likes it too.

She informs the name later to her mom who keeps herself very isolated as she feels terrible with Sudhir's hostile behaviour. Shivani you being happy is more important not whether you informing me later than your in-laws doesn't make any difference to me. Just be happy, it's not good for your health to cry so much as a young mom.

And when she calls her dad she says we have named the baby– AMEYA. Mr Girish says it's a nice name, hope she brings luck in your life. And don't worry about anything just be happy.

Mrs Rajeshwari gets very scared as Shivani cries almost every night with Sudhir's hostile behaviour calling her a irresponsible mother to the new born baby when she couldn't feed properly as she is new and the midwife says its takes time.

He says you are only bothered about your parents why don't you stay with them leave me and my baby alone.

Shivani just says my dad already left, do you want my mom to leave too, why are you behaving so hostile what's their fault they bought somany gifts to me and the baby.

Sudhir suddenly says what 's the big deal and I lend money to your brother and didn't even tell my parents about it. Shivani says you lend money, and he is going to return it to you in a month, don't shout loud my parents don't even have a clue about it, had they any clue they wouldn't have let Sharath ask us.

Mrs Rajeshwari rings Sharath and scolds him, why didn't he tell them and ask Shivani to pay, Sharath says as my cousin Rama sissy has given some, I thought brother inlaw can lend me as dad would scold me so much to change the university so abruptly.

Mrs Rajeshwari rings Mr Girish and asks him to pay off all the money including intrest to Sudhir's parents. This guy is making Shivani's life miserable, he is not applying visa for Ameya.

I don't know why he is doing this and his mom gives all stupid reasons for hurting Shivani.

Mr Girish pays off all the amount and Mrs Sunandha gives her account number to pay the amount. He just tells Shivani to apply Indian Visa to Ameya, you need a break that guy Sudhir has no empathy and makes a young mom like you shed tears everyday.

Shivani says to Sudhir now all the amount is paid off, can we apply Indian visa to Ameya, my mom is getting sick and she is suffering with Low Blood Pressure ever since her visa was in trouble during my pregnancy. Sudhir doesn't speak a word, and he threatens her that now,

I will do as my mom and sister bindu says. Just see the game, you people are acting very smart.

The very next day bindu rings Shivani and says if your mom is sick why don't you send her to India alone, why do you want to travel to India, you don't know how expensive the tickets are.

You need to get into a job that's what Sudhir bro wants from you. He is a very stubborn person I'm warning you, just do as he says.

Don't trigger his anger, start applying jobs, now that the baby is already 1 month old, don't worry if your mom doesn't want to stay our parents will come, but we all want you to get a job as soon as possible.

Shivani's mom says to Shivani, just relax and improve her health, and she says until I have the visa permit I will stay with you, but you don't get tensed already you are having nervous breakdown with these tensions getting dizzy.

I will speak to your mother in -law about your health getting worse by the day. Shivani rings Mrs Sunandha and she behaves as though nothing happened and she says, we got the amount from your father it's the exact amount don't worry. When Mrs Rajeshwari speaks to her regarding Shivani's woes and her nervous breakdown becuause of Sudhir's hostile behaviour she says, Shivani needs to get a job, if you want to stay there with her. Otherwise I will come, Sudhir is asking me to apply annual leave and come to take care of Ameya while shivani goes to work. Mrs Rajeshwari gets the fact that these people wont leave my Shivani at peace until she gets a job

Rahul comes to Sydney on vacation to see AMEYA

Rahul who is a out spoken guy without scorn in his mind, comes to see Ameya and he wants to spend some time with the family as they are the only immediate family he has in Australia.

Shivani doesn't show any signs of sadness as Sudhir warns all the time, don't even tell anyone about what happens in the house otherwise you will repent later. Rahul behaves well with Mrs Rajeshwari and shivani unlike Sudhir who is so hostile both of them feels a bit refreshed. He stays for few days and leaves to Melbourne and thanks Shivani's mom for the tasty food he gets to relish after he came to Australia.

Shivani tries to apply for jobs, but her resume doesn't even gets selected. when Shivani goes to shopping with her Sudhir says you won't be able to get a job even in a grocery store, what the hell do you think of yourself, be glad that I married you against my parents choice even when you all didn't even register the plot on your name.

Shivani thinks to herself, Stones and bricks can break my bones but negative words can't hurt me.

After things get bottled up Shivani asks Sudhir why is his behaviour so hostile towards his parents, you and your mom thought my dad would violate your rules, so he left to India. Sudhir doesn't answer anything and just leaves the house without answering her and he calls her and says ring my mom then only I will come home.

Mrs Rajeshwari speaks to Mrs Sunandha and pleads her that Shivani needs a break. We are not saying that she can laze around at home, but her health is not good, she is getting dizzy all the time with constant daunts from Sudhir.

Please tell him to apply Indian visa to Ameya and then both of them can have a break.

I will take the responsibility of Ameya, shivani can study some computer courses and then she can come back and search a job.

Moreover we are thinking to celebrate "CRADLE CEREMONY" to Ameya, Shivani can read Mrs Sunandha's mind so she tells her mom to say this and infact that's what Mr Girish alos wants to do for his only girl child's offspring.

She says I will speak to him and why don't you confront him. Shivani says mom don't even do what she says, first she will create fire and then fuels it more and more.

Sharath who rings his mom also says the same, we are stuck without visa to the baby don't confront him as she says sissy has a logic point in it, we all know sissy has sharp insight.

I feel very sad for sissy, she is fallen in a trap.

But I know she is very brave, she might cry today, but when the right time and her threshold is broken she will be assertive to all. Shivani says mom if you want to ask him the reason behind his hostile behaviour you can do it later, first we need to get a Indian visa. And don't worry toomuch about my future life, Worrying doesn't help at all, Logical thinking makes the difference, don't be sad lets go to the park with Ameya.

When Sudhir is at home just go to the Park and refresh yourself. He is very rough and also tough too. To irritate Shivani and her mom Sudhir starts to smoke heavily. Shivani tells him, he is spoiling his health, but he doesn't listen to her and shows his hostility to them.

Shivani starts to read Sudhir's scorn in his mind and she thinks twice that only way to get things done from him is being very pleasing to him, being assertive to him is like hitting your head to a wall.

Sudhir agrees to his mom and even Shivani says it would be a change to you too,

"CRADLE CEREMONY" for our princess would be great. Sudhir and Shivani get birth certificate to Ameya and then both go to apply Passport and Indian Visa to AMEYA.

Shivani says to her mom to eat well and don't stress toomuch, if you get sick, I feel very bad as you came to help me and Sudhir and his folks has made you also as targets, where I used to think that since I'm almost 7 yrs younger than him, he has taken me for granted. His mom and sister bindu are playing mind games with me since our wedding.

Sudhir doesn't reveal any information about when he is booking tickets to Shivani and Ameya and he keeps Shivani perplexed. Shivani rings her dad and says that they have got the Indian Visa to Ameya for a time period of three years too.

Shivani's mom says only way to get out of this negative environment is to fly back to India with Shivani and the baby.

Shivani gets a clear understanding that Sudhir only listens to his mom, and she is taking negative advantage of it.

She rings Mrs Sunandha and says that My dad wants to Celebrate Ameya's CRADLE CEREMONY, can you ask Sudhir to finalise the dates of our travel. He wants to get the invitation cards printed and select a date too.

Sudhir's mom who is always greedy about money and loves power and control, says to Sudhir to send Shivani and Ameya along with Shivani's mom.

Sudhir buys lots of toys and clothes to Ameya, he loves Ameya so much.

However, he doesn't know the fact that he is showing no empathy and respect to Shivani's parents.

The day when Shivani and her mom were about to leave to India, While Shivani is in the shower,

Shivani's mom says to Sudhir, we have always treated you like an elder son, I never wanted my only girl child to be married off overseas too.

But, since her dad said your family is very familiar and will take good care, we have married you off to our saviour child Shivani, she is very precious to us.

If you have any concerns about our behaviour you should have spoken to us or atleast to Shivani, but showing this hostility is not good, We came here as it was our duty as parents to help our only child's delivery. we won't visit your place again and cause inconvienience to you ever again, but please don't hurt our daughter. I am telling the same as how we would have told my son Sharath if he had behaved the same.

She is a young mom and we all saw how weak she became, you have made her cry almost everyday. you have no clue as what impact this stress will be on her emotional health at this vulnerable stage. She is very weak and fragile, her haemoglobin count always goes down when she is in stress.

Don't take out your frustration on us over my child. Now that you are also a father of a girl child, hope you will understand how sensitive girls are.

Sudhir doesn't say a word, as usual, while leaving he says to Shivani all what your mom has said to me, the outcome you will bear from my parents in India. My parents and sister won't leave you at peace, had not I supported you they all would have made your life hell, you don't know about my mom and bindu.

Shivani doesn't say a word, she just maintains her poise, she gives all the statements related to Centre Link Payments and the Baby Bonus amount to Sudhir and requests him to weigh the luggage.

Sudhir takes them to the airport and since he bought many toys to Ameya, he will have to pay some extra amount, to that he shouts at Shivani in the airport infront of his friends who come to the airport. Shivani tries to unload all the other stuff which she can buy in India and gives it to Sudhir as he had to pay some extra amount, Sudhir says I told you don't even touch them again, why don't you leave Ameya also and pack all your things and go. They board the flight on the final call notice with much chaos, Shivani's mom sheds tears.

FOUL GAME OF BIGOTRY STARTS

Shivani and Rajeshwari bring baby Ameya to India. All family and relatives of Shivani come to the airport and even Sudhir's mom comes to the airport, everyone ask about Shivani's health but Sudhir's mom doesn't even ask even once and behaves as though nothing happened in Sydey.

She keeps saying to all her kith and kin, she is lucky we couldn't even get visa when bindu had her baby, only after three months after delivery we went to Dublin.

Shivani's dad brings Shivani and the baby to Warangal, Dr. Rama Krishna who attends a Conference in AIIMS, New Delhi comes to MrGirish come and to see offspring of Shivani. All the kith and kin say Ameya totally resembles Shivani yet is much fair than Shivani and Sudhir.

Shivani who doesn't hide anything from her maternal uncle, says how much hostile Sudhir became, and his mom was sugar coating his hostility saying I need to get a job asap and the land that was gifted to her needs to be registered too.

Dr. Rama Krishna says Shivani don't worry about the land, it is always yours but I took a loan on it and bought the scanning machine, you need not worry about it. Just that you cant sell it or start any construction in it.

Shivani says I know that you all will do anything for me, but these people are very hostile and aggressive behind closed doors, Im afraid of my future and even Ameya's future too.

Sudhir comes to India and doesn't bother to ring Shivani, when he came and he sends his mom to bring Shivani and Ameya. Mrs Sunandha comes to their home to bring them, and she asks Mrs Rajeshwari as what made

Sudhir to get so angry, we all opposed the marriage, yet he only was adamant to marry her. Shivani's mom says that Shivani is bothered about Sudhir's choice of some mexican friends who are uncultured and have very rough and tough minds. How would it be if they plan to move to US.

Mrs Sunandha who always likes chaos in shivani's life and is very jealous about her, says you all did'nt even register the land you promised and now say that my son's choice of Mexican friends is not good.

Shivani's mom says Shivani is suffering with a lot of inferiority complex, when Sudhir daunts her on everything. She has lost her smile and confidence that was innate in her and he is using all his controlling traits on her which is making Shivani very stressful. Mrs Sunandha says in full rage, with aggression, I told him to leave his wife, but he doesn't listen and he still hears all these comments.

Shivani's mom becomes speechless, hearing her conversation, then Shivani's maternal grandmother, intervenes and says how could you say that, he needs to leave and desert our only golden child, when she has given birth to a baby girl as pious as goddess of eternal power.

Sudhir rings his mom to bring Shivani and Ameya, Sudhir's mom doesn't even give Shivani a chance to speak to Sudhir.

When they reach home, Sudhir puts up a grumpy angry face and doesn't even smile at Shivani, she doesn't even have a clue as why he is so hostile to her ever since Ameya is born.

Sudhir's parents start the conversation, and all three of them bombard shivani with nasty comments saying she is good enough only to have babies and she doesn't know the periodic cycle of her biological clock, for which Shivani feels very sad and stops speaking to all of them, Sudhir in a rage says I don't want to have her anymore in my life, what is she thinking about herself commenting about my Mexican friends. Adding more fuel to the fire Mrs Sunandha reverts all that shivani's mom spoke about her saying your in-laws are saying you are having inferiorty complex, as Shivani's brother and kith and kin are in US.

Shivani says to Sudhir's mom why are you filling his ears with lies, he already showed me worst days of motherhood mothering a infant calling me irresponsible. Mr Sudhakar tells to Sudhir, her dad is a show off he won't even celebrate Ameya's **CRADLE CEREMONY.**

Why should you pay the bills of vaccination to Ameya, send the bills to her dad, he didn't even pay the dowry on time, where is the sign on the land, these people have no manners, they don't keep their word.

Mr Sudhakar makes Shivani's life miserable saying the baby is crying because shivani is not taking good care of her.

Sudhir's mom keeps threatening Shivani that if you don't support Sudhir even when he is hostile to you, he will look for an extra marital affair. Such a thing has already happened to his maternal uncle Mr Srinivas. Your dad doesn't know but this is the reality the other day a lady who came to see Ameya is none other than the other woman in Mr Srinivas life, she has no kids, yet she is his defacto life partner even when he has a good wife and blessed with two sons. So, this a red flag to you better do as Sudhir says, otherwise your marital bliss will be a Mirage.

Shivani asks Sudhir with her innocence will you see another woman if I take a break to go to my parents home. Sudhir doesn't say a word, and Shivani gets perplexed by his silence and she feels dizzy, looses her conscious until Sudhir sprinkles water on her. Sudhir's mom doesn't even react, she says hire a car and send her back to her parents home, we just need you and Ameya.

Sudhir says this is what is happenin g to her since her pregnancy and she is getting weaker by the day. He gets water and tells Shivani that she needs to eat properly, Shivani says I'm feeling tensed,

I feel something bad is going to happen to our "Marriage".

Sudhir's mom then says to Shivani that there is some Religious ritual needed to calm down the chaos after Ameya is born. I have arranged a holy Puja for Ameya, as her birth time and star created a havoc to you.

Shivani doesn't believe in such things, but she thinks doing a puja is good and the Fire God is the one who blesses all. No god creates havoc, no child brings havoc to her mom, yes the mom becomes vulnerable as abusers take her for granted to abuse.

Shivani's mom says don't argue with them Shivani just listen to what they say, you are vulnerable now as Ameya needs youall her life, she is just a 6 months old baby. Don't panick we are in India, your dad will talk to his parents and he is arranging money to make Cradle Ceremony of Ameya a big feast. Mr Girish makes all the arrangements and Sharath tells his parents, don't compromise on anything, I have arranged my own funds for my fees its sissy who is important to us and her baby.

Celebrate the ceremony with grandeur. After Sissy she is the first girl child in our family.

CRADLE CEREMONY TO AMEYA ---

The Cradle is decorated with balloons and flowers of different colours

The baby was dressed in beautiful outfits and decked with gold.

Little Ameya looks like a angel fallen from heaven with her beautiful baby charm and dimples whenever she smiles.

Mr Girish makes all efforts, to make this ceremony a grandeur event. He makes it a feast for eyes to all kith and kin in a rich hotel in Warangal.

Mrs Sunandha gives a long list of gifts to Shivani's mom to give it to her relatives and says it our traditon. Mrs Rajeshwari who always obliges with her arranges all.

Yet, Sudhir's mom who knows how to create a chaos rings to Sudhir and says nobody is there to welcome us and you are nicely enjoying with your baby and wife. She goes to a Wrong Venue place.

Sudhir whose behaviour is unpredicatble shouts at Mr Girish in the Venue Place, you didn't even welcome my parents.

Mr Girish and his friends become speechless and Mr Nageshwar who arranged their match says Sudhir he is doing everything for your baby's Cradle Ceremony.

He has bought even a waist belt of gold to your baby. Your Parents went to the Wrong Venue place, what can he do. You should support your father in law, this is the ceremony of your offspring and learn to respect elders.

Mrs Sunandha who reaches the venue listens to this and says to Sudhir I thought there are two hotels of the same name. She never admits her mistake, that's her attitude, I am a guy's mom I have all Power and Control. Girls are vulnerable when they are married and they become weak once they have kids.

Sudhir leaves after a few days to Sydney and he starts to behave very hostile to Shivani. You need to go to my parents home with the baby.

I don't care whether you find hard to manage or not whether you have fever, my mom faced more than this, you are lucky. I just want you to be there otherwise when you come back to SYDNEY I won't even come to the airport to pick you.

The very next day on 21st oct 2007, Bindu rings Shivani and says don't think of taking the baby with you with a hope to rebuild your marital bliss. Only your job and perks can create it, otherwise you will lose your marriage and baby too. You will now see as what Sudhir is in reality.

If you want Sudhir to be happy you need to work hard earn money and listen to all that he says.

Mrs Sunandha says to Shivani in sarcastic way if you take the baby and not to go to work, you will fall pregnant once again. What else are you fit for, except having babies.

Shivani's parents listen to these words and say to Shivani, go and prove yourself these people will not leave you at peace if you don't listen to them.

BIGOTRY MAKES HER MOTHERHOOD VUNLERABLE

Shivani rings Sudhir and says your mom is saying I'm fit only to have babies, and you are saying you want Ameya with you. Sudhir says to Shivani what my mom and sister are saying is right. You are only fit for having babies. Are you credibile to get a job, had it ben anyone in your place, with no land registered and also with no job in hands. They would have deserted you, be thankful to me and my family.

Shivani joins a Software Testing crash course and completes it in a period of 15 days, Mrs Sunandha says leave the baby stop feeding your milk now, what's a big deal if you have more than enough to feed her. Bindu couldn't feed her son, isn't he healthy. Babies don't need mother's milk when they are 6 months of their age. Shivani needs medicines to stop feeding Ameya.

Ameya cries a lot when Shivani stops her feed forcibly and she gets constipated too. Shivani on other hand gets affected by fever with the medicine too.

Shivani says to her parents, I need to stand on my feet otherwise, I don't even know whether Sudhir will ever stay with me or desert me and my baby. Mrs Sunandha first says, I am not coming to the airport, then Sudhir rings her and says mom is coming to get Ameya's passport. Don't forget to get Ameya's passport. Shivani gives the passport to Mrs Sunandha and says if you want, you can keep Ameya with you as I don't even have the right to keep her with me.

She sheds tears, but Mrs Sunandha doesn't bother at all. Mrs Sunandha says I'm doing as my son is saying, why are you blaming me, let your parents enjoy with Ameya.

Shivani thinks, Sudhir is going to kill me with silent treatment if I even say one word now.

She just leaves Ameya and Prays to god that she shouldn't get constipated with Formula.

Her parents and maternal uncle shed tears and say take care. She takes pain killers which her medico uncle gives her. He says Shivani I will try to settle the Land issue, but be safe and ring us anyday we are here for you anytime.

She couldn't go to Sudhir's parents home due to her fever. Sudhir doesn't come to pick her from the airport though he is at home. Shivani knows from his voice that it's a punishment, so she takes ataxi and reaches home.

Sudhir makes Shivani cook the very night she comes, even when she is with mild fever as she forcibly stopped feeding Ameya.

He stops talking to her and says, if you want a family life, get a job quickly otherwise I don't have any interest to have you here while your parents are enjoying with Ameya. And your maternal uncle didn't transfer the papers of the land on your name.

Shivani becomes speechless, she cries every nightand starts missing Ameya. She doesn't know what to do as Sudhir imposes a condition that she has to speak to her parents and brother only when he is at home.

She feels alone as Mrs Sunandha, bindu and Sudhir keep talking all odd about her parents and maternal uncle as though they cheated them, for not registering the land on her name.

Shivani shows Sudhir that she has learnt Software Testing and can apply jobs in that arena. Kiran helps Shivani to collect Sample Resumes from his friends and he creates her Resume.

Sudhir who holds a different face outside home to his friends, says Shivani is so focussed on her career that's why she left Ameya at her Parents.

He takes help of his friend Jay to Review her resume. Shivani uplodas her resume in all job websites, but finds no results in her job search.

WORK EXPERIENCE AT NORTH SYDNEY

Mrs Sunandha and Mr Sudhakar once they know from Sudhir, that she is credible to get a job, start their plans to Visit Sydney. They keep saying try hard, we want to come once you get a job as your perks would add more money to finance our expenses in Sydney. We are not like your dad who visits and spends money when daughter is not having a job.

Shivani, one fine morning on the day of Sharath bday rings him on 1st nov 2007 and says bro, I am getting very stressed, my resume is not getting selected anywhere. Sharath says don't worry many companies even want fresher too.

She says Sudhir is not even speaking to me properly like before, he is all the time on phone talking to his mom who is literally killing me with words.

Sharath says sissy, you got to overcome all these hurdles, you know that they are not going to change why are you expecting empathy from them. Don't stress yourself --- stress doesn't yield any result and take care of your health. Some companies advertise jobs directly without a consultancy too.

Shivani on the same day afternoon looks at a job advertisment on seek.com.au from a Start-upCompany, Software Development Agency at North Sydney @ PACIFIC HIGHWAY.

They want freshers and the selection process would be followed by a PYCHOMETRIC TEST.

Shivani fills the entry and answers to most of the questions, all of them are based on Analytical Thinking.

Shivani tells Sudhir the same, after filling the questionnaire. After two days Shivani gets a call from the CTO, Recruiter Angela.

We are looking for a junior Business analyst who is good at debugging and also with good analytical writing skills. You have been selected to attend the interview.

Shivani feels happy she tells her mom that may be the discord in her marital lifewill end, if she gets a job. Mrs Rajeswhari says offer your prayers to Goddess Shakti and go to the interview, she knows how to care of you and empower you. You just need work hard with dedication

Shivani has never been to North Sydney though she heard it's the beautiful place in Sydney with high cost of living. She saw the place in Indian Movies.

Sudhir knows every corner of New South Wales, he drops Shivani at Pacific Highway smiles at her almost after 7 months of his hostile behaviour and says "ALL THE BEST", give your best shot. It's for Ameya's future remember that.

Shivani gets dressed in a simple business shirt and she wears a business coat for the first time.

She fills confidence in her and says, to herself this job is very important to my marital bliss and my baby. I have to give my best shot and prove them I am credible to work for them.

She loves the ambience of the Office Suite and the view of Sydney CBD looks beautiful from all the windows.

Shivani will be interviewed by Recruiter Angela, Richard and Ratnam, they ask her questionsone at a time. Shivani answers with confidence and her innervoice keeps saying to her, God this job is very important to me. Last question they ask is What is the best way to convince a client. Shivani answers – Effective Communication and Negotiation.

They ask her fill a form to rate her Communicating, Thinking and Analyzing skills in a 1 to 10 scale.

Then they ask her some Technical questions too and ask her where she does she see herself in 5 years. Shivani says "I want to excel as a Senior Business Analyst".

I believe Competency, discipline and endeavour can make any employee grow and excel in their career. They offer her some snacks and tea and ask her to wait for 10 minutes in the Visitors room

After their meeting, Angela says to her, we have interviewed almost 200 applicants and you are now selected in the top 20.

We congratulate you on your achievement and the final round is scheduled to next week. We have your contact number in your Resume, we will ring you a day before the interview time is scheduled for you.

Shivani feels very happy, yet she follows all Interview tips given on Slide share. com and maintains her poise and leaves the place.

Shivani loves the place and she rings Sudhir, saying I'm selected for the next round and I am among 20 who applicants who were selected from 200. I want to shop for a while is it ok to you, the plaza is very interesting than in Ashfield and Burwood.

Sudhir says don't be on cloud nine, you didn't even get the job, catch the next train and go home to prepare for the next round. Shivani knows when Sudhir gets angry she can't convince him at all. His silent treatment will be horrible. Shivani takes the train and goes home.

She gets call from Angela and she asks to bring Shivani's Passport too to check her Eligibilty to work. Shivani takes her Passport to the interview and she attends the final round successfully.

Angela introduces the Board of Directors of the Company and the list of their Clients and Agencies. They ask her if she is available to take calls from the clients on weekends. Shivani obliges with all their requirements.

After a Meeting, Angela says we have come to a Conclusion to appoint you as our Junior Business Analyst and we have decided to pay you 40, 000 auz$.

Are you happy with payment, as it's an entry level job, we can't pay you more than this.

You have to be a quick learner and also understand the work culture quickly as you would be dealing with Clients from Fortune Five Hundred Companies too.

Shivani feels very happy and informs Sudhir after she comes out of the building. Sudhir says congrats and he says abruptly now we will invite my parents who can enjoy their trip to Sydney. They want you to come only when you get a job as you already know they don't even like you.

Shivani doesn't even get affected by his words, because she strongly believes that an arranged marriage takes place with approval of all family members.

Yet Shivani feels very anxious when she hears her in-laws are coming as she knows how hostile they are and how much they daunt her.

Mrs Sunandha says Sudhir has sent us papers and we have passport of Ameya. Mr Sudhakar asks Shivani how much is the pay when she says its 40k, he says in a sarcastic way, may be they don't feel you are fit for more pay, that's why they are paying you this less.

Shivani doesn't even understand how a dentist, five years older be compared to a fresher like her My arena of work and my branch of engineering don't even coincide with each other.

She rings Sharath and says bro you are just amazing your advise worked well, Now I'm employed as Junior Buisness Analyst @ Startup in North Sydney.

She rings Kiran too and he feels happy yet he says to her never ever allow Sudhir to raise his hand at you as Violence doesn't stop Shivani. But big challenge I am happy to have Ameya with me, but my in-laws are coming, you know how hostile they are. My father in-law always compares me to his Dental science daughter bindu. And my mil wants me as a slave nothing less and nothing more, she doesn't leave a single word left to intimidate me.

Sharath says sissy you know that they are all a team and brother inlaw Sudhir is not understanding your vulnerability.

You just do your duty, I know how hard it is for you, but we can't help it. Now you have a baby girl and you need Marriage as a social status and for Ameya too.

Shivani a day before Sudhir's parents come says that I know how easy it's going to be to you as you will take leave.

But, this is my new arena of work and even I'm a fresher in Sydney.

I need my space and need to update my skills to live up to the expectations of my Employer. Sudhir doesn't say a word and says to her, I'm going out for a while, I need my space too. Don't ring me or text me "Sorry messages" until I come home. Shivani yet with her innocence rings him and texts him she will never ever speak a word about his parents or sister to him. Yet, he doesn't respond at all. And comes home late in the midnight.

Next morning Shivani gets a call from bindu, Shivani thinks may be bindu rang to congratulate her for getting a job. But she daunts her saying that shivani doesn't like her parents visiting Sydney.

You have no clue, how much patience we are showing even when your folks didn't register the land officially on your name.

Better be on your feet and don't even bother about financial matters. Shivani doesn't speak a word, as she gets startled is it Sudhir's mom speaking or bindu, or they both are same. She cries a lot all night as nobody spoke to her and intimidated her so much.

Sudhir doesn't speak a word when Shivani is crying and says, better be on your feet. You don't know all these days how I saved you from them.

Shivani just says may be she is rich that's why she is so proud of it. Sudhir gets fumed up and walks out of the house. Shivani thinks what is this life??.

I feel like I'm living like a unwanted wife here in my own marital home. This Sudhir is showing his power, of course he is powerful.

Sudhir comes home after 2 hrs and says some of my friends are saying how come she gets a job which pays only 40k.

Shivani doesn't feel bad about what he says, because he is always daunting her on some or the other other point. It has become a habit to them. To demean her on some or the other issue.

INFANT AMEYA GETS TO WITNESS UGLY VIOLENCE

Sudhir's parents bring little Ameya forcibly from Shivani's parents, the baby cries a lot in the flight.

When she arrives at the airport, Ameya doesn't even come close to Mrs Sunandha and she says her first word "Ma" when shivani holds her. Shivani feels very happy and feels atleast she can be happy with Ameya close to her. Inspite of severe daunting from Sudhir's mom and his sister, Shivani cooks very well for her inlaws.

Shivani tries to impress them with all the recipies she know. Sudhir takes them to Canberra and to other places, too. Whereever they go, his parents crack silly jokes saying, Ameya came to her dad, now you go and stay with your dad.

Shivani finds those words intimidating, but still maintains her poise. Bindu calls them everyday and she keeps asking about Shivani's behaviour with them day to day. Shivani finds it very insulting, and she feels bindu is bullying her since she has a dental assistant job. Bindu tries to write the same exam, P.G Diploma in Trinity college of

Dublin, for ages and Mrs Sunandha says she is finding hard to study and manage the kid.

Shivani gets her appointment letter to join work on 2nd jan 2008. They don't even congratulate Shivani for getting a job, and start daunting about the land that is not registered on her name.

Shivani wakes up early, offers her prayers to god and prepares breakfast to all. Sudhir takes official leave to enjoy with Ameya and his parents.

Shivani just remembers what Sharath and her parents tell her, focus on your work, leave all their words into air.

By god's grace you got a job in the arena of Software, prove yourself, you can do it said Sharath. Shivani loves the ambience of the place and she is the youngest employee in the office. Everyone see her as a fresher. Angela likes Shivani's Sportive attitude and also her Intuition into the field of Advesrting. But, Angela says Shivani the outfits you are wearing don't suit Buisness Meetings. You need branded shirts and branded shoes. You need them on business meetings. We liase with big clients Shivani, this is Sydney not India.

There is a shop in Westfield called E-Sprit, you need some Business Shirts when we have our meetings with Clients.

Shivani comes home and tells Sudhir the same, Angela is saying I need branded Business Shirts, can we an buy @ E-Sprit. Sudhir's parents who always compare their life in India to their son's life ask Sudhir how much does the Shirts she is asking cost, Sudhir says it will be almost 80-120.

Mrs Sunandha screams on the top of the voice, you didn't even get your first pay check and now you are demanding so much.

I don't know why my son married you. Shivani gets fumed up and says to Sudhir, can't you balance your parents and me. I'm your wife and mother of Ameya.

Suddenly Sudhir's dad screams on the top of his voice, had I got a daughter like you I would have chopped her head off, and he raises his hand against Shivani to hit her. Shivani gets scared and says to Sudhir your parents made my life miserable and now this is what you are doing??

Shivani says those are just shirts, not gold or a party in five star hotel. My dad spent more than RS 5 Lakhs all together for the ceremony and also for the jewellery he bought for Ameya and me. I would have got 100 business shirts or more with that money.

Sudhir gives one tight slap on shivani's face and says don't utter a single word.

I'm going to beat you so much that you won't be able to go to work tomorrow. Shivani doesn't say a word and sleeps in her room. Sudhir comes after a while and says better be on your feet. Tell your Angela to buy those by herself, if she can't see you in these shirts.

Shivani says had this been your sister would you do the same. Sudhir gets fumed up and beats Shivani black and blue, she tries to defend herself, but he is like 20 kgs more than her and is 6 inches taller than her.

Shivani gets deeply wounded and she cries all night. The body pains intensify as she is just a new mom of 8 months old Ameya.

Shivani is a saviour child, her haemoglobin count goes low when in stress says the doctor during her preganancy, but he doesn't care after Ameya is born.

Sudhir's mom hears cries of Shivani in pain and knocks the door. Instead of confronting Sudhir she says, if anything happens to her we will be in trouble.

Shivani doesn't know what to do, she just thinks it's better I end my life, than I live with these people. God, I never saw anyone so violent than them. Sudhir's dad says you will kill my son one day, get out of his room, he sleeps next to Sudhir.

Mrs Sunandha says this girl has no manners, she is behaving like a teenager I want branded shirts. The baby is crying and she doesn't bother, Shivani finds unable to walk, she still manages to take Ameya and she holds her tight and cries.

Ameya stops crying and touches Shivani's wounds and looks at her. Mrs Sunandha grabs Amyea and says now don't make the baby like you. She is my grand daughter, go to India and leave both her and my son.

Shivani wakes up 4:00 in the morning and she has a warm bath to get relieved from the body pains. She spends more time in the bathroom as she finds that place safe from bullying an to cry in silence.

Sudhir wakes up at 7:30 am and says common get ready and go to work. Shivani says to him, I'm sick today with body pains and bruises.

I don't want to work too. They want confident and happy employees and dress according to business attire. These Corporate jobs are not for submissive women like me, who will be beaten on a drop of a hat. I will tell them I am unfit to work for them and resign the job.

Mrs Sunandha gets aggressive and says if you don't go to work, it's better we all move back to India. Sudhir will resign his job too and will open a grocery store.

I used to wake up early morning at 4 :00 am and catch a bus and go to work and teach the kids.

Look at you, you have all the luxuries, we didn't have half of what you have.

Shivani gets scared as she knows the stubborn nature of Sudhir, his behaviour is unpredictable. He will do as his parents say, he is making her a punching bag ever since Ameya is born. She just says I will go to work, I can't handle every day chaos in India.

Sudhir says I will drop you at the station, put a smile on your face. You are almost 7 years younger than me. you got to listen to what I say, why did you give back answers to me and my parents.

You know that your Mama has a loan on the land they gifted you, so only your work can add some perks to our life.

We don't even know whether he will give it to you or not. He is not your dad, and your dad is still in financial crisis.

Shivani says Sudhir I'm his only niece, he will not do injustice to me. And Sharath will soon get a placement, he is in his training period.

Whatever my dad has will be mine, we have lands in our native village too. Sudhir says Shivani you are ignorant and innocent, my parents and I are fighting for you, to get what you want from your family.

Shivani doesn't know that she is being abused as she is 25yrs old with a 8 months old infant baby girl, and she has to go to work. That's what her family tells her, you need to stand on your feet otherwise they will daunt you all your life.

We need to save for Ameya, you know the life style in Sydney only if both of us work then only we can live here. Moreover I bought a land in Hyderabad too. Don't make me angry again and loose your job, if they make out, you have a problem at home. They will think you are unfit for work and rest is in your hands.

Sudhir smiles at Shivani, but Shivani feels very scared as she has a meeting and even Angela is very senior to her and she is the CTO of the Company. What will she answer to Angela about the business shirts and the branded shoes. Yet, she says to herself,

I will give my best Presentation about the Ratings scale and the Evaluation. Rest my destiny will decide.

Shivani enters the board room, gives her presentation to the Client from Pfizer who views it online from America. Richard, Ratnam and Angela watch it. Richard gets impressed by the way Shivani has explained the ratings to the Client.

SHIVANI'S RAPPORT WITH HER CTO, ANGELA

Angela who is a very intuitive person, observes bruises on Shivani's hands, when Shivani gets into the Ladies room. She observes Shivani trying to cover them under her sleeves and cries as nobody ever has hurt her so much in her life to that extent and with worse verbal abuse.

She wipes her tears and cries in silence. Yet, she feels I can't quit this life, I have a baby girl and it's a divine duty to brave all this for her.

Angela asks Shivani during lunch break, if you don't mind can you tell me who did this to you??. Shivani doesn't say a word and when she insists she will keep it confidential, she says my husband beat me last night when I asked about the branded shirts @E-Spirit.

Angela says how can he do that to you? You are his wife and mother of his child. Shivani with her innocence says, he told me not to tell anyone in the office, otherwise I will loose my job.

Angela hugs shivani and says you are just 25 yrs old and innocent, and these people at your home are seeing you as a Corporate slave. Tell him that I told him he will loose his job, if you report this issue to the cops.

Shivani says, Cops I can't do it. He will divorce me, his mom says even if I utter a single word against them. Angela just tells her, shivani you are intelligent but have courage to be assertive to them. You have good analytical writing and your language skills are good.

Shivani tries to be assertive and Sudhir as usual beats her, she remains calm and doesn't even cry loud. He beats her in rage and then rubs balm on her when she cries in silence.

Shivani just tells Angela abusers should feel the shame, why should she report to cops when his parents are at home. I'm a die heart hindu woman and to me marriage is sacred. Let them abuse as much as they want. God is counting my tears and I'm angry on God why he is not changing my life ever since my baby is born.

My in-laws want me to report to cops, so that we start life like them from the scratch. My husband is also a scapegoat, but he is getting prejudiced now. All this is weaving from my sil in Dublin.

She is a dental assistant an her husband is less educated than her and he has some Visa consultancy. So, she is jealous of my husband's mechanical intellect. That is why they want me to suffer more.

Angela applauds shivani and says shivani truly your perspective about life is amazing. One day you will shine and show you that beyond this innocent child at heart there is a warrior princess.

Shivani gets her salary after one month of her endeavour. She feels happy and shares it with Sudhir, hey I got my first pay, Sudhir says don't be so excited it's peanuts that's all.

Shivani asks him can I use the pay to buy some nice clothes to Ameya. Sudhir says "your wish".

Angela becomes like a friend to Shivani, she shops with her, and they buy new clothes for the baby too.

Shivani shows Angela her childhood pics and even Ameya's pictures too. Angela becomes more of a mentor to her.

Angela takes Shivani to the most expensive Restaurant at North Sydney. They discuss about work during lunch. become good friends. Shivani gets inspired by Angela, her good technical skills.

After a week Angela leaves to London for a Company meeting. Shivani works under supervision of the CEO Ratnam.

He asks Shivani if she can provide the papers regarding her Permanent Visa application, as they need those papers as a part of their recruitment process.

Sudhir's mom starts complaining that Shivani has no concern for the baby and she is speaking to her parents in their absence when they go to the park.

Sudhir confronts Shivani why is she not going to park, and does she need any punishment for that too. Shivani gets scared and says why don't you all kill me at once, than torture me day to day.

Sudhir says now I wont sign the papers, lets see what you do, Shivani cries a lot, as its her right as his wife and mom of his child.

Sudhir's dad says, do as we say and then only you will get a approval for P.R. Shivani doesn't know what to do she just tells Sudhir, what you are doing to me is injustice, that you should know.

SHIVANI'S INLAWS CREATE COGNITIVE RIFT

I have hundreds of issues at work, I don't even know the basics of Business Analysis, I'm not a computer student. yet, my writing skills and presentation skills are keeping my job. Angela is out of Country, my CEO is examining my work.

Sudhir's parents say to Sudhir look how proud is?that she is working in a software company and you are just a Mechanical engineer, that's why she is not listening to you.

Look at the Mexican lady who came today Rosy she is milky fair and she is doing such hardwork and is so nice in her attitude. Shivani says did Rosy meet your parents when I'm at work??

Why didn't you tell me? Sudhir says what has that got to do with you not being good to my parents.

Shivani says, Sudhir your mom is praising a office and bathroom cleaner. Did you tell them what is her job??, Shivani gets angry and says your parents are just obsessed by fair complexion.

Like they got a fair bridegroom for your sister they want a milky fair bride for you. Death is easier than this life, my parents are stupid to make me suffer and listen to this crap. Shivani's mom says Sudhir we are leaving, book our tickets. Sudhir says I will also come with you.

Let her go to work and enjoy her freedom in Sydney. She has become a Corporate Woman, she is no more your wife. Sudhir's dad says when we reach India, we will call your dad reveal all that you did to us. Let us see how much he is going to scold you. You think you are too good than anyone.

Shivani faints and becomes unconscious, as stress makes her loose her conscious and abuse and stress make her more weak by the day. Sudhir starts to panick, he cries and says I don't know what to do? I never listened to my parents and this chaos is making me crazy.

Shivani wakes up after a while and she decides to see a doctor. Sudhir insists that he or his mom will come with him. Shivani says, no need then, I can't speak a word, if you are with me. I have to speak about my low blood pressure. The doctor should know about it.

I will ring my Dr. Mama and ask him what to do, Sudhir's mom says what's a big deal in stress, why do you need to ring them. Its normal stress, what's a big deal in it.

You just need a chance to speak to your people, and they are so cunning, they didn't even sign the papers of the land.

SUDHIR'S PARENTS TAKE AMEYA FROM HER FORCIBLY

Sudhir's parents plan a trip to Melbourne. They tell Shivani, your company is very small when compared to Sudhir's one, just take a leave. We want to visit Melbourne.

Shivani tells Sudhir that she can't take a leave, Angela is in London and there is some rift of difference in opinion among the directors.

Everybody in the office are working on a major issue, regarding a client. Taking off this time, is like red flag to your job. Sudhir's mom again intervenes, she is doing wantedly all this. Why can't she take a day off on Friday?.

Shivani says I can't take one, you speak to my CEO, I already told you he comes on Friday to the office. He is very different to Angela. Angela knows me well, but he doesn't even know.

He saw bruises on my hand and even asked me, why are you taking so much risk and working.

Some Indian men just don't like their wives taking up Corporate jobs, can't see you like this everyday.

You are the youngest in this firm, I'm advising you tell him to seek professional help for his anger issues. You didn't submit your PR application yet.

Sudhir says go to work and come in the afternoon, to the embassy. Shivani says ok, and she takes permission from office to apply PR at the embassy.

Sudhir comes there and he looks angry, Shivani just asks him did you all have lunch?

Suddenly Sudhir shouts at her, I am going to beat you with a shoe, what the hell do you think of yourself.

Go to your office, I'm not coming with you, do hell with your PR. Shivani doesn't know what to do, she asks if she can have an appointment with embassy next week.

She reaches Office and she behaves as though nothing happened. She tries to maintain her poise so that her CEO doesn't call her once again and ask how things are at home.

The very next day, Rahul comes to Sydney, Shivani doesn't say a word to Rahul, though he makes out that something is wrong. Shivani is not happy at all. Shivani leaves to work as usual and Rahul, Sudhir and his parents go around the city with Ameya.

Sudhir gets a call that his fathers' mom has passed away. Sudhir comes to Shivani and hugs her and cries a lot. Shivani doesn't know what do, one minute he says, get out of my life and other minute he becomes closer to her.

She consoles him, and says she went with her blessing on us, she likes you a lot. Don't be sad, just be glad she went without any illness. She was a nice woman.

Sudhir's mom becomes so angry when Shivani says I want Ameya with me, I have decided to keep her with me. I am going to resign my job.

Even Sudhir is so attached to her, he will not be happy if she is not there. Sudhir's mom says, you want to escape work, and enjoy life with my son.

I am taking her back, go to work. Don't create a scene infront of Rahul. Ameya cries a lot, that night. Shivani says

Sudhir if I need to have this job, I should have to leave to work early.

We have a board meeting today, I got a call from my Rebecca, CEO is in Sydney today. Sudhir says don't act smart, first arrange everything to my parents and then leave to work.

Sudhir doesn't tell Shivani, but he books a week trip to BANKOK to his parents and all of their passports are with the travel agent. So, Shivani takes Rahul and Sudhir's parents, to the airport. She calls Rebecca in the office and explains the situation.

Rebecca is the new secretary appointed to CEO Ratnam. She says, the meeting is at 10:30 am make sure you are on time. The client is coming online from PFIZER.

Shivani says, yes I will be on time, I wont miss the meeting. I need to prepare the minutes too. So, will be there soon.

Sudhir keeps ringing Shivani and he doesn't listen anything she says, Sudhir will I be able to reach office at 10:30 am. Sudhir doesn't say a word and disconnects the call.

Angela tells Shivani before she leaves to London, that if she wants to make a stand in the company, she has to negotiate effectively, as her presentation skills are good. And everybody in the office like that in her.

Sudhir cancels the ticket and brings a new ticket for his parents and Ameya. Ameya holds Shivani tight and cries "Ma". Shivani gets tears in her eyes as Ameya gets constipated and Sudhir's mom doesn't care about it. She bows to them, but Sudhir's mom shows hostility infront of Rahul.

Shivani thinks what's new about it, did she ever be nice to me?? Sudhir says now I will drop you, at the station next to to your office.

Shivani looks at the time it will be 10: 00 am. She knows that Pfizer is a very big client and if they get disappointed, she will be the first lay off in the company who are having lot of chaos in-between directors and their offsprings.

Shivani reaches the office, and gets the Company laptop and reaches the board room. Ratnam is standing there, shivani gets so scared to see him very serious. He says, we shouldn't have appointed a young mom as a B.A, they have thousands of issues and their last priority is their work. Rebecca stands there, and doesn't say a word, she just says all the best Shivani.

Shivani starts her monthly presentation, and the Client from Pfizer asks her why is the ratings going wrong in RO. Shivani gets so confused, she just has Ameya in her mind and says.

RO is working good may be you haven't checked well this time. Can you please check the tally count?

The client says, we are not impressed by the RO precision this week. We need a data record of all ratings by tomorrow. And also we want the Minutes prepared too.

SHIVANI MEETS SUSHMA -- SHE HELPS HER WHEN ANGELA IS AWAY

Shivani doesn't know what to do, as she has no knowledge of mind mapping, Angela used to manage everything. She used to make corrections. It will take more two weeks for Angela to come.

Ratnam is slicing her here and Sudhir is slicing her at home. Did you talk to your mama about the land?? this is what he says, God he married me or the land, whats that piece of land. It was my play area, how can my grandfather's dream for me, be betrayed by mama. These people have no empathy at all.

Sushma looks at Shivani wiping her tears and comes close to her. Hey Shivani, I know you we met at a common function and even in RPA you said to me take care – I was in the delivery room. You came with some Aussie woman. Shivani says Sushma, yes I do remember you, I came to your son's cradle ceremony by the way how old is he now?? Sushma says he is 1 an half years old.

How about you?? Shivani says my Ameya is 8 months old, and is not with me.

Why are you so sad then? Shivani says my mentor is away and there is big challenge ahead to me.

Sushma works at a Finacial firm and she is almost 3 years older than Shivani, she says hey chill, don't worry lets do it, don't be sad.

Shivani takes help of Sushma in designing the mind maps, as sushma is very good at logics.

Her mind is filled with tension about the land loan and also abuse at home. Shivani and Sushma meet every day at the food court. Shivani tells her about her problems with Sudhir and his behaviour.

Sushma says don't worry just come home with Sudhir sometime. Sudhir knows Sushma's husband and they invite them for dinner.

Sudhir and Shivani go to Sushma's place there they meet their lovely son -Nitya, Shivani finds him so cute, and she gets reminded of Ameya. After coming home, shivani says to Sudhir, it would have been good if I would have kept Ameya with me instead of this work and pressure. Ratnam is not Angela and he has started lay offs as the Company is making changes of their H.Q to Sandiego, Richard is going, she says.

Sudhir says Shivani you know me well, don't start all this all over again. I will get angry and you will again say pain, bruises and scars.

Shivani takes help of Sushma and uses her writing skills to make the presentations. Angela comes from London, and they have a exchange of words as Ratnam wants someone who is versatile and even good at Mind maps too in Shivani's place.

Angela tells him that yes the Company is a startup and he can do whatever he want to do. But, Shivani can write a good report, and her outspoken skills are giving Clients a clear understanding of their Performance Review and the RO. She takes time to derive a mind map, but she will get there soon. They get muddled up with various other issues too, regarding financial tie ups and the stake holders shares. Angela takes Shivani for lunch and says I have a bad experience with them, they are not even paying my travel expenses of the board meeting in London.

Shivani you got be very careful while CEO is in the city, he is after layoffs and new recruitment strategy. Shivani gets scared, if she gets a pink slip, will she ever get a job?? Her marital life will suffer a major blow.

Shivani says to Sudhir, I may loose my job, Ratnam is after my layoff, he wants a replacement.

He is using some new strategies in the company and stake holders are going away.

Sudhir doesn't say a word to comfort shivani, and on Ameya's bday Shivani's parents invite Sudhir's parents. Sudhir's mom rings Sudhir and complains, your inlaws have no manners, Shivani's dad went to a political meeting and he is not at home yet.

Sudhir says to Shivani who comes home tired from work, look what your folks are doing to my parents. what the hell does your dad think of himelf?. He didn't even register the land on your name. And your job is in risk, we don't have any money. Shivani says, when the loan is finished they will register and it is close to my home.

What's the big deal there, whether its registered or not as of now. They are celebrating Ameya's bday, your parents didn't put a penny into it. And what's the big deal, if my dad has gone out. Your parents find reasons to complain.

Sudhir gets fumed up and smacks Shivani, common now say a word against them, I swear on god I'm going to beath you to death. Will you take it if your sister's husband does the same to her. Anyways he is henpecked so you are giving me tough time right.

Bindu calls Sudhir and she hears shivani saying, I just don't get it how could you beat me so much on the drop of a hat and why did you marry me??

If your parents were against this marriage? I thought it was a arranged marriage with all their approval, I never saw you or your family ever before. Bindu keeps adding more fuel to the fire, saying bro, I think you need to decide about this girl. Give the phone to her, my husband wants to talk to her. You know how good he is at speaking, she says. Sudhir says do as my sister says otherwise I will dump you here.

Shivani speaks to Jagan, he says to her better listen to what I say.

Your parents have created a havoc in your marriage by not giving the land to you. If you want to fix it, better be away from them. Stop all communications with them, do you even know what your position would be in India, if sudhir deserts you.

Shivani doesn't know what to do, whether to choose family or work. She just thinks, I must give my best as they are very keen about my perks.

Shivani leaves to work with fear in her eyes, and there she finds that the company has given her pink slip as she is Victimized by abuse at home. That is the reason, Ratnam has given to the directors, saying it's a danger to her life at home and we can't risk our Start-up's reputation.

Angela hugs Shivani and with tears in her eyes too, she says any day anywhere in the world, you want a reference, then call me. I will give you reference. Here take this book, this is the life story of the CEO of Cover Girl, who build her life over nothing.

Shivani feels so bad, and she cries a lot, she doesn't know what to do, she calls her mom and says, my company has given me pink slip because of abuse. Can I come to India?? I am broken.

Mr Girish says, my reputation comes first to me than anything, once you come here that guy and his family will desert you. Try one more job, you have to try harder.

Shivani doesn't know what to do, she walks away with the book in her hand, first time in her life, she faced a failure as it was the job she got with first interview.

SHIVANI SUCCUMBS TO MEDICATION AS HER ANXIETY MAKES HER VERY VULNERABLE. — DEC 2012

Sudhir takes big advantage of Shivani's vulnerability when he knows Sushma is leaving. Sushma's mom who is a qualified English lecturer says, you don't need to brave all this for your family's reputation. Abuse has no excuse, and being a teacher, I am telling you, Life is not Survival. You even worked here; you need to address this issue very assertively to your parents. I just can't get it how can your husband's mom who is a social teacher is weaving such ugly violence while her daughter who is a dentist is enjoying life.

Sushma asks Shivani to keep her sons's favourite fish bowl with her. Sudhir stalks her even when he has less friendship ties with Sushma's husband. He intervenes when shivani says ok; you will not take good care of it. Shivani's resentment towards his coward violent attitude bursts out. She says yes "I can't take care of Ameya and even a fish too". He doesn't speak a word, when anyone is around. When nobody is there he targets Shivani behind closed doors.

Shivani doesn't feel bad all the time, when sushma leaves because her teachers always told her, you are so good that anybody can become your friend. She takes Ameya to the playground and she meets a sweet and kind woman from India. Her name is Harika, she has two daughters and she hears Shivani speaking to her parents with the old phone, when Ameya is very busy playing. She says, is there is any problem, I see you shedding tears, Shivani explains her situation. She also says, she is looking for a job, but since she resigned her previous one, she isn't able to get any.

Harika shows her empathy and says whenever you feel like you can't handle things at home. Do please come to my home. Don't feel bad about it, Ameya is so cute and one day things will fall in place.

Ameya joins Ballet and she finds a new friend Sofia whose mom is a Doctor. Shivani doesn't tell her anything straightway, they have play days and when she invites Shivani to her home in Haberfield. Shivani takes off her jacket. Dr. Krishna observes Shivani's bruises turned blue on her hands. She feels embarssed but as Krishna is a doctor she says don't feel guilt of being abused. You can tell me what is happening.

Shivani explains the situation, she also says what is the price of Social stigma and how stereotype her dad is. Ameya's childhood and her anxiety issues. Dr. Krishna says Shivani you don't need to keepthis volcano of anxiety issues in your head. It will become chronic, just see your doctor and she will give you medication for this.

Shivani explains how her in-laws weaved rumours, when she took medication for her Nervous Weakness. Shivani says I don't feel low when I am out with friends and even people with empathy. Only when Sudhir beats me, abuses me verbally and his family weaves violence. That's when I feel like ending my life. I am very sportive Krishna and I braved worse than this. Don't you think mindfulness would help me? I don't want to fall for medication. Krishna says try it I feel sad, you are almost 8 yrs younger than me and going through this.

Shivani tries to brave medication each day, but one day while she is in the shower, she observes that her mind got freeze. She knows this is a terrible condition of Anxiety. She comes out, when Sudhir has finished his dinner; she says I think my brain is damaged. I am feeling anxious and getting freeze sometimes. I know this is a terrible situation of Nervous Weakness. Sudhir gets sacred, when she says I don't care even if you don't show me Ameya or not. I feel like my head is spinning around. There is such a pain in my head, I can't explain in words. I hate you, your parents and if my dad comes in front of me I would say "YOU ARE A STEEREOTYPE, LIVE IN YOUR COMFORT ZONE".

Sudhir hugs Shivani and says, if you want you can speak to your doctor mama. Shivani says what he will say; he will start crying or ask me to see a NueroPhysician or a psychologist. Sudhir says sleep on my shoulder you will be ok, medication will have side effects.

Shivani says that you and your family and even my parents should know before putting me in such vulnerable shoes. Shivani tries to sleep, but she feels like she will lose her Cognition and will become In -cognitive. She doesn't feel like sleeping, she then throws up and feels restless. She wakes up and gets ready to see the doctor. Ameya has a bowel problem, she is in the bathroom. You please take care of her, I will go alone. Sudhir takes care of Ameya, when Shivani is off to shopping.

I need to see the doctor; Shivani goes to the doctor, when Ameya is with Sudhir. She first cries a lot and says I don't feel like living, I am getting freeze. I think I can't brave this anymore doctor. I told my husband to tell this wonderful news of their weaving violence outcome to his family.

Shivani says, I can fill any questionnaire. The doctor says shivani still I feel your Cognition is good. Isn't mindfulness helping you. Shivani says I am using Mindfulness but still I am getting freeze while cooking, bathing, and even sometimes ironing clothes. Suddenly any sound, I get scared, I feel like each day is a nightmare.

The doctor says Shivani, take this medication, Shivani reads the name, its Olanzapine (0.25 mg). Rather than medication, your husband should change his behaviour. Shivani says not only my husband, his family and even my family too. They abuse me and my parents watch it in silence. All my dad wants is just his name, which won't stay even a day if I give up in life.

She takes the medicine and comes home. Sudhir expects her to cook even in that condition too. He starts grumbing I don't know what is making you so restless to this tablets. Shivani says, I am not taking it as a fun. It's the outcome of your abuse from 2008. Shivani makes Vegrice and a curry. She asks him to give it to Ameya and she is off to sleep.

Sudhir says why you are giving so much trouble to yourself and to me and Ameya. You can't live without speaking to your parents, don't challenge your brain. I won't give any divorce to you. Just stay in Hyderabad and I will come once in 3 months. You are just on a wild goose chase. Shivani says; do whatever you want to, I am sleeping please let me sleep. Where does divorce apply to a dead person, do you think there is any life left in me.

When Shivani takes the dose next day, she throws up and she can't digest the next one. Shivani doesn't know what to do, why is the small dosage not going into her tummy. She finds an idea, she takes the tablet with juice. And feels good, the trembling of hands and legs stop. Sudhir starts grumbling, my mom at your age used to cook three meals and go to school. Anyways these anxiety and depression are for rich people like you and not for hardworking women. Do you want me to apply Disabilty care leave? Shivani doesn't say a word, if you have any human concern on me, please goes from this room. I braved this for almost 2 years with your violence and divorce threats and your family daunting me each day.

I was going to get struck by a vehicle on the road that is why I took the medication. The doctor will send a letter, to see a Therapist. Since Ameya has school holidays, no big deal about waking up early.

Mrs Sunandha rings Sudhir and he talks to her about Shivani's condition. She says if you sit idle at home and also don't be in good terms with sister-in-law, this is what happens. Sudhir asks Shivani to speak, she refuses to do so. MrsSunandha says I' m not lazy like she is, I have to go to school. Her dad and maternal uncle might have raised her with privileges, but I had no such things. Shivani doesn't say a word, she thinks now she is jealous of my Privileged childhood too.

She and her daughter bindu have wrecked my marital life and even Motherhood too. Vow she is simply outstanding with her irrational thoughts. Sudhir says now see what she is going to do to you and your fame. Good let her do, and shout loud that my son's wife is on ant suicidal because of the inhuman stressors we have given her. Sudhir makes her so vulnerable saying what if Ameya comes in touch with those medication.

Shivani says is Ameya not in danger zone in your home, where your dad who has Parkinson's takes almost 7 medicines a day and he leaves them everywhere. But, I have kept a separate box and even explained Ameya, that she should think that box as a Danger box. She can't even reach the height of the shelf, where I myself use a chair to get to the box.

After a week Sunitha rings Shivani and says what happened to you? Why didn't you come to my home in School Holidays. Shivani says I was sick, now I'm ok. Sunitha says my husband said that kids can have nice time at the Darling Harbour. Why don't you bring Ameya. Shivani says let me ask Sudhir. After he comes from work, shivani asks Sudhir if she can take Ameya with Hasitha. Sudhir says ok, she prepares his lunch and says we will be home by evening.

She says I'm not lazy, it's just 0.25mg and the only side effect would be weight gain. I'm always below my BMI, so maybe it will compensate. Shivani takes Ameya. Sudhir rings her and demeans her saying you are spoiling their family time. Shivani says I didn't intrude, she invited so I came, and it's for Ameya.

Shivani explains Sunitha how much he and his family have troubled her and how she was about to meet an accident. She says when will he change Shivani? I don't know shivani says, now I got used to this as social stigma would be worse. Sunitha comforts shivani about her medication when she says I'm not guilty of taking it, as I braved it for almost 2 years.

Sunitha says why can't he send you to India? His parents are heartless she adds. My mother-in- law says I'm lazy so he is abusing me and also I fell for Antisuicidal. I am angry with my parents, especially my Dad who can't negotiate with my in-laws. Sunitha says did you tell them. Shivani says no I didn't and I don't want to speak to them either. My parents silence is the real trigger for this Violence. Sudhir says I am spoiling your family time.

Sunitha says he is very suspicious that you might share your woes with me, so he is saying this. Don't worry you are not giving me any trouble.

Shivani says after a week I have appointment with Therapist, as I am on Suicide alert. Sunitha says think about Ameya, and don't succumb to it.

Shivani and sunitha share some good time and they return home. Shivani takes Ameya each day to the playground, she starts cleaning and cooking when Ameya is colouring. Ameya starts to draw as Shivani used to do when she was at her age. God don't make a Dejavou with Ameya, she should have a wonderful life in future. I saved her childhood with bruises and scars; you know what happened to me.

The doctor makes a schedule with a Therapist and she gives her referral. She is a CBT therapist. I have checked your Psychopathology Shivani you can't cause harm to anyone. It is zero. Don't worry about what your husband and his family say. Shivani says will the dosage decrease by doctor, because when my child has bowel problem I'm unable to attend her needs at night. The doctor says Shivani once you start the ttherapy, things will gradually change. Don't try to brave the medication, take the medicine very early then you will be alert. Don't think you are misfit, I know how much Cognition you have and how much will power you possess.

Shivani checks with Sudhir his roster and then arranges her therapy sessions. She explains the therapist what all happened ever since her marriage, and how vulnerable is her motherhood.

The therapist understands her fragile situation and says you say you are privileged in India. You don't need to stay in this violent situation, I'm quite sure once you are away from this danger zone, you won't need any medication.

Shivani says, I can't quit. I have hope, faith and also I can't see my marriage as a failure and go to India with these labels of bad mother. Giving a dysfunctional childhood to my child. She says look for Volunteer work to get back on your feet.

And do have a support system when you are in trouble. Spend time with friends and don't bottle up your feelings. Just don't forget to take your medication. This is a small dosage; it doesn't affect your cognition it will save your brain. You will come out of this very soon. OCD is not a severe anxiety disorder. It's inhuman stressors and your vulnerability that is making you prone to this.

RAHUL COMES TO VISIT SYDNEY WITH HIS WIFE--- April 2013

Shivani gains weight and Sudhir says look at yourself, you are looking like a Gunny bag. Shivani doesn't feel bad as she knows that the doctor said soon she will start to lose weight. After Ameya's bday a week later in the Easter holidays, Rahul plans to visit Sydney with his wife.

Sudhir tells Shivani to cook all needed for Rahul and his wife. Shivani tells Sudhir, don't make me a fool infront of the new girl. If you don't like me, it's ok. I have accepted this kind of hatred from you ever since Ameya is born. But don't intimidate me in front of them.

Sudhir slaps Shivani when she tries to tell him about his behaviour. She doesn't discuss the topic again and completes her chores for the day and goes to sleep. The very next day, she arranges everything for them to have dinner. Rahul likes Shivani's cooking and his wife says Sissy you can cook really well.

They plan to visit lot many places, and even when she is finding difficult with the medication and the hectic work, she does everything to make them feel home. Shivani finds no pleasure in anything with Sudhir making her feel very guilt of using medication. Look at his wife, she is his mom's selection and he is lucky to have her, she is working now as a dental assistant. Shivani thinks, I resigned my dream job at HCF because of your family and you weaving violence. Good, she is intelligent, beautiful and well-mannered. Shivani says I am happy for them. Did I beg you to marry me? You should have married your mom's choice. I just finished my graduation when I got married to you.

I am in a trap as my dad selected you and you made me a punching bag to your family too. His rude behaviour could be seen easily by Rahul and his wife. He doesn't even bother to offer her anything to eat unless Ameya reminds him sometimes. Shivani just thinks that these are the ethics and values his mom has given him. Abuse and silence a wife after she gives birth to a baby girl.

Shivani feels scared of water sports and her anxiety triggers with his intimidating behaviour. Sudhir says if you don't come, Ameya won't, and don't be a spoil sport. Shivani feels as though it's a challenge to her. Rahul and his wife don't even have a clue as what is she going through. She drowns in the water and she doesn't know to swim. She shouts for help, but Sudhir doesn't come after her. She gets pushed away by the water and she feels that may be God's call has come to escape her from this hell.

Suddenly a life Saviour jumps in and brings her out. She doesn't speak for few minutes and they ask Sudhir to take care of her. She swallowed a lot of water. Rahul's wife says sissy why are you so scared, nothing happened. She says, I'm scared of water from my childhood I don't enjoy water sports. You people carry on; I will wait for you here.

Her legs and hands start shivering, a lady who sits beside her says, what happened your hands are shivering? Shivani says I forgot to take my medication today for anxiety. She holds her hand and says don't worry, everything will be ok. She says that she is taking this pill to brave abuse.

I thought may be god wanted me to come out of that living hell as a water accident as I promised myself that I won't kill myself. She hugs her and says I feel very sorry for you, and you don't need to think about Suicide. Life is beautiful, if you can be assertive to abuse. I can't take break in life that's the problem

If I go to India even when I am sick, I get outcast and deserted by my husband and his family. I am just surviving this as violence is weaved by his sister and mother too.

Whenever she is in sheer need of empathy, she finds someone who can comfort her. She feels so good about Empathy in Aussie women. And also gets a clear idea that Morality and Empathy has no barriers.

Rahul says we need to make sure sis-in-law is happy. She looks very sad, let's plan a dinner at Indian Restaurant. Shivani doesn't ask Sudhir to take her anywhere. Rahul's wife observes Shivani crying in the washroom. She says Sissy I think you have a major issue; I have been observing Ameya's dad rude behaviour towards you. Why don't you tell your parents to fix this, if it's out of your control? Shivani says she is restricted to speak to her parents.

She comforts her when she says you people are there he is not beating. Otherwise he beats even if I be assertive to him and his family. It's silence, violence or threat of Divorce. I am braving all this for Ameya's functional childhood and it's almost 9 years of our wedding. And now he and his family are not sparing me even when I have succumbed to this abuse and label me as a bad mother.

His parents and sister support his abusive behaviour and even weave violence too. It's getting late Ameya needs me in the toilet, you go now. If not Sudhir will say I told you everything about him and his family's abusive behaviour.

Swetha comes to the dinner table and she behaves as though nothing happened. Shivani gives a good clean to Ameya changes her dress and packs everything. She maintains very good hygiene to Ameya, even when Sudhir says she is no good for her.

Next day Rahul and his wife leave to Melbourne. They just plan a three day visit. Shivani smiles at them while leaving and whatever moments Sudhir is happy, she just lives in those moments. Rahul and his wife say you must also visit Melbourne Ameya, tell dad to plan to Melbourne.

She attends few more sessions of CBT and her therapist says, you are doing much better than before. Shivani reveals that she worked as Quality Assurance Analyst in HCF. And she resigned the job because of Domestic Violence. The therapist Helen says, one in 4 four women in Auz suffer Domestic Violence, and some even lose their life.

The therapist says bring your husband once with you. Because he needs to understand that the stressors are the main reason of your anxiety.

You are a very Cognitive Person. Sometimes men don't value their wives and later repent when abuse takes a toll on their lives. He is really ignorant person to give trouble to an intelligent pious woman like you.

SHIVANI MEETS HER TEAM MATE SHEETAL AT ART WORKSHOP—MAY 2013

Shivani takes Ameya to a free Art Workshop organised by the Council at a Famous Library. They do have" Women Empowerment" Classes too for Young mothers. Shivani applies it online and she attends the classes.

Shivani finds Sheetal with her 6 year old son, who comes to the Workshop?

Shivani thinks she didn't change much over the years; rather than she has gained some weight. Shivani says if I'm not mistaken you worked as Senior Programmer Analyst at HCF. Sheetal says yes, I am still working there. Shivani says I worked for a short period as Quality Analyst I'm Shivani,

I worked in your team. Sheetal says Oh yes Shivani! Long-time I forgot you, you have a adorable baby girl right. Yes, now she is in her year1. She is in Big School now. I never thought you would return to Sydney. How is family life Shivani? She says it's not that bad, but took a toll on my health.

Sheetal says I don't know why you are dragging this Marriage so much? Shivani says for Functional Childhood of Ameya. I just can't break her childhood into bits and pieces. He is not abusive to Ameya, but treats me more like her Nanny less like his wife. Sheetal asks what happened to your health. Shivani says I am in the Spectrum of OCD and on Olanzapine 0.25 mg. Sheetal says Holy Goodness!! We worked at Nuero Project and you are now taking this medication. Shivani says I don't know I tried to brave this cycle of abuse, but finally succumbed to medication. I am taking CBT from a Family Counsellor. Sheetal says don't be guilt of taking medication, and therapy will build Confidence in you. Abuse should be at Guilt not innocents. I pity your husband's empathy.

Shivani, your husband has no empathy and his family are weavers of violence. Take my number we have bought a home close to CBD. Shivani takes her no, she shows her Ameya. Sheetal says vow she is grown into a beautiful girl and is just like you. Sheetal says to her son Ashish to give some toffees to Ameya. Ameya likes Ashish, she gives her painting to him. Sheetal says Ameya is "Creative" like you.

Just look for your happiness in Ameya. And I'm telling you again don't risk your life, just call the cops if he beats you. Tell his sister that their threats from Dublin have been recorded by a Q.A recorder and if you submit them to the concerned authorities. They will call her for debriefing.

Shivani feels embarrassed to become a victim as she can't sustain to witness it. Now, she is even experiencing it in a most ugly shape.

DR.RAMA KRISHNA SHEDS TEARS WHEN HE COMES TO SYDNEY – OCT 2013

Shivani attends the sessions and she reads in Wikipedia that Generic drugs don't cause so much of weight gain. She asks the doctor, if she can go for them. The doctor says you can ask the Pharmacist and they can advise you about it. Her peers start to notice some change in Shivani. She starts avoiding people who know Sudhir.

She starts the generic drugs, avoids bread as it has yeast in it and starts to do lot of walking. The CBT also brings some change in her as she attends regular sessions after the school holidays for Ameya. She drops Ameya at the Ballet Classes and walks to the therapist. Each she gets reminded of Mr Jagan and Bindu who provoked Sudhir to destroy her career and also her marital bliss.

Ameya likes dancing and Shivani takes even Sofia, daughter of Dr. Krishna to the classes. Both of them get to meet each other and Krishna gives a lot of comfort to Shivani. She says you are improving, better try hard with your job search. The swelling of your face has reduced too. Good you chose generic they are cost effective and also have less chemical composition.

Sudhir still takes on Shivani whenever she asks him to let her live with freedom, not Independence. Being together doesn't mean always you set some irrational rules. In which part of Hindu marriage is abuse allowed. Who says that once you are a mom you should endure abuse and be isolated from all? She tries to be assertive to him, but he used his power to smack her then walk out of home. Mrs Sunandha calls her, bombards her with abusive words, saying only if you keep quiet, he will come.

Shivani thinks Mrs Sunanadha is behind all this foul play because her bindu has a henpecked husband. She says to Sudhir that Sheetal at HCF says, what I am enduring is Human Resources Exploitation and not Hinduism. Sudhir says people at my firm also say you are lazy and a nagger. Shivani thinks it's of no use to speak to him when he is using his Chauvinism.

Bindu calls Sudhir and even speaks for long to Ameya. One day shivani says to Sudhir let Ameya finish her dinner and speak to bindu what's so urgent there. Bindu says your wife doesn't want me to speak to Ameya, fair enough this is what I get to hear, she has become a headache in the family. Sudhir says to Shivani now pick up the phone and call bindu and say sorry.

Shivani says whatever she has done I am enduring now with even medication. I don't feel like speaking to her, and even if I ring her she will not pick up because she is so egoistic. A dentist without empathy is what she is, am I doing the same to my younger brother's wife.

Sudhir slaps shivani hard and says now I want you to cook for me Chapathi, I am not going to eat rice. Shivani says it's already 9:30pm and Ameya is off to sleep. Sudhir says decision is yours, whether chapathi now or you want me to leave. Sudhir always threatens shivani to leave the house. Shivani sometimes feels that he should be taken first to a NeuroPsychiatrist. Something is wrong with him, not with her.

She makes the Chapathi and the curry; he eats and goes to sleep. She packs his lunch for the next day and keeps it in the fridge. He wakes up early and takes his lunch box. Sudhir doesn't like shivani to ask him when he is coming home, whenever she asks at what time you will finish your work. He says when my employer is not asking, why you are asking me. Shivani thinks it's all the fault of upbringing and inducing Chauvinism by weaving violence.

Shivani doesn't bother much about it and she starts to read Wikipedia and search to find a job. He calls her and says, there is one job at my firm, are you willing to apply. Shivani say ok, I will tailor my Resume, and send it to you. She thinks it's the best to do, but when she looks at the job profile it says 24/7 shifts. Shivani says to him, already you work in late night shifts. What will happen to Ameya, if I work on shifts? She will have tough time, and don't you think I can get any other work other than this. Sudhir says for the potential you have, this is the best you can get. Shivani applies for it and they call her.

They just ask her if she has any experience working in shifts. Shivani says "No "I don't have any experience, yet I think I can manage. Sudhir asks her "Did you answer them well; Shivani says they asked me if I worked in the night shift, and I said no. Sudhir says I know why you did this, because you don't want to work unless I allow you to speak to your parents. Shivani says, why do you bring this parents stuff each day. You are the one who speaks to your parents and sister each day, and they give you marvellous ideas to abuse me.

Sudhir says I am doing everything for Ameya. If both of us work, she will have everything she needs. Shivani gets fumed up and says I am braving anxiety and meeting all needs of you and Ameya. Each day I feel like ending my life and you are accusing me of not providing enough money for Ameya.

One day shivani forgets to bring her keys of the apartment; she cooks lunch and goes to the Mall. She buys groceries and returns home. When she looks in her bag, she finds her keys missing. She doesn't know what to do; she has to stay outside until Sudhir comes. She rings Sunitha if she is at home. Sunitha says, you can stay at my home until Sudhir returns from work. She says ok, I have even prepared lunch for him, so nothing to worry. On the way, he rings Sudhir and says that she forgot the keys and going to stay at Sunitha's home until he returns from work You can have your lunch too, as I prepared everything. Ring me when you are home.

Sunitha says you are much better Shivani, you can brave this. Shivani says the doctor has decreased my dosage, now it's only one tablet a day.

Sunitha says don't bother too much, you have always been thin, so you might be feeling bit different when you gained some extra pounds.

She says may be, but Sudhir is daunting me each day. I feel like going to India, but he will outcast me if I go there. He makes me walk on egg shells each day and his family is making my motherhood a living hell. Sunitha says don't worry too much, God will teach them good lessons. Shivani says hope so, I don't wish anything bad to them, but they are not allowing me to live at peace.

Ameya has no OCI and also she is not having Indian Visa too. Sunitha, says how can he do this to you, already they all troubled you so much in 2008. You are very courageous than you think you are, you will brave this and they will learn a lesson. She says don't worry toomuch and spoil your health, have lunch with me peacefully. Sunitha always has a warm heart to Shivani and says to eat something like a sister.

She says ring your parents, Shivani says its waste of time to talk to my Dad, he says come to India alone, I will send you to America. We have somany family members who can help you. Even my maternal grandpa who is a advocate at High court says if you can't bring Ameya with you come alone. They are not getting me right, I want a happy family not Success in life. And how can I leave "Ameya", she is my life. Had I chosen success, I wouldn't resign my job at HCF. They feared for my life and I gave up because of Domestic Violence.

She calls her mom and she says Shivani Dad did tell to his maternal uncle and he even shed tears at their home. Yet, he says that Sudhir's dad asked him to be out of this and humiliated him. So, he says he is helpless too. Your mother in-law is saying to all in her family that you don't have a job so the chaos is because of that. Don't ask Sudhir as things will turn worse.

Shivani's mom starts crying. Shivani says I am tired of crying mom, don't make me weak, crying doesn't bring a solution. Don't ask Sudhir that his mom is spreading rumours about you not having a job. Shivani says no mom I won't "I feel that Mr Srinivas is also supporting them." My mother-in-law is the toughest lady in the world who sans

Empathy and even sympathy antoo. Sunitha says "I will give her Moral Support".

Shivanii rings Sudhir if he is home, he says "I am". Shivani says sunitha he is sounding very rude, I think his suspicion will start, that I came to talk to you about my family issues. Sunitha says just be confident, he draws answers from you. You didn't do anything wrong, they are doing wrong by abusing and silencing you. This is very inhuman.

Shivani comes home and she observes that Sudhir hasn't eaten anything. Shivani says why you didn't eat lunch it's your favourite recipe. I am hungry I am eating "Do you want me to serve food to you"? Sudhir says nothing, shivani thinks now something is going in his mind. His mom and sis won't leave me alone until she sees me dead.

Shivani observes two days he doesn't eat at home. One day, she feels like telling Sunitha about his silent treatment. He comes home and sees shivani speaking to Sunitha, that he is not eating at home.

Shivani fears and says it's my cousin Usha, he comes and checks the phone no, he abuses her so much and says, I have work to do. You sit and complain on me and my family. Shivani texts him and rings him that she will never reveal anything to anyone. Sudhir says I don't believe you, you didn't learn a lesson when I sent you to India in 2008.

Your family has no values; they didn't teach you that you have to keep your problems inside the house. Shivani says I don't have access to speak to my parents. Sudhir says don't worry "You stay with them in India forever". Shivani cries a lot, and makes sure he eats at home. For the next consecutive 3 months he cooks on his own.

On Oct 20th, Dr. Rama Krishna comes to Sydney after their family Round trip to Australia. He rings Shivani to meet her. He says they have a Ferry Ride at night, but they have chosen to meet her than go to the ride. Shivani says to her aunt that Sudhir is not eating at home and is not speaking to her; life is like a hell to her.

Her aunt says Shivani we have given the land, jewellery your parents gave somcuch. We told them how you weak you became. Seriously I feel so bad my child; I have seen you as a Princess of our family. But, trust God one day Mrs Sunandha's game will be ripped by him.

Shivani's maternal aunt says, your mama spoke to Sudhir and he has said he will be at home, tomorrow. Sudhir, rings his mom to say that Dr. mama is in Sydney. She takes authority and tell him let them come and see what is his niece doing without a job.

Shivani says did you ask them for dinner. Sudhir says, he said he will come only for an hour. Shivani says "You can tell him my flaws". Sudhir says I am not a weak person to discuss my family issues with outsiders. Except my parents and sister, everybody is an outsider to me to discuss my family issues.

Shivani just gets some ice-cream, she feels so bad, he gave me life, and even a land worth a fortune to some middle class people. Yet, I can't even have freedom to invite him to dinner. His House His Rules, you break one, you will be beaten black and blue and then threaten with divorce.

Dr. Rama Krishna comes to their home by a taxi, and says to Sudhir the place is very close, he need not come to the hotel to pick them. He brings somany gifts to Shivani and Ameya. Shivani's cousins say Ameya is just like Sissy in her intellect and speech. Ameya says Dr. Grandpa look at my toys and this is my art.

Dr. Rama Krishna says to his wife isn't Ameya so creative like Shivani. Sudhir behaves very modest to them, but talks very less. Shivani feels I can't get this man, he likes to speak to his mom and sister for ages. He doesn't even speak to such a good doctor for a second. I don't know when he will come out his PARONIA. Shivani offers ice-cream to all and when she offers Sudhir, he says first he denys and Dr. Rama Krishna says why don't you eat it. He gives a angry look to Shivani and he eats it. Dr. Rama Krishna asks Ameya all about her school and her friends. All in shivani's family adore Ameya so much.

He always looks Shivani's reflection in Ameya. His wife says Ameya, you must study like your mom, she was very good at studies. Ameya says Mom doesn't work, shivani's youngest cousin, yes because she has to look after you. When you were in India she worked in HCF.

Sudhir doesn't say a word, ameya says she is so excited to see their hotel in CBD. She says thank you grandpa and granny for the gifts. Shivani's cousins adore ameya so much and say you have to eat a lot. Momma was a good food- lover. We used to have a lot of parties, his mom adds saying, now her life completely changed. She is no more that smiling doll, something always bothers her. Sudhir doesn't even give a thought to what she says about shivani. Because she is the only person in shivani's famly who is very assertive to Sudhir's parents. She always says to Dr. Rama Krishna, this guy is abusing our princess because his mom and sister can't digest her happiness.

Sudhir drops them at the hotel, and shivani shares her woes, she feels like she could stay one day with her maternal uncle and his family. He sheds tears when shivani cries in silence. Just go to counselling I don't know what this curse to you is. This guy is like a silent killer, he is eating you slice by slice. Shivani requests Sudhir can you please eat now atleast. Sudhir says if you ask me again, I will drop you here and you can catch a Taxi and come home.

The very next morning Shivani's maternal uncle and his family leave to India. After few days she tries to explain him how fragile she is, she gets burst out of her stress and says "GOD IS COUNTING MY TEARS OF DESPAIR", don't forget your sister also has a baby girl now. Whatever Ameya is witnessing seeing my vulnerability, God will revert it to your sister. He beats her so much, how dare you talk about my sister, and in pouring rain he pushes her out of the house.

She feels so intimidated, and goes to shopping at 7:00 pm. She feels like reporting to the Cops that he has pushed her out of home. But, he comes after her to the Mall with Ameya, and says lets us get some groceries. When she gets freeze and Ameya asks Sudhir what happened. He says Mom is in Coma, you know all brain is dead, that stage. Lazy people who don't maintain good terms with husband and family get cursed by God in this way.

Shivani doesn't even ask why he pushed, because she knows her tragic situation. And his mom always says whenever shivani says Sudhir is behaving so violent. Sunandha says report to cops, he will lose his job and you guys can live on me and my bindu's earnings. She is so proud of her teacher job and her daughter's earnings too.

BINDU AND SUDHIR PLAN MRS SUNANDHA'S RETIREMENT FUNCTION – DEC 2013

Shivani rings Mrs Sunandha and says, we don't have visa for Ameya, my P.R is about to expire. He is beating me and not eating food. What can we do?? She first acts like I don't know all this he is such a secretive person. I thought you guys are doing well. And don't tell him you called me. Shivani feels like asking, don't you have any freedom to speak to others and live with Respect. But she feels like she has get out of this hell. So, she says if you have sympathy on me and Empathy on Ameya, you will ask him to send to India when you are retiring.

Sudhir and bindu discuss about the gift they are going to give it Mrs Sunanadha. Sudhir says bindu want to talk to you about the gift. Shivani says, what do I know, I am not that good at selecting anything. Sudhir says, I will let you know by evening. Sudhir says now here is the deal, you will speak to bindu and then to my Vani aunty. Then I will allow you to speak to your parents and also to go to their home.

Mrs Sunandha though she plans everything according to her wish and will says "I am not having any celebration". When you guys are fighting with each other, but I want to advise you that it's not good to tell your family problems to anyone. Shivani says, then why does he beat me so much and doesn't allow me to speak to my parents. Already you lost your intelligence, what will you do except taking care of Ameya.

Mrs Sunandha says there are millions like you, who are enduring this what's the big deal, men have several issues,

wife should endure all their anger. For this time I will ask him to eat what you have cooked.

Shivani thinks, yes this is a power game and she knows all, even when I didn't say, anyways these people love Negative drama. Sudhir acts as though his mom is the only Anchor shivani has in the world. Her blood keeps boiling inside, but she doesn't speak a word. Common you abusers weave and act more drama, her inner voice says. Shivani looses all respect for Sudhir and his family. She feels that they are the worst people behind their good masks outside home.

Shivani applies her P.R renewal and Sudhir calls her and abuses her so much, if yours is finished is done right. Why would you bother about Ameya, even a step-mother doesn't behave so rude to her. Even a psychotic woman feeds her baby properly. Look at her she doesn't eat at all, you don't know you raise a child, he says I don't know what a curse you are to me and my family.

Shivani applies Ameya's visa and she gets in few days Visa to India. Then she renewals her visa too. Mrs Sunandha rings her and says bindu is coming, bring all of your jewellery. Shivani feels what a big deal has let this woman take all my jewellery and its control.

Now with this bruises and scars I am tired. Shivani gets very tanned as Olanzapine makes her skin very sensitive to Sun, even when she applies Sunscreen. Whenever Shivani goes to any party, Sindhu always asks Shivani, why are you wearing all old dresses, Shivani says it's been 3 years I have been to India. I didn't get any new ones. She doesn't speak to anyone, because her motive is to brave this anxiety and get back on her feet.

Sudhir asks Shivani to apply only 3 months Visit visa to Ameya as she has her school re-opened in February. Shivani collects all Ameyas' yearly reports and both attend the Parents and Teachers Meeting.

Ameya is doing good and she is very intuitive says her teacher. She doesn't eat her lunch, she always skips it.

Shivani says that is what my major concern is, she doesn't eat at home too. Sudhir doesn't say anything about it. Shivani on their way back to home says, you and your family say I have not raised Ameya up to the mark and don't give her food. Now the teacher says the same, only up to Year1, teachers monitor whether kids are eating their lunch. Sudhir says now don't start it again, and spoil my mood.

Sudhir invites his friends for dinner, Shivani cooks all items according to his list. Sunitha also comes to their home with her husband and family. She asks if she needs any help, shivani says no I can manage, please monitor whether Ameya is eating. Shivani and sunitha don't give a clue to other friends as what pain shivani is enduring with weaving Violence from Dublin and India.

Ameya's eating habits and also her bowel syndrome makes her tired always; she doesn't know how to tell her to drink more water. She tries all means, looks in the internet. Sometimes she even prepares Pizza at home. Sudhir doesn't like it, he makes a big deal out of everything. Shivani still tries to make Ameya love food she makes at home. She gives her flavoured drinks, by adding Oranges to her water.

Sudhir asks Shivani to book tickets for all three of them. He says he will come in January. Shivani does accordingly, she packs basic items and she feels good that she is going to India with Ameya. Sudhir finally gives permission to speak

to her parents and he says if my mom doesn't come to the airport, your dad can come and pick you and Ameya.

Shivani rings her Dad and says I don't have any good clothes to wear, Can you bring some cash to the airport, if I have to go with Sudhir's mom. Shivani's dad says it's ok, don't worry I will get you money. Shivani's mom says, I will bring dresses to you and even cash, if you don't like some of them, as you say you have gained weight.

SHIVANI COMES TO INDIA WITH AMEYA TO ATTEND MRS SUNANDHA'S RETIREMNET CEREMONY – 25TH DEC 2013

Shivani thinks that since it will be late in the night, Sudhir's mom won't come to pick her from the airport. But, to her ill fate she comes at late night and she has to wait for her for hours in the Airport. Mr Girish and his friend Rahman arrange a Welcome Note to Shivani and Ameya. As soon as she clears customs, Rahim and Girish come to her and help her with Ameya and her luggage. Looking at Shivani, her mom and paternal aunt shed tears, the way she has become so tanned and vulnerable.

She lands at the airport and Ameya starts crying that she has cramps in her stomach. Shivani's paternal aunt says, let's go to our home, it's closely. Suddenly Sunandha rings shivani's mom and says I am coming to pick them from the airport. They have to come to my home, bindu and jagan have come.

Shivani says Mom manage somehow I don't want to go with her and stay with that abusive bindu and jagan. Shivani

takes the clothes parcel and the money. Ameya doesn't go close to shivani's mom and dad though they have raised her. Shivani says to her dad let's go to our home.

Shivani's dad who is a Stereotype says "Wait she is coming", don't get into new trouble. I did speak to her brother Srinivas and he said this time, he will talk to the entire family as what have they achieved abusing you so much. Why is bindu and jagan again involving and weaving violence from Dublin. Mrs Sunandha comes to the car park and she starts grumbling at Girish and his wife. Saying where is shivani and ameya. Girish's sister says, shivani took ameya to the bathroom she was crying so much.

Mrs Sunandha rings Sudhir and says, your wife doesn't want to come to our house I guess her whole family is here to take her. Shivani's aunt says why are you jumping into conclusion, we didn't say we have come to take shivani and ameya. They are your family Sunandha says I'm dying with this shivani, she has no time management and doesn't know to manage ameya.

Shivani brings ameya from the bathroom, she gives a nice clean to her and gets her dressed in new clothes which shivani's mom has got for her. Mr Girish, says it's too late in the night. Let us all stay at my sister's home tonight since both of them are sick, they have jet lag.

Sudhir's mom says I will ask Sudhir what he says. She doesn't allow shivani to speak to him and says Sudhir is on rage, he is saying if she goes to Warangal, she need not come to Sydney. After a while, Mr Girish brings Ameya some fruit drink and gives her a teddy bear. Suddenly Ameya says Nana, shivani's aunty says ameya is just like our little shivani. When Shivani's mom makes her drink some juice,

she says Nani. Both of them hug Ameya and she says I want to come to your home. I don't want to go with her, she is so rude.

Shivani says I want to explain him, the stomach cramps shivani is having and my panic attacks too. She speaks to him, but he screams at her and says, my sister and her family have come to India. Just do as my mom says. Shivani's mom requests her that its 2:00am and both of them are sick, why don't you stay at your sisters' house close to the city?.

Sudhir's mom says ok, I will come with them, you guys carry on. In the middle of their journey, she says to the driver common divert the road. Shivani consoles Ameya who says "Mom this car is bad". We should not have come with her, she is very rude. Mrs Sunandha tries to touch Ameya, she shouts and screams, you are so rude. Nana and Nani are good they don't shout like you.

Sunandha gets fumed up and says if you shout once again, I will drop you and your mom on the road. Ameya starts crying, she says I want to go to Nana. Shivani whispers in her ears, that if she doesn't listen to what she says "We will be in trouble with dad". Ameya likes Sudhir but she is scared of him too. She knows that he smacks her sometimes with a comb too. And can stop talking to her for a day. So, being a innocent child she always gets perplexed as how to keep a big secret that her mom is abused and silenced.

They reach Sudhir's home town at 4:00 am and Ameya cries a lot with stomach cramps. Shivani says "Namasthe to Sudhir'dad who becomes with Parkinsons. She observes that he is losing his cognition by the day as Mrs Sunandha even confuses him too. But, Sudhir's dad doesn't support shivani even he knows she is getting abused and silenced. He is the one who raised his hand against her and gave licence to sudhir from Silence to Violence and the Cycle is taking a nasty turn by the day.

Shivani feels very tired and she throws up as she couldn't attend Ameya's bathroom needs each hour. Mrs Sunandha says, she is asking you and is not letting me in. Ameya shouts Granny is rude, I want to go to Nani. Mrs Sunandha threatens Ameya, if you shout more this is my home and your dad is my son. I will tell your dad to put you in a hostel. Ameya gets scared by the word hostel, because she can't sleep without Shivani by her side and also she is very dependent on her for everything. Shivani whispers, ameya let me tell you a story of a Princess. Ameya loves Shivani's creative stories.

But she asks her will we go to Nana, shivani says yes, we will ask Dad and go, now princess shouldn't scream in the toilet. When do good kids scream? "Ameya says I scream you Scream for an Ice-cream." Right answer, see then this is not the right place to scream. It is bad manners, to wake up everyone at this early hour by screaming in the toilet.

She weaves a story in her mind and she tells her a new one each day. Ameya says to Sunandha, my mom is so nice and kind. Why does Dad beat Mom? You are his parents why don't you say to stop beating mom. My teacher told me that beating is bad, we need to tell her if someone does that to her.

But, mom is not a kid, she even worked her cousin said, why does Dad beat Mom?. Sunandha gets very angry and says who is teaching you all this, is your mom. Ameya says no, Mom says Dad is good and we should understand that

he is tired from work. My teacher told us about abuse. I am now in a big school.

Mom says we shouldn't speak about Nana, Nani and Chinnu mama to dad. But, why should she speak to you all and Bindu aunty and uncle? Sunandha gives a angry look at shivani, she says to Ameya, let's go to sleep. Ameya, says I want you to sleep, she doesn't allow Sunandha to touch her. Sudhir's dad comes and tries to squeeze ameya's cheeks. She doesn't like it and Sunandha pushes him like a servant, keep away from my son's daughter. Shivani gets scared by the way Sunandha treats Sudhir's dad. Yet she can't forget the way he abused her so much. He is very selfish and shed crocodile tears.

Shivani and Ameya go to sleep and shivani wakes up at 8:00 am. Sudhir rings his mom and even when shivani wants to speak to him. She says, don't need to, are you so irresistible to speak to your husband. Shivani feels very embarrassed, she just wants Sudhir to send Ameya'slatest Eye Screening test reports. Shivani doesn't bring the box of her anxiety medication. Because she knows what Mrs Sunandha will do?

She keeps saying to Sudhir that Ameya is scared of Shivani. Why doesn't she have patience with the child? Shivani gets shocked; Sudhir says you know right these days she is on some stupid medicine. I keep telling her not to take it, she says I have to.

After a while Sudihr says give the phone to shivani, she speaks to him in a private room. She says I am not being rude to ameya, your mom was threatening her, how can she say such bitter lies. Sudhir says, don't ever dare to speak about my mom, whatever she does you have to accept it.

Now, see the real feast for you is when my sister and her husband come. Shivani says, I am used to it and braved it, I have been taught to be civilized not vandalized.

MRS SUNANDHA USES BIGOTRY TO CREATE AND WEAVE RUMOURS ON SHIVANI'S ANXIETY –

They have a party among Sudhir's relatives; she says to shivani that she bought a sari for her. Then again she says, I don't know where I lost it. Now let me check whether you have some good stuff. Shivani opens her suitcase, she brings all her old saris to give it to her mom or anyone and buy new ones.

Mrs Sunandha says you don't have any new stuff. All relatives there will ask so many questions. Shivani says I don't want to come. Ameya and I will stay at home as she is still having Jet lag. Ameya always has problem with her stomach cramps. She gets tired and sleeps in the evening. Mrs Sunandha puts party clothes to Ameya and she takes her to the party. Shivani gets so tensed as what if she wakes up and cries in the middle of their journey.

Sudhir rings shivani and says, my mom might be ashamed to introduce you to my relatives, that is why she took ameya with them. Anyways you say, you don't like family parties so good for you. Shivani says, I know how much you are enjoying by giving me such trouble and anxiety.

Yet, I am younger than you, so I do respect your age but not your callous attitude. This is not sense of humour. It is

killing hope of a Mother too who was once called NLC of HCF. Whenever Sudhir says something assertive, Sudhir says I don't want to hear your daily soap dialogues.

Shivani says I don't watch daily soaps. You and your family in collaboration with Jagan and his Paranoid family have made an NLC fail and God will prove it one day. Even J.K Rowling suffered a catastrophic Marriage, and was even clinically depressed. But when she healed and bounced back she became a "BILLONAIRE". And to me she is my inspiration.

Psychological disorder is not Psychotic, I worked in the Neuro-Science Project, and I know even the chemical composition of my medicine. No big deal even doctors have endured this and bounced back, I have seen many patients of my Dr. Mama gone through the worse and even healed.

His good deeds will be re-paid by God. I will heal and brave all this once nobody in my kith and kin will be ashamed of me. I braved and I am braving ugly violence for their reputation. Had this been a marriage of my choice, I wouldn't have been this patient with you and your family.

But I am not Clincally depressed. Dr. Helen told you that its inhuman stressors created and I couldn't fit into your archaic rules, where I am a free spirit person. Each day and moment I took this life as a challenge, yet I don't regret because I come from a School of Courage. I already braved half of the dosage.

Ameya doesn't wake up in the party too, as Ameya has no good sleep for about 2 days with jet lag and also with stomach cramps. Sunandha comes home, shivani makes some less spicy curry for Ameya to eat. The very next day

one of Sudhir's cousin rings to Sunandha and he says my wife lavanya wants to speak to shivani.

Shivani calls her sissy because she is quite older than and they hairom the same home town. She is also related to shivani even through her Paternal Family. Lavanya asks shivani if her fever is down., shivani says I had jet lag sissy not fever. Susheel wants to speak. Susheel calls her Sis-in –law though shivani is even younger than his own sister. Shivani with due respect says, I am younger than your sister Nischitha.

You can call me shivani, and please do consider me as one more sister too. Susheel says ok Shivani I have mentioned that way because Sudhir bro is elder to me. Anyways it's been ages we haven't met and even your parents too. Shivani says yes time flies and family obligations. Susheel says now that we are here settled in India for good, you have to come to visit us. Shivani says, yes with pleasure, when sudhir comes too.

The very next day Bindu and Jagan come with their family, shivani speaks to them very well as she knows that they fuel more violence. Mr Jagan says in a saracsatic way, you have made a fool of yourself by not being in goodt terms with us. Now, you are suffering with anxiety, this is what God does when you don't listen to Powerful people. Shivani feels like giving one tight slap on his face and call the cops to arrest him.

Shivani struggles a lot with Ameya's health and they enjoy their suffering. Bindu, says I am a doctor, I know how to fix your problem. Ameya in an assertive tone says you are a dentist not a doctor. My friend Sofia's mom is a doctor. She told me and mom what to do. You only check people's

teeth. Suddenly Jagan shouts on Shivani saying, Shut your Ameya's mouth. How dare she speak to bindu like that?

Ameya comes crying to shivani, she says to her "Momma they are rude", we will go to Nana. Bindu says hey Ameya, your jagan uncle was joking. Come and play with Sakhi. Ameya feels bad when they treat shivani bad. Mrs Sunandha sees shivani crying and instead of consoling her she says I will tell sudhir to keep you away from our family. You don't even need to go to Sydney too.

The next day shivani hears bindu and sunandha speaking to her cousin in U.S saying shivani lost her cognition. Shivani feels very bad about it, and she comes to sunandha and says why don't you all kill me at once, than to spread rumours about my cognition. Suddenly Jagan intervenes and says shivani we are all good, we are saying everything to your wellbeing.

What's a big deal if your dad is saying to Mr Srinivias that we are giving trouble to you and you are suffering each day? So bindu and her mom are revealing the reason behind the chaos. Shivani in an assertive tone says Prove that I'm incognitive and then weave rumours about my Cognition. So, pathetic you all are, I will ask Sudhir how far is it good to speak about a young mother this way. Sunandha says you want to create rift between bro and sister once again. I will not spare you thistime if you create any scene in my function. I am already having tough time with Sudhir's dad ailing health, because he thinks toomuch about Sudhir and his future.

Rjeshwari calls Sunandha and wishes her on her retirement. Then only she invites them, she is such a controlling woman who doesn't want shivani to heal and be

happy. She just wants her bindu to shine. Shivani's mom says Shivani did put on some weight, I was just thinking what dress have you purchased for her. Sunandha says bindu and shivani will wear sari. Shivani has plenty here, with her it's a small get-together we don't need to be a show off. Rajeshwari who always wants the best to shivani and sharth's wife still purchases some new dresses for Shivani.

Sunandha brings icecreams and toffies to ameya to attract her towards her, so that she has control over shivani and sudhir. Shivani always warns her not to give ameya somany junk foods. Yet, she says you are jealous of ameya, Shivani says me and jealous of ameya. I had a wonderful childhood very privileged than Ameya. My dad and his family is not abusive like you all are.

Ameya slowly gets attracted to Sunandha and bindu as one gives ice creams and the other gives video games to play. Mrs Sunandha on purpose asks Shivani to serve food to Jagan. Shivani feels so bad, when he shows his weird looks on her. Shivani starts to suspect Jagan's behaviour as he speaks of vulgarism on T.V so open to everyone. His questions always involve sharath and his properties and then Dr. Rama Krishna and his super speciality hospital. Shivani tries to avoid his presence and takes ameya out for shopping.

When she goes to out, she calls Rajeshwari and says I want to come out of this hell. Do take me to home after this silly function. This woman is celebrating as though she has won President's award. Mom I don't want to stay here, that Jagan's attitude is very vulgar. Rajeshwari says, don't panick shivani you just need to spend few days with them, just do meditation when you feel stress.

Sunandha says you didn't bring the parcel your mom gave. Shivani's dresses are in the parcel, she feels that what sunandha is saying is wrong. She might have hidden them as she hates me wearing new dresses and wants to see me in her shoes. She said she bought some new saris to both bindu and her. But, she then says she lost them.

On the day of her retirement Sunandha asks shivani to wear a sari and she gives a new dress to bindu. Shivani feels I will not complain now let my parents see what mind games she has played and my dad hates to see me in old clothes. This attitude of theirs will trigger my dad's anger and will be good to him and his stereotype attitude.

Ameya says mom you look old and bindu aunty looks good. Sunandha says, your dad is unlucky to have a ugly woman as his wife. Ameya says mom looks beautiful in her marriage picture. Dad says mom was beautiful, that is why he married her. My teacher says we shouldn't say to anyone they are not beautiful.

Krishna aunty who is a doctor said to me that mom is sick as dad beats mom, so she lost her charm. Jagan says you are very beautiful Ameya, I love your eyes, come and sit beside me. Ameya says you yelled at my mom I will not speak to you. I will complain to my dad about you when we go to Nana. My Nana is very nice and he bought so many dresses to me and mom. This is my special teddy from U.S my sharath mama sent me and I keep it with me always, Nana gave me this in the airport.

Shivani will be forced to say good words about Mrs Sunandha, she just says, she is a good teacher. Shivani feels like she is walking on thorns and doesn't want to stay at their place. She often feels that its not her real brave and assertive

behaviour. She feels like she is enslaved in Marriage. She writes in her book all her feelings which are bottled up deep inside her heart.

I can't imagine what my life is bringing day to day walking on these thorns each single day.

Is there any ray of hope in this swamp of despair and family violence each day?

I was born as a saviour child and raised as a princess with all privileges given by a famous doctor and an Entrepreneur.

I think my dad made a bad deal one business day with an engineer and I became the target of Money, Power and Control grilled each day?

God I know you are seeing this negative drama each day aren't you bored to see my tears, bruises and scars every day.

Your saviour child who is a young mom is getting diced and sliced, by abuse every single day.

Show me the way and take me to the healing land I know that you are not offline today.

Shivani's dad says to Sunandha that he wants Ameya and Shivani to come to their home. He says it's been three years they have come and we want them to come with us. Sunandha asks Shivani and Ameya packs all her stuff to leave to their home.

Shivani says, I don't know mom, again Sudhir will start his silence and violence if I don't tell him. Sunandha takes shivani to another side of the hall and threatens her that you can't leave bindu came to spend time with you. You know temperament of Sudhir and rest is in your hands. Shivani says to her dad she will come after two days. Just send the car you don't need to cancel your business trips because of me.

Shivani's dad always shows empathy to Sudhir's dad and when he is about to stumble down he says Shivani hold your father-in-law. Shivani looks at her dad and says, these people are spilling venom in my life and I have to be a devoted daughter-in-law. I wish my dad has some intuitive outlook like all his cousins have. Shivani holds him, suddenly Sunandha screams at her when shivani's mom is watching. Shivani just leaves the palce and says to Sunandha I am not your servant.

Shivani says see this is what I get to take care of him as a devoted wife of Sudhir. Dad is gone too dramatic after few words of sugar coated venom. He forgets my pain and believes all people are so honest and gentle like him. I feel like locking dad in one room and teach him what gullibility looks like in real world. Bindu comes and says mom is tired that is why shouted at shivani. Shivani says I got used to this cold attitude didn't your husband shout at me and Ameya. All her relatives think shivani is in trouble. Because, they know how aggressive and manipulative both bindu and sunandha are.

SHIVANI REVEALS HER PAIN, SUFFERING TO HER KITH AND KIN—jan2014

Shivani's parents invite sudhir to come to attend a holy rtual for their marital bliss and for Ameya's health at a temple. Sudhir controls shivani's every move and all her kith and kin observe how much he is using his "Power and Control". When her family asks him to stay for a night with

his family, Mrs sunandha plays her mind game and asks him not to stay for the night.

He does the same as his mom; he says we are going to meet Dr. Rama Krishna and then once they start off, he tells the driver to divert the route to his home town. Shivani gets reminded of sudhir's mom impromptu manipulation. She gets a clear idea, that he is so tough like his mom and this is her feedback.

After few days MrGirish comes to take Shivani and Ameya for a new land registration. Sunandha and bindu play mind games with shivani's stuff. They refuse to give Ameya's Eye test reports. Dr. Rama Krishna asks shivani to get Ameya's eye test reports. Sudhir goes to Hyderabad and shivani comes to Warangal. All of her kith and kin gather and they shed tears to see their lovely princess all worn out with abuse

She reveals to her family how they have abused and silenced her and says that her label is "Incognitive Mother". Dr. Rama Krishna hugs shivani and he cries tears of blood. I raised you with my hands; these people are after your life.

Shivani doesn't cry as much as her family does, she says Mama when violence takes an ugly shape, God will intervene. You have given me the best and now you people are adding one more property to my inheritance. But, they are playing a very dangerous game with your high profile status they have abused and silenced your princess.

I am going to sign and give this letter to you, if anything happens to me, all my belongings and also these properties will be given to Ameya only when she is 18 years old. Since they have a abusive record in NSW medicare, they will not have Ameya with them. I am not a fool dad, I have recorded

even bindu and jagan fuelling violence. Simple if ameya has to suffer so does bindu and her family too.

Everybody in her maternal and paternal family says Princess you don't need to stay with that guy who is a mooma's boy of a Manipulative Parents and very conniving Sister and brother-in-law. Shivani says to her dad that jagan's attitude is very vulgar.

He has very bad eyes on us and some mantras he keeps chanting when we are around. He yelled at ameya and me too. Her grand ma and her mama cry so much.

Mr Girish says that Sudhir's maternal uncle is not aware of everything, shivani says dad you are so ignorant. They all are a team and I was a good catch that Mr Srinivas cant utter a single word before my inalws and sudhir. And his favourite is bindu and jagan. They all say that Marriage is just a label, you are abused and enslaved.

You don't need to stay with this guy and family shivani. We won't force you anymore we know how much you have sacrificed for Ameya and our reputation. Shivani says "Dad I don't believe you". Within days you will be stringed by social stigma and start chaos at home. You only said even if I were to die, it's at my marital home. Now, I am doing the same, I don't believe you. Now if I back off, they will bombard all of you that they are so good people to let an in cognitive woman as their family member. You don't know this game I understood it, but one day I will break it too.

I can see that my father-in-law is getting for all that he has done to me. Shivani's paternal aunties say we are afraid that you might end up like him. Shivani says, no aunty don't ever think that way, he is very scornful and paranoid that is why he is the stage of delusion and slowly he will get

into psychosis too. My mom-in-law plays mind games with him too. Yet, I don't empathize with him as he is one with crocodile heart and tears.

Shivani says I am suffering like" Mother India "during the regime of British Colonization. Same archaic procedures are being used against me. I just pity them now, I don't even hate them. I know that one day God will show me the way and heal me. I saw miracles happen to me and ameya.

I was in deep sleep and the wind blew so strong the balcony door smashed, I was sleeping on the couch, after taking my medicine. Ameya was at school and Sudhir at work. The door slashed down and broke into pieces, yet nothing happened to me, even there were glass piece on the floor underneath the couch I was sleeping.

Ameya hurt her head, stitches on her head and nothing happened to her skull too. I was drowned in water, and swallowed a lot, thought I will end my life. Yet the life saviour came and saved me. I saw that god was sending his messengers to save me when I was about to meet death. One in four women experience Domestic Violence in Australia and some even die too.

I can put him behind the bars and do you why I didn't do it, because his mom wants him to be her slave in her retirement days. She says, he doesn't need any work to do there and if I complain to the cops, he will lose his job. Such a pathetic idiotic approach his parents have towards him. She says ring the cops and you guys can come over and live on my money or my daughter's money. His family's intentions are worse than him mama. He is a scapegoat; I have read al lot about this kind of phenomenon. He cries after he beats me and then again does the same.

Shivani's mama takes her to the Nuero Physician, Dr. Samuel, says except inhuman stressors our princess cognition is perfect. I am unable to believe how she can be so brave and courageous even when they are abusing her beyond human threshold. I can bet you buddy she doesn't need any medication, if she heals her emotional and physical wounds and stays here with us.

He says that fellow her husband needs Counselling, he doesn't know that he is abusing another Xerox brain, phantom intellect of Dr. Rama Krishna. Dr. Ram Krishna says shivani doesn't want to give up, she doesn't want the taboo of social stigma on her.

She would have been a doctor like you, look at her intuition and her knowledge about her medication. She is even telling you that she changed from dosage to dosage with CBT and also telling you that she is using generic brand, because of low chemical composition. She knows each bit of her medication and she has read a lot about CBT and about anxiety disorders.

I will tell you, that her intellect is far more than they ever imagine and her courage is far more than we can ever expect and anticipate. She is a rare combo of beauty, brains and courage. I respect you shivani for great sacrifice you have made for ameya and to your family's reputation. you have such commitment to marriage and he is behaving inhuman to you. This guy is the most unlucky one to abuse a Beautiful Princess with high intellect and warrior Courage.

The problem with her suicidal thoughts is because of inhuman stressors and weaving violence. These people should be behind the bars, because this guy has hurt shivani's head, there are injuries on her skull too.

Dr. Rama Krishna cries a lot, and says because of some stupid drama in that Jagan family, he hurt her onto the washing machine.

Shivani tells uncle he hurt me on my head several times. Yes princess your skull has injuries, but hypothalamus is perfect. Keep this report with you and don't ever show it to them. When we need to punish them, they will not have a word to say about your cognition. It was my mistake by not being assertive to that family in 2008. My princess is being abused and beaten black and blue.

Shivani says something is very fishy about this mantras and rings. I need to get a clear understanding exactly what are their cruel intentions. Shivani says to her grandma "I want to know what my Star sign is". My in-laws blame my zodiac sign for chaos. There is something going on very bad at Mr Jagan's home on us. I don't say it's Occult worship, yet I can say Evil Eye black magic.

I know mama that you won't believe in this stuff, but there is negative energy and negative vibes used in that home in Ongole. She Visits the temple and tells him what has happened to her ever since Ameya is born She shows him the stone anywhere in the bin. These people know that you are beyond perfection.

She askshim is my Zodaic sign a havoc to marital bliss? The priest says shivani what is the meaning of your name—SHIVANI (GODESS OF ETERNAL POWER) – DURGA DEVI. Yes Shivani I can bet on my life and say your star is similar to the Warrior Princess of the Kakatiya Dynasty, RUDRAMA DEVI – SAME STARS SAME INTELLECT, SAME COURAGE, SAME MORALS. SAME PREVILEGES.

You will heal one day in such a way that the WORLD WILL KNOW WHO YOU ARE. I know your birth history you are a saviour child born with blessings of this SHAKTHI GODESS. You are very charming. You are a beauty with brains and courage. Your husband will one day repent so much for his flaws that he will fall on your feet.

From that day onwards, their downfall starts and your Credibility begins. He says you are blessed by the Eternal Power of Shakthi, the goddess has saved you and she will save you, you have a long life Shivani.

You are born to rewrite and to heal mental disorders in women suffered by adversity. Don't cry anymore, walk with confidence and remember to recite "DURGA CHALISA". And be careful with your honesty. Just play Gulliblity with gullible people. Your credibility will make your abusers shiver with your eternal power.

Your faith in Hanuman will save and is a sacred saviour to you. When your intuition says that you are in danger immediately escape and seek help. You also have to brave very tough situations ahead. But nothng will happen to you once you escape and brave tough situations.

You will not look back in life, you will be transformed into a Beautiful Warrior Princess. You braved suffering, and injustice that could easily kill 8 women in a row. You will never ever Commit Suicide, because I know that the Goddess will save you. She will repay all your tears and triple your credibility. I don't advertise myself as a Astrologer, This temple is from Centuries, women like you have battles in their life. Your beautiful life starts from 2016. Being good and braving hurdles will pay you good.

CHAPATER 5

SHIVANI SUCCUMBS TO MEDICATION AS HER ANXIETY MAKES HER VERY VULNERABLE.--- DEC 2012

Sudhir takes big advantage of Shivani's vulnerability when he knows Sushma is leaving. Sushma's mom who is a qualified English lecturer says, you don't need to brave all this for your family's reputation. Abuse has no excuse, and being a teacher, I am telling you, Life is not Survival. You even worked here; you need to address this issue very assertively to your parents. I just can't get it how can your husband's mom who is a social teacher is weaving such ugly violence while her daughter who is a dentist is enjoying life.

Sushma asks Shivani to keep her sons's favourite fish bowl with her. Sudhir stalks her even when he has less friendship ties with Sushma's husband. He intervenes when shivani says ok; you will not take good care of it. Shivani's resentment towards his coward violent attitude bursts out. She says yes "I can't take care of Ameya and even a fish too". He doesn't speak a word, when anyone is around. When nobody is there he targets Shivani behind closed doors.

Shivani doesn't feel bad all the time, when sushma leaves because her teachers always told her, you are so good that anybody can become your friend. She takes Ameya to the playground and she meets a sweet and kind woman from India. Her name is Harika, she has two daughters and she hears Shivani speaking to her parents with the old phone, when Ameya is very busy playing. She says, is there is any problem, I see you shedding tears, Shivani explains her situation. She also says, she is looking for a job, but since she resigned her previous one, she isn't able to get any.

Harika shows her empathy and says whenever you feel like you can't handle things at home. Do please come to my home. Don't feel bad about it, Ameya is so cute and one day things will fall in place.

Ameya joins Ballet and she finds a new friend Sofia whose mom is a Doctor. Shivani doesn't tell her anything straightway, they have play days and when she invites Shivani to her home in Haberfield. Shivani takes off her jacket. Dr. Krishna observes Shivani's bruises turned blue on her hands. She feels embarssed but as Krishna is a doctor she says don't feel guilt of being abused. You can tell me what is happening.

Shivani explains the situation, she also says what is the price of Social stigma and how stereotype her dad is. Ameya's childhood and her anxiety issues. Dr. Krishna says Shivani you don't need to keepthis volcano of anxiety issues in your head. It will become chronic, just see your doctor and she will give you medication for this.

Shivani explains how her in-laws weaved rumours, when she took medication for her Nervous Weakness. Shivani says I don't feel low when I am out with friends and even people with empathy. Only when Sudhir beats me, abuses me verbally and his family weaves violence. That's when I feel like ending my life. I am very sportive Krishna and I braved worse than this. Don't you think mindfulness would help me? I don't want to fall for medication. Krishna says try it I feel sad, you are almost 8 youngers than me and going through this.

Shivani tries to brave medication each day, but one day while she is in the shower, she observes that her mind got freeze. She knows this is a terrible condition of Anxiety. She comes out, when Sudhir has finished his dinner; she says I think my brain is damaged. I am feeling anxious and getting freeze sometimes. I know this is a terrible situation of Nervous Weakness. Sudhir gets sacred, when she says I don't care even if you don't show me Ameya or not. I feel like my head is spinning around. There is such a pain in my head, I can't explain in words. I hate you, your parents and if my dad comes in front of me I would say "YOU ARE A STEEREOTYPE, LIVE IN YOUR COMFORT ZONE".

Sudhir hugs Shivani and says, if you want you can speak to your doctor mama. Shivani says what he will say; he will start crying or ask me to see a NueroPhysician or a psychologist. Sudhir says sleep on my shoulder you will be ok, medication will have side effects.

Shivani says that you and your family and even my parents should know before putting me in such vulnerable shoes. Shivani tries to sleep, but she feels like she will lose her Cognition and will become In -cognitive. She doesn't feel like sleeping, she then throws up and feels restless. She wakes up and gets ready to see the doctor. Ameya has a bowel problem, she is in the bathroom. You please take care of her, I will go alone. Sudhir takes care of Ameya, when Shivani is off to shopping.

I need to see the doctor; Shivani goes to the doctor, when Ameya is with Sudhir. She first cries a lot and says I don't feel like living, I am getting freeze. I think I can't brave this anymore doctor. I told my husband to tell this wonderful news of their weaving violence outcome to his family.

Shivani says, I can fill any questionnaire. The doctor says shivani still I feel your Cognition is good. Isn't mindfulness helping you. Shivani says I am using Mindfulness but still I am getting freeze while cooking, bathing, and even sometimes ironing clothes. Suddenly any sound, I get scared, I feel like each day is a nightmare.

The doctor says Shivani, take this medication, Shivani reads the name, its Olanzapine (0.25 mg). Rather than medication, your husband should change his behaviour. Shivani says not only my husband, his family and even my family too. They abuse me and my parents watch it in silence. All my dad wants is just his name, which won't stay even a day if I give up in life.

She takes the medicine and comes home. Sudhir expects her to cook even in that condition too. He starts grumbing I don't know what is making you so restless to this tablets. Shivani says, I am not taking it as a fun. It's the outcome of your abuse from 2008. Shivani makes Vegrice and a curry. She asks him to give it to Ameya and she is off to sleep.

Sudhir says why you are giving so much trouble to yourself and to me and Ameya. You can't live without speaking to your parents, don't challenge your brain. I won't give any divorce to you. Just stay in Hyderabad and I will come once in 3 months. You are just on a wild goose chase. Shivani says; do whatever you want to, I am sleeping please let me sleep. Where does divorce apply to a dead person, do you think there is any life left in me.

When Shivani takes the dose next day, she throws up and she can't digest the next one. Shivani doesn't know what to do, why is the small dosage not going into her tummy. She finds an idea, she takes the tablet with juice. And feels good, the trembling of hands and legs stop. Sudhir starts grumbling, my mom at your age used to cook three meals and go to school. Anyways these anxiety and depression are for rich people like you and not for hardworking women. Do you want me to apply Disabilty care leave? Shivani doesn't say a word, if you have any human concern on me, please goes from this room. I braved this for almost 2 years with your violence and divorce threats and your family daunting me each day.

I was going to get struck by a vehicle on the road that is why I took the medication. The doctor will send a letter, to see a Therapist. Since Ameya has school holidays, no big deal about waking up early.

Mrs Sunandha rings Sudhir and he talks to her about Shivani's condition. She says if you sit idle at home and also don't be in good terms with sister-in-law, this is what happens. Sudhir asks Shivani to speak, she refuses to do so. MrsSunandha says I' m not lazy like she is, I have to go to school. Her dad and maternal uncle might have raised her with privileges, but I had no such things. Shivani doesn't say a word, she thinks now she is jealous of my Privileged childhood too.

She and her daughter bindu have wrecked my marital life and even Motherhood too. Vow she is simply outstanding with her irrational thoughts. Sudhir says now see what she is going to do to you and your fame. Good let her do, and shout loud that my son's wife is on ant suicidal because of the inhuman stressors we have given her. Sudhir makes her so vulnerable saying what if Ameya comes in touch with those medication.

Shivani says is Ameya not in danger zone in your home, where your dad who has Parkinson's takes almost 7 medicines a day and he leaves them everywhere. But, I have kept a separate box and even explained Ameya, that she should think that box as a Danger box. She can't even reach the height of the shelf, where I myself use a chair to get to the box.

After a week Sunitha rings Shivani and says what happened to you?Why didn't you come to my home in School Holidays. Shivani says I was sick, now I'm ok. Sunitha says my husband said that kids can have nice time at the Darling Harbour. Why don't you bring Ameya. Shivani says let me ask Sudhir. After he comes from work, shivani asks Sudhir if she can take Ameya with Hasitha. Sudhir says ok, she prepares his lunch and says we will be home by evening.

She says I'm not lazy, it's just 0.25mg and the only side effect would be weight gain. I'm always below my BMI, so maybe it will compensate. Shivani takes Ameya. Sudhir rings her and demeans her saying you are spoiling their family time. Shivani says I didn't intrude, she invited so I came, and it's for Ameya.

Shivani explains Sunitha how much he and his family have troubled her and how she was about to meet an accident. She says when will he change Shivani? I don't know shivani says, now I got used to this as social stigma would be worse. Sunitha comforts shivani about her medication when she says I'm not guilty of taking it, as I braved it for almost 2 years.

Sunitha says why can't he send you to India? His parents are heartless she adds. My mother-in- law says I'm lazy so he is abusing me and also I fell for Antisuicidal. I am angry with my parents, especially my Dad who can't negotiate with my in-laws. Sunitha says did you tell them. Shivani says no I didn't and I don't want to speak to them either. My parents silence is the real trigger for this Violence. Sudhir says I am spoiling your family time.

Sunitha says he is very suspicious that you might share your woes with me, so he is saying this. Don't worry you are not giving me any trouble.

Shivani says after a week I have appointment with Therapist, as I am on Suicide alert. Sunitha says think about Ameya, and don't succumb to it.

Shivani and sunitha share some good time and they return home. Shivani takes Ameya each day to the playground, she starts cleaning and cooking when Ameya is colouring. Ameya starts to draw as Shivani used to do when she was at her age. God don't make a Dejavou with Ameya, she should have a wonderful life in future. I saved her childhood with bruises and scars; you know what happened to me.

The doctor makes a schedule with a Therapist and she gives her referral. She is a CBT therapist. I have checked your Psychopathology Shivani you can't cause harm to anyone. It is zero. Don't worry about what your husband and his family say. Shivani says will the dosage decrease by doctor, because when my child has bowel problem I'm unable to attend her needs at night. The doctor says Shivani once you start the therapy, things will gradually change. Don't try to brave the medication, take the medicine very early then you will be alert. Don't think you are misfit, I know how much Cognition you have and how much will power you possess.

Shivani checks with Sudhir his roster and then arranges her therapy sessions. She explains the therapist what all happened ever since her marriage, and how vulnerable is her motherhood.

The therapist understands her fragile situation and says you say you are privileged in India. You don't need to stay in this violent situation, I'm quite sure once you are away from this danger zone, you won't need any medication.

Shivani says, I can't quit. I have hope, faith and also I can't see my marriage as a failure and go to India with these labels of bad mother. Giving a dysfunctional childhood to my child. She says look for Volunteer work to get back on your feet.

And do have a support system when you are in trouble. Spend time with friends and don't bottle up your feelings. Just don't forget to take your medication. This is a small dosage; it doesn't affect your cognition it will save your brain. You will come out of this very soon. OCD is not a severe anxiety disorder. It's inhuman stressors and your vulnerability that is making you prone to this.

RAHUL COMES TO VISIT SYDNEY WITH HIS WIFE--- April 2013

Shivani gains weight and Sudhir says look at yourself, you are looking like a Gunny bag. Shivani doesn't feel bad as she knows that the doctor said soon she will start to lose weight. After Ameya's bday a week later in the Easter holidays, Rahul plans to visit Sydney with his wife.

Sudhir tells Shivani to cook all needed for Rahul and his wife. Shivani tells Sudhir, don't make me a fool infront of the new girl. If you don't like me, it's ok. I have accepted this kind of hatred from you ever since Ameya is born. But don't intimidate me in front of them.

Sudhir slaps Shivani when she tries to tell him about his behaviour. She doesn't discuss the topic again and completes her chores for the day and goes to sleep. The very next day, she arranges everything for them to have dinner. Rahul likes Shivani's cooking and his wife says Sissy you can cook really well.

They plan to visit lot many places, and even when she is finding difficult with the medication and the hectic work, she does everything to make them feel home. Shivani finds no pleasure in anything with Sudhir making her feel very guilt of using medication. Look at his wife, she is his mom's selection and he is lucky to have her, she is working now as a dental assistant. Shivani thinks, I resigned my dream job at HCF because of your family and you weaving violence. Good, she is intelligent, beautiful and well-mannered. Shivani says I am happy for them. Did I beg you to marry me? You should have married your mom's choice. I just finished my graduation when I got married to you.

I am in a trap as my dad selected you and you made me a punching bag to your family too. His rude behaviour could be seen easily by Rahul and his wife. He doesn't even bother to offer her anything to eat unless Ameya reminds him sometimes. Shivani just thinks that these are the ethics and values his mom has given him. Abuse and silence a wife after she gives birth to a baby girl.

Shivani feels scared of water sports and her anxiety triggers with his intimidating behaviour. Sudhir says if you don't come, Ameya won't, and don't be a spoil sport. Shivani feels as though it's a challenge to her. Rahul and his wife don't even have a clue as what is she going through. She drowns in the water and she doesn't know to swim. She shouts for help, but Sudhir doesn't come after her. She gets pushed away by the water and she feels that may be God's call has come to escape her from this hell.

Suddenly a life Saviour jumps in and brings her out. She doesn't speak for few minutes and they ask Sudhir to take care of her. She swallowed a lot of water. Rahul's wife says sissy why are you so scared, nothing happened. She says, I'm scared of water from my childhood I don't enjoy water sports. You people carry on; I will wait for you here.

Her legs and hands start shivering, a lady who sits beside her says, what happened your hands are shivering? Shivani says I forgot to take my medication today for anxiety. She holds her hand and says don't worry, everything will be ok. She says that she is taking this pill to brave abuse.

I thought may be god wanted me to come out of that living hell as a water accident as I promised myself that I won't kill myself. She hugs her and says I feel very sorry for you, and you don't need to think about Suicide. Life is beautiful, if you can be assertive to abuse. I can't take break in life that's the problem

If I go to India even when I am sick, I get outcast and deserted by my husband and his family. I am just surviving this as violence is weaved by his sister and mother too.

Whenever she is in sheer need of empathy, she finds someone who can comfort her. She feels so good about Empathy in Aussie women. And also gets a clear idea that Morality and Empathy has no barriers.

Rahul says we need to make sure sis-in-law is happy. She looks very sad, let's plan a dinner at Indian Restaurant. Shivani doesn't ask Sudhir to take her anywhere. Rahul's wife observes Shivani crying in the washroom. She says Sissy I think you have a major issue; I have been observing Ameya's dad rude behaviour towards you. Why don't you tell your parents to fix this, if it's out of your control? Shivani says she is restricted to speak to her parents.

She comforts her when she says you people are there he is not beating. Otherwise he beats even if I be assertive to him and his family. It's silence, violence or threat of Divorce. I am braving all this for Ameya's functional childhood and it's almost 9 years of our wedding. And now he and his family are not sparing me even when I have succumbed to this abuse and label me as a bad mother.

His parents and sister support his abusive behaviour and even weave violence too. It's getting late Ameya needs me in the toilet, you go now. If not Sudhir will say I told you everything about him and his family's abusive behaviour.

Swetha comes to the dinner table and she behaves as though nothing happened. Shivani gives a good clean to Ameya changes her dress and packs everything. She maintains very good hygiene to Ameya, even when Sudhir says she is no good for her.

Next day Rahul and his wife leave to Melbourne. They just plan a three day visit. Shivani smiles at them while leaving and whatever moments Sudhir is happy, she just lives

in those moments. Rahul and his wife say you must also visit
Melbourne Ameya, tell dad to plan to Melbourne.

She attends few more sessions of CBT and her therapist
says, you are doing much better than before. Shivani reveals
that she worked as Quality Assurance Analyst in HCF. And
she resigned the job because of Domestic Violence. The
therapist Helen says, one in 4 four women in Auz suffer
Domestic Violence, and some even lose their life.

The therapist says bring your husband once with you.
Because he needs to understand that the stressors are the
main reason of your anxiety.

You are a very Cognitive Person. Sometimes men don't
value their wives and later repent when abuse takes a toll on
their lives. He is really ignorant person to give trouble to an
intelligent pious woman like you.

SHIVANI MEETS HER TEAM MATE SHEETAL AT ART WORKSHOP—MAY 2013

Shivani takes Ameya to a free Art Workshop organised
by the Council at a Famous Library. They do have" Women
Empowerment" Classes too for Young mothers. Shivani
applies it online and she attends the classes.

Shivani finds Sheetal with her 6 year old son, who
comes to the Workshop?

Shivani thinks she didn't change much over the years;
rather than she has gained some weight. Shivani says if I'm
not mistaken you worked as Senior Programmer Analyst at
HCF. Sheetal says yes, I am still working there. Shivani says
I worked for a short period as Quality Analyst I'm Shivani,

I worked in your team. Sheetal says Oh yes Shivani! Long-time I forgot you, you have a adorable baby girl right. Yes, now she is in her year1. She is in Big School now. I never thought you would return to Sydney. How is family life Shivani? She says it's not that bad, but took a toll on my health.

Sheetal says I don't know why you are dragging this Marriage so much? Shivani says for Functional Childhood of Ameya. I just can't break her childhood into bits and pieces. He is not abusive to Ameya, but treats me more like her Nanny less like his wife. Sheetal asks what happened to your health. Shivani says I am in the Spectrum of OCD and on Olanzapine 0.25 mg. Sheetal says Holy Goodness!! We worked at Nuero Project and you are now taking this medication. Shivani says I don't know I tried to brave this cycle of abuse, but finally succumbed to medication. I am taking CBT from a Family Counsellor. Sheetal says don't be guilt of taking medication, and therapy will build Confidence in you. Abuse should be at Guilt not innocents. I pity your husband's empathy.

Shivani, your husband has no empathy and his family are weavers of violence. Take my number we have bought a home close to CBD. Shivani takes her no, she shows her Ameya. Sheetal says vow she is grown into a beautiful girl and is just like you. Sheetal says to her son Ashish to give some toffees to Ameya. Ameya likes Ashish, she gives her painting to him. Sheetal says Ameya is "Creative" like you.

Just look for your happiness in Ameya. And I'm telling you again don't risk your life, just call the cops if he beats you. Tell his sister that their threats from Dublin have been recorded by a Q.A recorder and if you submit them to the concerned authorities. They will call her for debriefing.

Shivani feels embarrassed to become a victim as she can't sustain to witness it. Now, she is even experiencing it in a most ugly shape.

DR.RAMA KRISHNA SHEDS TEARS WHEN HE COMES TO SYDNEY – OCT 2013

Shivani attends the sessions and she reads in Wikipedia that Generic drugs don't cause so much of weight gain. She asks the doctor, if she can go for them. The doctor says you can ask the Pharmacist and they can advise you about it. Her peers start to notice some change in Shivani. She starts avoiding people who know Sudhir.

She starts the generic drugs, avoids bread as it has yeast in it and starts to do lot of walking. The CBT also brings some change in her as she attends regular sessions after the school holidays for Ameya. She drops Ameya at the Ballet Classes and walks to the therapist. Each she gets reminded of Mr Jagan and Bindu who provoked Sudhir to destroy her career and also her marital bliss.

Ameya likes dancing and Shivani takes even Sofia, daughter of Dr. Krishna to the classes. Both of them get to meet each other and Krishna gives a lot of comfort to Shivani. She says you are improving, better try hard with your job search. The swelling of your face has reduced too. Good you chose generic they are cost effective and also have less chemical composition.

Sudhir still takes on Shivani whenever she asks him to let her live with freedom, not Independence. Being together doesn't mean always you set some irrational rules. In which part of Hindu marriage is abuse allowed. Who says that once you are a mom you should endure abuse and be isolated from all? She tries to be assertive to him, but he used his power to smack her then walk out of home. Mrs Sunandha calls her, bombards her with abusive words, saying only if you keep quiet, he will come.

Shivani thinks Mrs Sunanadha is behind all this foul play because her bindu has a henpecked husband. She says to Sudhir that Sheetal at HCF says, what I am enduring is Human Resources Exploitation and not Hinduism. Sudhir says people at my firm also say you are lazy and a nagger. Shivani thinks it's of no use to speak to him when he is using his Chauvinism.

Bindu calls Sudhir and even speaks for long to Ameya. One day shivani says to Sudhir let Ameya finish her dinner and speak to bindu what's so urgent there. Bindu says your wife doesn't want me to speak to Ameya, fair enough this is what I get to hear, she has become a headache in the family. Sudhir says to Shivani now pick up the phone and call bindu and say sorry.

Shivani says whatever she has done I am enduring now with even medication. I don't feel like speaking to her, and even if I ring her she will not pick up because she is so egoistic. A dentist without empathy is what she is, am I doing the same to my younger brother's wife.

Sudhir slaps shivani hard and says now I want you to cook for me Chapathi, I am not going to eat rice. Shivani says it's already 9:30pm and Ameya is off to sleep. Sudhir says decision is yours, whether chapathi now or you want me to leave. Sudhir always threatens shivani to leave the house. Shivani sometimes feels that he should be taken first to a NeuroPsychiatrist. Something is wrong with him, not with her.

She makes the Chapathi and the curry; he eats and goes to sleep. She packs his lunch for the next day and keeps it in the fridge. He wakes up early and takes his lunch box. Sudhir doesn't like shivani to ask him when he is coming home, whenever she asks at what time you will finish your work. He says when my employer is not asking, why you are asking me. Shivani thinks it's all the fault of upbringing and inducing Chauvinism by weaving violence.

Shivani doesn't bother much about it and she starts to read Wikipedia and search to find a job. He calls her and says, there is one job at my firm, are you willing to apply. Shivani say ok, I will tailor my Resume, and send it to you. She thinks it's the best to do, but when she looks at the job profile it says 24/7 shifts. Shivani says to him, already you work in late night shifts. What will happen to Ameya, if I work on shifts? She will have tough time, and don't you think I can get any other work other than this. Sudhir says for the potential you have, this is the best you can get. Shivani applies for it and they call her.

They just ask her if she has any experience working in shifts. Shivani says "No "I don't have any experience, yet I think I can manage. Sudhir asks her "Did you answer them well; Shivani says they asked me if I worked in the night shift, and I said no. Sudhir says I know why you did this, because you don't want to work unless I allow you to speak to your parents. Shivani says, why do you bring this parents stuff each day. You are the one who speaks to your parents and sister each day, and they give you marvellous ideas to abuse me.

Sudhir says I am doing everything for Ameya. If both of us work, she will have everything she needs. Shivani gets fumed up and says I am braving anxiety and meeting all needs of you and Ameya. Each day I feel like ending my life and you are accusing me of not providing enough money for Ameya.

One day shivani forgets to bring her keys of the apartment; she cooks lunch and goes to the Mall. She buys groceries and returns home. When she looks in her bag, she finds her keys missing. She doesn't know what to do; she has to stay outside until Sudhir comes. She rings Sunitha if she is at home. Sunitha says, you can stay at my home until Sudhir returns from work. She says ok, I have even prepared lunch for him, so nothing to worry. On the way, he rings Sudhir and says that she forgot the keys and going to stay at Sunitha's home until he returns from work You can have your lunch too, as I prepared everything. Ring me when you are home.

Sunitha says you are much better Shivani, you can brave this. Shivani says the doctor has decreased my dosage, now it's only one tablet a day.

Sunitha says don't bother too much, you have always been thin, so you might be feeling bit different when you gained some extra pounds.

She says may be, but Sudhir is daunting me each day. I feel like going to India, but he will outcast me if I go there. He makes me walk on egg shells each day and his family is making my motherhood a living hell. Sunitha says don't worry too much, God will teach them good lessons. Shivani says hope so, I don't wish anything bad to them, but they are not allowing me to live at peace.

Ameya has no OCI and also she is not having Indian Visa too. Sunitha, says how can he do this to you, already they all troubled you so much in 2008. You are very courageous than you think you are, you will brave this and they will learn a lesson. She says don't worry toomuch and spoil your health, have lunch with me peacefully. Sunitha always has a warm heart to Shivani and says to eat something like a sister.

She says ring your parents, Shivani says its waste of time to talk to my Dad, he says come to India alone, I will send you to America. We have somany family members who can help you. Even my maternal grandpa who is a advocate at High court says if you can't bring Ameya with you come alone. They are not getting me right, I want a happy family not Success in life. And how can I leave "Ameya", she is my life. Had I chosen success, I wouldn't resign my job at HCF. They feared for my life and I gave up because of Domestic Violence.

She calls her mom and she says Shivani Dad did tell to his maternal uncle and he even shed tears at their home. Yet, he says that Sudhir's dad asked him to be out of this and humiliated him. So, he says he is helpless too. Your mother in-law is saying to all in her family that you don't have a job so the chaos is because of that. Don't ask Sudhir as things will turn worse.

Shivani's mom starts crying. Shivani says I am tired of crying mom, don't make me weak, crying doesn't bring a solution. Don't ask Sudhir that his mom is spreading rumours about you not having a job. Shivani says no mom I won't "I feel that Mr Srinivas is also supporting them." My mother-in-law is the toughest lady in the world who sans

Empathy and even sympathy antoo. Sunitha says "I will give her Moral Support".

Shivanii rings Sudhir if he is home, he says "I am". Shivani says sunitha he is sounding very rude, I think his suspicion will start, that I came to talk to you about my family issues. Sunitha says just be confident, he draws answers from you. You didn't do anything wrong, they are doing wrong by abusing and silencing you. This is very inhuman.

Shivani comes home and she observes that Sudhir hasn't eaten anything. Shivani says why you didn't eat lunch it's your favourite recipe. I am hungry I am eating "Do you want me to serve food to you"? Sudhir says nothing, shivani thinks now something is going in his mind. His mom and sis won't leave me alone until she sees me dead.

Shivani observes two days he doesn't eat at home. One day, she feels like telling Sunitha about his silent treatment. He comes home and sees shivani speaking to Sunitha, that he is not eating at home.

Shivani fears and says it's my cousin Usha, he comes and checks the phone no, he abuses her so much and says, I have work to do. You sit and complain on me and my family. Shivani texts him and rings him that she will never reveal anything to anyone. Sudhir says I don't believe you, you didn't learn a lesson when I sent you to India in 2008.

Your family has no values; they didn't teach you that you have to keep your problems inside the house. Shivani says I don't have access to speak to my parents. Sudhir says don't worry "You stay with them in India forever". Shivani cries a lot, and makes sure he eats at home. For the next consecutive 3 months he cooks on his own.

On Oct 20th, Dr. Rama Krishna comes to Sydney after their family Round trip to Australia. He rings Shivani to meet her. He says they have a Ferry Ride at night, but they have chosen to meet her than go to the ride. Shivani says to her aunt that Sudhir is not eating at home and is not speaking to her; life is like a hell to her.

Her aunt says Shivani we have given the land, jewellery your parents gave somcuch. We told them how you weak you became. Seriously I feel so bad my child; I have seen you as a Princess of our family. But, trust God one day Mrs Sunandha's game will be ripped by him.

Shivani's maternal aunt says, your mama spoke to Sudhir and he has said he will be at home, tomorrow. Sudhir, rings his mom to say that Dr. mama is in Sydney. She takes authority and tell him let them come and see what is his niece doing without a job.

Shivani says did you ask them for dinner. Sudhir says, he said he will come only for an hour. Shivani says "You can tell him my flaws". Sudhir says I am not a weak person to discuss my family issues with outsiders. Except my parents and sister, everybody is an outsider to me to discuss my family issues.

Shivani just gets some ice-cream, she feels so bad, he gave me life, and even a land worth a fortune to some middle class people. Yet, I can't even have freedom to invite him to dinner. His House His Rules, you break one, you will be beaten black and blue and then threaten with divorce.

Dr. Rama Krishna comes to their home by a taxi, and says to Sudhir the place is very close, he need not come to the hotel to pick them. He brings somany gifts to Shivani and Ameya. Shivani's cousins say Ameya is just like Sissy in her intellect and speech. Ameya says Dr. Grandpa look at my toys and this is my art.

Dr. Rama Krishna says to his wife isn't Ameya so creative like Shivani. Sudhir behaves very modest to them, but talks very less. Shivani feels I can't get this man, he likes to speak to his mom and sister for ages. He doesn't even speak to such a good doctor for a second. I don't know when he will come out his PARONIA. Shivani offers ice-cream to all and when she offers Sudhir, he says first he denys and Dr. Rama Krishna says why don't you eat it. He gives a angry look to Shivani and he eats it. Dr. Rama Krishna asks Ameya all about her school and her friends. All in shivani's family adore Ameya so much.

He always looks Shivani's reflection in Ameya. His wife says Ameya, you must study like your mom, she was very good at studies. Ameya says Mom doesn't work, shivani's youngest cousin, yes because she has to look after you. When you were in India she worked in HCF.

Sudhir doesn't say a word, ameya says she is so excited to see their hotel in CBD. She says thank you grandpa and granny for the gifts. Shivani's cousins adore ameya so much and say you have to eat a lot. Momma was a good food- lover. We used to have a lot of parties, his mom adds saying, now her life completely changed. She is no more that smiling doll, something always bothers her. Sudhir doesn't even give a thought to what she says about shivani. Because she is the only person in shivani's famly who is very assertive to Sudhir's parents. She always says to Dr. Rama Krishna, this guy is abusing our princess because his mom and sister can't digest her happiness.

Sudhir drops them at the hotel, and shivani shares her woes, she feels like she could stay one day with her maternal uncle and his family. He sheds tears when shivani cries in silence. Just go to counselling I don't know what this curse to you is. This guy is like a silent killer, he is eating you slice by slice. Shivani requests Sudhir can you please eat now atleast. Sudhir says if you ask me again, I will drop you here and you can catch a Taxi and come home.

The very next morning Shivani's maternal uncle and his family leave to India. After few days she tries to explain him how fragile she is, she gets burst out of her stress and says "GOD IS COUNTING MY TEARS OF DESPAIR", don't forget your sister also has a baby girl now. Whatever Ameya is witnessing seeing my vulnerability, God will revert it to your sister. He beats her so much, how dare you talk about my sister, and in pouring rain he pushes her out of the house.

She feels so intimidated, and goes to shopping at 7:00 pm. She feels like reporting to the Cops that he has pushed her out of home. But, he comes after her to the Mall with Ameya, and says lets us get some groceries. When she gets freeze and Ameya asks Sudhir what happened. He says Mom is in Coma, you know all brain is dead, that stage. Lazy people who don't maintain good terms with husband and family get cursed by God in this way.

Shivani doesn't even ask why he pushed, because she knows her tragic situation. And his mom always says whenever shivani says Sudhir is behaving so violent. Sunandha says report to cops, he will lose his job and you guys can live on me and my bindu's earnings. She is so proud of her teacher job and her daughter's earnings too.

BINDU AND SUDHIR PLAN MRS SUNANDHA'S RETIREMENT FUNCTION – DEC 2013

Shivani rings Mrs Sunandha and says, we don't have visa for Ameya, my P.R is about to expire. He is beating me and not eating food. What can we do?? She first acts like I don't know all this he is such a secretive person. I thought you guys are doing well. And don't tell him you called me. Shivani feels like asking, don't you have any freedom to speak to others and live with Respect. But she feels like she has get out of this hell. So, she says if you have sympathy on me and Empathy on Ameya, you will ask him to send to India when you are retiring.

Sudhir and bindu discuss about the gift they are going to give it Mrs Sunanadha. Sudhir says bindu want to talk to you about the gift. Shivani says, what do I know, I am not that good at selecting anything. Sudhir says, I will let you know by evening. Sudhir says now here is the deal, you will speak to bindu and then to my Vani aunty. Then I will allow you to speak to your parents and also to go to their home.

Mrs Sunandha though she plans everything according to her wish and will says "I am not having any celebration". When you guys are fighting with each other, but I want to advise you that it's not good to tell your family problems to anyone. Shivani says, then why does he beat me so much and doesn't allow me to speak to my parents. Already you lost your intelligence, what will you do except taking care of Ameya.

Mrs Sunandha says there are millions like you, who are enduring this what's the big deal, men have several issues,

wife should endure all their anger. For this time I will ask him to eat what you have cooked.

Shivani thinks, yes this is a power game and she knows all, even when I didn't say, anyways these people love Negative drama. Sudhir acts as though his mom is the only Anchor shivani has in the world. Her blood keeps boiling inside, but she doesn't speak a word. Common you abusers weave and act more drama, her inner voice says. Shivani looses all respect for Sudhir and his family. She feels that they are the worst people behind their good masks outside home.

Shivani applies her P.R renewal and Sudhir calls her and abuses her so much, if yours is finished is done right. Why would you bother about Ameya, even a step-mother doesn't behave so rude to her. Even a psychotic woman feeds her baby properly. Look at her she doesn't eat at all, you don't know you raise a child, he says I don't know what a curse you are to me and my family.

Shivani applies Ameya's visa and she gets in few days Visa to India. Then she renewals her visa too. Mrs Sunandha rings her and says bindu is coming, bring all of your jewellery. Shivani feels what a big deal has let this woman take all my jewellery and its control.

Now with this bruises and scars I am tired. Shivani gets very tanned as Olanzapine makes her skin very sensitive to Sun, even when she applies Sunscreen. Whenever Shivani goes to any party, Sindhu always asks Shivani, why are you wearing all old dresses, Shivani says it's been 3 years I have been to India. I didn't get any new ones. She doesn't speak to anyone, because her motive is to brave this anxiety and get back on her feet.

Sudhir asks Shivani to apply only 3 months Visit visa to Ameya as she has her school re-opened in February. Shivani collects all Ameyas' yearly reports and both attend the Parents and Teachers Meeting.

Ameya is doing good and she is very intuitive says her teacher. She doesn't eat her lunch, she always skips it.

Shivani says that is what my major concern is, she doesn't eat at home too. Sudhir doesn't say anything about it. Shivani on their way back to home says, you and your family say I have not raised Ameya up to the mark and don't give her food. Now the teacher says the same, only up to Year1, teachers monitor whether kids are eating their lunch. Sudhir says now don't start it again, and spoil my mood.

Sudhir invites his friends for dinner, Shivani cooks all items according to his list. Sunitha also comes to their home with her husband and family. She asks if she needs any help, shivani says no I can manage, please monitor whether Ameya is eating. Shivani and sunitha don't give a clue to other friends as what pain shivani is enduring with weaving Violence from Dublin and India.

Ameya's eating habits and also her bowel syndrome makes her tired always; she doesn't know how to tell her to drink more water. She tries all means, looks in the internet. Sometimes she even prepares Pizza at home. Sudhir doesn't like it, he makes a big deal out of everything. Shivani still tries to make Ameya love food she makes at home. She gives her flavoured drinks, by adding Oranges to her water.

Sudhir asks Shivani to book tickets for all three of them. He says he will come in January. Shivani does accordingly, she packs basic items and she feels good that she is going to India with Ameya. Sudhir finally gives permission to speak

to her parents and he says if my mom doesn't come to the airport, your dad can come and pick you and Ameya.

Shivani rings her Dad and says I don't have any good clothes to wear, Can you bring some cash to the airport, if I have to go with Sudhir's mom. Shivani's dad says it's ok, don't worry I will get you money. Shivani's mom says, I will bring dresses to you and even cash, if you don't like some of them, as you say you have gained weight.

SHIVANI COMES TO INDIA WITH AMEYA TO ATTEND MRS SUNANDHA'S RETIREMNET CEREMONY – 25TH DEC 2013

Shivani thinks that since it will be late in the night, Sudhir's mom won't come to pick her from the airport. But, to her ill fate she comes at late night and she has to wait for her for hours in the Airport. Mr Girish and his friend Rahman arrange a Welcome Note to Shivani and Ameya. As soon as she clears customs, Rahim and Girish come to her and help her with Ameya and her luggage. Looking at Shivani, her mom and paternal aunt shed tears, the way she has become so tanned and vulnerable.

She lands at the airport and Ameya starts crying that she has cramps in her stomach. Shivani's paternal aunt says, let's go to our home, it's closely. Suddenly Sunandha rings shivani's mom and says I am coming to pick them from the airport. They have to come to my home, bindu and jagan have come.

Shivani says Mom manage somehow I don't want to go with her and stay with that abusive bindu and jagan. Shivani

takes the clothes parcel and the money. Ameya doesn't go close to shivani's mom and dad though they have raised her. Shivani says to her dad let's go to our home.

Shivani's dad who is a Stereotype says "Wait she is coming", don't get into new trouble. I did speak to her brother Srinivas and he said this time, he will talk to the entire family as what have they achieved abusing you so much. Why is bindu and jagan again involving and weaving violence from Dublin. Mrs Sunandha comes to the car park and she starts grumbling at Girish and his wife. Saying where is shivani and ameya. Girish's sister says, shivani took ameya to the bathroom she was crying so much.

Mrs Sunandha rings Sudhir and says, your wife doesn't want to come to our house I guess her whole family is here to take her. Shivani's aunt says why are you jumping into conclusion, we didn't say we have come to take shivani and ameya. They are your family Sunandha says I'm dying with this shivani, she has no time management and doesn't know to manage ameya.

Shivani brings ameya from the bathroom, she gives a nice clean to her and gets her dressed in new clothes which shivani's mom has got for her. Mr Girish, says it's too late in the night. Let us all stay at my sister's home tonight since both of them are sick, they have jet lag.

Sudhir's mom says I will ask Sudhir what he says. She doesn't allow shivani to speak to him and says Sudhir is on rage, he is saying if she goes to Warangal, she need not come to Sydney. After a while, Mr Girish brings Ameya some fruit drink and gives her a teddy bear. Suddenly Ameya says Nana, shivani's aunty says ameya is just like our little shivani. When Shivani's mom makes her drink some juice,

she says Nani. Both of them hug Ameya and she says I want to come to your home. I don't want to go with her, she is so rude.

Shivani says I want to explain him, the stomach cramps shivani is having and my panic attacks too. She speaks to him, but he screams at her and says, my sister and her family have come to India. Just do as my mom says. Shivani's mom requests her that its 2:00am and both of them are sick, why don't you stay at your sisters' house close to the city?.

Sudhir's mom says ok, I will come with them, you guys carry on. In the middle of their journey, she says to the driver common divert the road. Shivani consoles Ameya who says "Mom this car is bad". We should not have come with her, she is very rude. Mrs Sunandha tries to touch Ameya, she shouts and screams, you are so rude. Nana and Nani are good they don't shout like you.

Sunandha gets fumed up and says if you shout once again, I will drop you and your mom on the road. Ameya starts crying, she says I want to go to Nana. Shivani whispers in her ears, that if she doesn't listen to what she says "We will be in trouble with dad". Ameya likes Sudhir but she is scared of him too. She knows that he smacks her sometimes with a comb too. And can stop talking to her for a day. So, being a innocent child she always gets perplexed as how to keep a big secret that her mom is abused and silenced.

They reach Sudhir's home town at 4:00 am and Ameya cries a lot with stomach cramps. Shivani says "Namasthe to Sudhir'dad who becomes with Parkinsons. She observes that he is losing his cognition by the day as Mrs Sunandha even confuses him too. But, Sudhir's dad doesn't support shivani even he knows she is getting abused and silenced. He is the one who raised his hand against her and gave licence to sudhir from Silence to Violence and the Cycle is taking a nasty turn by the day.

Shivani feels very tired and she throws up as she couldn't attend Ameya's bathroom needs each hour. Mrs Sunandha says, she is asking you and is not letting me in. Ameya shouts Granny is rude, I want to go to Nani. Mrs Sunandha threatens Ameya, if you shout more this is my home and your dad is my son. I will tell your dad to put you in a hostel. Ameya gets scared by the word hostel, because she can't sleep without Shivani by her side and also she is very dependent on her for everything. Shivani whispers, ameya let me tell you a story of a Princess. Ameya loves Shivani's creative stories.

But she asks her will we go to Nana, shivani says yes, we will ask Dad and go, now princess shouldn't scream in the toilet. When do good kids scream? "Ameya says I scream you Scream for an Ice-cream."Right answer, see then this is not the right place to scream. It is bad manners, to wake up everyone at this early hour by screaming in the toilet.

She weaves a story in her mind and she tells her a new one each day. Ameya says to Sunandha, my mom is so nice and kind. Why does Dad beat Mom? You are his parents why don't you say to stop beating mom. My teacher told me that beating is bad, we need to tell her if someone does that to her.

But, mom is not a kid, she even worked her cousin said, why does Dad beat Mom?. Sunandha gets very angry and says who is teaching you all this, is your mom. Ameya says no, Mom says Dad is good and we should understand that

he is tired from work. My teacher told us about abuse. I am now in a big school.

Mom says we shouldn't speak about Nana, Nani and Chinnu mama to dad. But, why should she speak to you all and Bindu aunty and uncle? Sunandha gives a angry look at shivani, she says to Ameya, let's go to sleep. Ameya, says I want you to sleep, she doesn't allow Sunandha to touch her. Sudhir's dad comes and tries to squeeze ameya's cheeks. She doesn't like it and Sunandha pushes him like a servant, keep away from my son's daughter. Shivani gets scared by the way Sunandha treats Sudhir's dad. Yet she can't forget the way he abused her so much. He is very selfish and shed crocodile tears.

Shivani and Ameya go to sleep and shivani wakes up at 8:00 am. Sudhir rings his mom and even when shivani wants to speak to him. She says, don't need to, are you so irresistible to speak to your husband. Shivani feels very embarrassed, she just wants Sudhir to send Ameya'slatest Eye Screening test reports. Shivani doesn't bring the box of her anxiety medication. Because she knows what Mrs Sunandha will do?

She keeps saying to Sudhir that Ameya is scared of Shivani. Why doesn't she have patience with the child? Shivani gets shocked; Sudhir says you know right these days she is on some stupid medicine. I keep telling her not to take it, she says I have to.

After a while Sudihr says give the phone to shivani, she speaks to him in a private room. She says I am not being rude to ameya, your mom was threatening her, how can she say such bitter lies. Sudhir says, don't ever dare to speak about my mom, whatever she does you have to accept it.

Now, see the real feast for you is when my sister and her husband come. Shivani says, I am used to it and braved it, I have been taught to be civilized not vandalized.

MRS SUNANDHA USES BIGOTRY TO CREATE AND WEAVE RUMOURS ON SHIVANI'S ANXIETY –

They have a party among Sudhir's relatives; she says to shivani that she bought a sari for her. Then again she says, I don't know where I lost it. Now let me check whether you have some good stuff. Shivani opens her suitcase, she brings all her old saris to give it to her mom or anyone and buy new ones.

Mrs Sunandha says you don't have any new stuff. All relatives there will ask so many questions. Shivani says I don't want to come. Ameya and I will stay at home as she is still having Jet lag. Ameya always has problem with her stomach cramps. She gets tired and sleeps in the evening. Mrs Sunandha puts party clothes to Ameya and she takes her to the party. Shivani gets so tensed as what if she wakes up and cries in the middle of their journey.

Sudhir rings shivani and says, my mom might be ashamed to introduce you to my relatives, that is why she took ameya with them. Anyways you say, you don't like family parties so good for you. Shivani says, I know how much you are enjoying by giving me such trouble and anxiety.

Yet, I am younger than you, so I do respect your age but not your callous attitude. This is not sense of humour. It is

killing hope of a Mother too who was once called NLC of HCF. Whenever Sudhir says something assertive, Sudhir says I don't want to hear your daily soap dialogues.

Shivani says I don't watch daily soaps. You and your family in collaboration with Jagan and his Paranoid family have made an NLC fail and God will prove it one day. Even J.K Rowling suffered a catastrophic Marriage, and was even clinically depressed. But when she healed and bounced back she became a "BILLONAIRE". And to me she is my inspiration.

Psychological disorder is not Psychotic, I worked in the Neuro-Science Project, and I know even the chemical composition of my medicine. No big deal even doctors have endured this and bounced back, I have seen many patients of my Dr. Mama gone through the worse and even healed.

His good deeds will be re-paid by God. I will heal and brave all this once nobody in my kith and kin will be ashamed of me. I braved and I am braving ugly violence for their reputation. Had this been a marriage of my choice, I wouldn't have been this patient with you and your family.

But I am not Clincally depressed. Dr. Helen told you that its inhuman stressors created and I couldn't fit into your archaic rules, where I am a free spirit person. Each day and moment I took this life as a challenge, yet I don't regret because I come from a School of Courage. I already braved half of the dosage.

Ameya doesn't wake up in the party too, as Ameya has no good sleep for about 2 days with jet lag and also with stomach cramps. Sunandha comes home, shivani makes some less spicy curry for Ameya to eat. The very next day

one of Sudhir's cousin rings to Sunandha and he says my wife lavanya wants to speak to shivani.

Shivani calls her sissy because she is quite older than and they hairom the same home town. She is also related to shivani even through her Paternal Family. Lavanya asks shivani if her fever is down., shivani says I had jet lag sissy not fever. Susheel wants to speak. Susheel calls her Sis-in –law though shivani is even younger than his own sister. Shivani with due respect says, I am younger than your sister Nischitha.

You can call me shivani, and please do consider me as one more sister too. Susheel says ok Shivani I have mentioned that way because Sudhir bro is elder to me. Anyways it's been ages we haven't met and even your parents too. Shivani says yes time flies and family obligations. Susheel says now that we are here settled in India for good, you have to come to visit us. Shivani says, yes with pleasure, when sudhir comes too.

The very next day Bindu and Jagan come with their family, shivani speaks to them very well as she knows that they fuel more violence. Mr Jagan says in a saracsatic way, you have made a fool of yourself by not being in goodt terms with us. Now, you are suffering with anxiety, this is what God does when you don't listen to Powerful people. Shivani feels like giving one tight slap on his face and call the cops to arrest him.

Shivani struggles a lot with Ameya's health and they enjoy their suffering. Bindu, says I am a doctor, I know how to fix your problem. Ameya in an assertive tone says you are a dentist not a doctor. My friend Sofia's mom is a doctor. She told me and mom what to do. You only check people's

teeth. Suddenly Jagan shouts on Shivani saying, Shut your Ameya's mouth. How dare she speak to bindu like that?

Ameya comes crying to shivani, she says to her "Momma they are rude", we will go to Nana. Bindu says hey Ameya, your jagan uncle was joking. Come and play with Sakhi. Ameya feels bad when they treat shivani bad. Mrs Sunandha sees shivani crying and instead of consoling her she says I will tell sudhir to keep you away from our family. You don't even need to go to Sydney too.

The next day shivani hears bindu and sunandha speaking to her cousin in U.S saying shivani lost her cognition. Shivani feels very bad about it, and she comes to sunandha and says why don't you all kill me at once, than to spread rumours about my cognition. Suddenly Jagan intervenes and says shivani we are all good, we are saying everything to your wellbeing.

What's a big deal if your dad is saying to Mr Srinivias that we are giving trouble to you and you are suffering each day? So bindu and her mom are revealing the reason behind the chaos. Shivani in an assertive tone says Prove that I'm incognitive and then weave rumours about my Cognition. So, pathetic you all are, I will ask Sudhir how far is it good to speak about a young mother this way. Sunandha says you want to create rift between bro and sister once again. I will not spare you thistime if you create any scene in my function. I am already having tough time with Sudhir's dad ailing health, because he thinks toomuch about Sudhir and his future.

Rjeshwari calls Sunandha and wishes her on her retirement. Then only she invites them, she is such a controlling woman who doesn't want shivani to heal and be

happy. She just wants her bindu to shine. Shivani's mom says Shivani did put on some weight, I was just thinking what dress have you purchased for her. Sunandha says bindu and shivani will wear sari. Shivani has plenty here, with her it's a small get-together we don't need to be a show off. Rajeshwari who always wants the best to shivani and sharth's wife still purchases some new dresses for Shivani.

Sunandha brings icecreams and toffies to ameya to attract her towards her, so that she has control over shivani and sudhir. Shivani always warns her not to give ameya somany junk foods. Yet, she says you are jealous of ameya, Shivani says me and jealous of ameya. I had a wonderful childhood very privileged than Ameya. My dad and his family is not abusive like you all are.

Ameya slowly gets attracted to Sunandha and bindu as one gives ice creams and the other gives video games to play. Mrs Sunandha on purpose asks Shivani to serve food to Jagan. Shivani feels so bad, when he shows his weird looks on her. Shivani starts to suspect Jagan's behaviour as he speaks of vulgarism on T.V so open to everyone. His questions always involve sharath and his properties and then Dr. Rama Krishna and his super speciality hospital. Shivani tries to avoid his presence and takes ameya out for shopping.

When she goes to out, she calls Rajeshwari and says I want to come out of this hell. Do take me to home after this silly function. This woman is celebrating as though she has won President's award. Mom I don't want to stay here, that Jagan's attitude is very vulgar. Rajeshwari says, don't panick shivani you just need to spend few days with them, just do meditation when you feel stress.

Sunandha says you didn't bring the parcel your mom gave. Shivani's dresses are in the parcel, she feels that what sunandha is saying is wrong. She might have hidden them as she hates me wearing new dresses and wants to see me in her shoes. She said she bought some new saris to both bindu and her. But, she then says she lost them.

On the day of her retirement Sunandha asks shivani to wear a sari and she gives a new dress to bindu. Shivani feels I will not complain now let my parents see what mind games she has played and my dad hates to see me in old clothes. This attitude of theirs will trigger my dad's anger and will be good to him and his stereotype attitude.

Ameya says mom you look old and bindu aunty looks good. Sunandha says, your dad is unlucky to have a ugly woman as his wife. Ameya says mom looks beautiful in her marriage picture. Dad says mom was beautiful, that is why he married her. My teacher says we shouldn't say to anyone they are not beautiful.

Krishna aunty who is a doctor said to me that mom is sick as dad beats mom, so she lost her charm. Jagan says you are very beautiful Ameya, I love your eyes, come and sit beside me. Ameya says you yelled at my mom I will not speak to you. I will complain to my dad about you when we go to Nana. My Nana is very nice and he bought so many dresses to me and mom. This is my special teddy from U.S my sharath mama sent me and I keep it with me always, Nana gave me this in the airport.

Shivani will be forced to say good words about Mrs Sunandha, she just says, she is a good teacher. Shivani feels like she is walking on thorns and doesn't want to stay at their place. She often feels that its not her real brave and assertive

behaviour. She feels like she is enslaved in Marriage. She writes in her book all her feelings which are bottled up deep inside her heart.

I can't imagine what my life is bringing day to day walking on these thorns each single day.

Is there any ray of hope in this swamp of despair and family violence each day?

I was born as a saviour child and raised as a princess with all privileges given by a famous doctor and an Entrepreneur.

I think my dad made a bad deal one business day with an engineer and I became the target of Money, Power and Control grilled each day?

God I know you are seeing this negative drama each day aren't you bored to see my tears, bruises and scars every day.

Your saviour child who is a young mom is getting diced and sliced, by abuse every single day.

Show me the way and take me to the healing land I know that you are not offline today.

Shivani's dad says to Sunandha that he wants Ameya and Shivani to come to their home. He says it's been three years they have come and we want them to come with us. Sunandha asks Shivani and Ameya packs all her stuff to leave to their home.

Shivani says, I don't know mom, again Sudhir will start his silence and violence if I don't tell him. Sunandha takes shivani to another side of the hall and threatens her that you can't leave bindu came to spend time with you. You know temperament of Sudhir and rest is in your hands. Shivani says to her dad she will come after two days. Just send the car you don't need to cancel your business trips because of me.

Shivani's dad always shows empathy to Sudhir's dad and when he is about to stumble down he says Shivani hold your father-in-law. Shivani looks at her dad and says, these people are spilling venom in my life and I have to be a devoted daughter-in-law. I wish my dad has some intuitive outlook like all his cousins have. Shivani holds him, suddenly Sunandha screams at her when shivani's mom is watching. Shivani just leaves the palce and says to Sunandha I am not your servant.

Shivani says see this is what I get to take care of him as a devoted wife of Sudhir. Dad is gone too dramatic after few words of sugar coated venom. He forgets my pain and believes all people are so honest and gentle like him. I feel like locking dad in one room and teach him what gullibility looks like in real world. Bindu comes and says mom is tired that is why shouted at shivani. Shivani says I got used to this cold attitude didn't your husband shout at me and Ameya. All her relatives think shivani is in trouble. Because, they know how aggressive and manipulative both bindu and sunandha are.

SHIVANI REVEALS HER PAIN, SUFFERING TO HER KITH AND KIN—jan2014

Shivani's parents invite sudhir to come to attend a holy rtual for their marital bliss and for Ameya's health at a temple. Sudhir controls shivani's every move and all her kith and kin observe how much he is using his "Power and Control". When her family asks him to stay for a night with

his family, Mrs sunandha plays her mind game and asks him not to stay for the night.

He does the same as his mom; he says we are going to meet Dr. Rama Krishna and then once they start off, he tells the driver to divert the route to his home town. Shivani gets reminded of sudhir's mom impromptu manipulation. She gets a clear idea, that he is so tough like his mom and this is her feedback.

After few days MrGirish comes to take Shivani and Ameya for a new land registration. Sunandha and bindu play mind games with shivani's stuff. They refuse to give Ameya's Eye test reports. Dr. Rama Krishna asks shivani to get Ameya's eye test reports. Sudhir goes to Hyderabad and shivani comes to Warangal. All of her kith and kin gather and they shed tears to see their lovely princess all worn out with abuse

She reveals to her family how they have abused and silenced her and says that her label is "Incognitive Mother". Dr. Rama Krishna hugs shivani and he cries tears of blood. I raised you with my hands; these people are after your life.

Shivani doesn't cry as much as her family does, she says Mama when violence takes an ugly shape, God will intervene. You have given me the best and now you people are adding one more property to my inheritance. But, they are playing a very dangerous game with your high profile status they have abused and silenced your princess.

I am going to sign and give this letter to you, if anything happens to me, all my belongings and also these properties will be given to Ameya only when she is 18 years old. Since they have a abusive record in NSW medicare, they will not have Ameya with them. I am not a fool dad, I have recorded

even bindu and jagan fuelling violence. Simple if ameya has to suffer so does bindu and her family too.

Everybody in her maternal and paternal family says Princess you don't need to stay with that guy who is a mooma's boy of a Manipulative Parents and very conniving Sister and brother-in-law. Shivani says to her dad that jagan's attitude is very vulgar.

He has very bad eyes on us and some mantras he keeps chanting when we are around. He yelled at ameya and me too. Her grand ma and her mama cry so much.

Mr Girish says that Sudhir's maternal uncle is not aware of everything, shivani says dad you are so ignorant. They all are a team and I was a good catch that Mr Srinivas cant utter a single word before my inalws and sudhir. And his favourite is bindu and jagan. They all say that Marriage is just a label, you are abused and enslaved.

You don't need to stay with this guy and family shivani. We won't force you anymore we know how much you have sacrificed for Ameya and our reputation. Shivani says "Dad I don't believe you". Within days you will be stringed by social stigma and start chaos at home. You only said even if I were to die, it's at my marital home. Now, I am doing the same, I don't believe you. Now if I back off, they will bombard all of you that they are so good people to let an in cognitive woman as their family member. You don't know this game I understood it, but one day I will break it too.

I can see that my father-in-law is getting for all that he has done to me. Shivani's paternal aunties say we are afraid that you might end up like him. Shivani says, no aunty don't ever think that way, he is very scornful and paranoid that is why he is the stage of delusion and slowly he will get

into psychosis too. My mom-in-law plays mind games with him too. Yet, I don't empathize with him as he is one with crocodile heart and tears.

Shivani says I am suffering like" Mother India "during the regime of British Colonization. Same archaic procedures are being used against me. I just pity them now, I don't even hate them. I know that one day God will show me the way and heal me. I saw miracles happen to me and ameya.

I was in deep sleep and the wind blew so strong the balcony door smashed, I was sleeping on the couch, after taking my medicine. Ameya was at school and Sudhir at work. The door slashed down and broke into pieces, yet nothing happened to me, even there were glass piece on the floor underneath the couch I was sleeping.

Ameya hurt her head, stitches on her head and nothing happened to her skull too. I was drowned in water, and swallowed a lot, thought I will end my life. Yet the life saviour came and saved me. I saw that god was sending his messengers to save me when I was about to meet death. One in four women experience Domestic Violence in Australia and some even die too.

I can put him behind the bars and do you why I didn't do it, because his mom wants him to be her slave in her retirement days. She says, he doesn't need any work to do there and if I complain to the cops, he will lose his job. Such a pathetic idiotic approach his parents have towards him. She says ring the cops and you guys can come over and live on my money or my daughter's money. His family's intentions are worse than him mama. He is a scapegoat; I have read al lot about this kind of phenomenon. He cries after he beats me and then again does the same.

Shivani's mama takes her to the Nuero Physician, Dr. Samuel, says except inhuman stressors our princess cognition is perfect. I am unable to believe how she can be so brave and courageous even when they are abusing her beyond human threshold. I can bet you buddy she doesn't need any medication, if she heals her emotional and physical wounds and stays here with us.

He says that fellow her husband needs Counselling, he doesn't know that he is abusing another Xerox brain, phantom intellect of Dr. Rama Krishna. Dr. Ram Krishna says shivani doesn't want to give up, she doesn't want the taboo of social stigma on her.

She would have been a doctor like you, look at her intuition and her knowledge about her medication. She is even telling you that she changed from dosage to dosage with CBT and also telling you that she is using generic brand, because of low chemical composition. She knows each bit of her medication and she has read a lot about CBT and about anxiety disorders.

I will tell you, that her intellect is far more than they ever imagine and her courage is far more than we can ever expect and anticipate. She is a rare combo of beauty, brains and courage. I respect you shivani for great sacrifice you have made for ameya and to your family's reputation. you have such commitment to marriage and he is behaving inhuman to you. This guy is the most unlucky one to abuse a Beautiful Princess with high intellect and warrior Courage.

The problem with her suicidal thoughts is because of inhuman stressors and weaving violence. These people should be behind the bars, because this guy has hurt shivani's head, there are injuries on her skull too.

Dr. Rama Krishna cries a lot, and says because of some stupid drama in that Jagan family, he hurt her onto the washing machine.

Shivani tells uncle he hurt me on my head several times. Yes princess your skull has injuries, but hypothalamus is perfect. Keep this report with you and don't ever show it to them. When we need to punish them, they will not have a word to say about your cognition. It was my mistake by not being assertive to that family in 2008. My princess is being abused and beaten black and blue.

Shivani says something is very fishy about this mantras and rings. I need to get a clear understanding exactly what are their cruel intentions. Shivani says to her grandma "I want to know what my Star sign is". My in-laws blame my zodiac sign for chaos. There is something going on very bad at Mr Jagan's home on us. I don't say it's Occult worship, yet I can say Evil Eye black magic.

I know mama that you won't believe in this stuff, but there is negative energy and negative vibes used in that home in Ongole. She Visits the temple and tells him what has happened to her ever since Ameya is born She shows him the stone anywhere in the bin. These people know that you are beyond perfection.

She askshim is my Zodaic sign a havoc to marital bliss? The priest says shivani what is the meaning of your name—SHIVANI (GODESS OF ETERNAL POWER) – DURGA DEVI. Yes Shivani I can bet on my life and say your star is similar to the Warrior Princess of the Kakatiya Dynasty, RUDRAMA DEVI – SAME STARS SAME INTELLECT, SAME COURAGE, SAME MORALS. SAME PREVILEGES.

You will heal one day in such a way that the WORLD WILL KNOW WHO YOU ARE. I know your birth history you are a saviour child born with blessings of this SHAKTHI GODESS. You are very charming. You are a beauty with brains and courage. Your husband will one day repent so much for his flaws that he will fall on your feet.

From that day onwards, their downfall starts and your Credibility begins. He says you are blessed by the Eternal Power of Shakthi, the goddess has saved you and she will save you, you have a long life Shivani.

You are born to rewrite and to heal mental disorders in women suffered by adversity. Don't cry anymore, walk with confidence and remember to recite "DURGA CHALISA". And be careful with your honesty. Just play Gulliblity with gullible people. Your credibility will make your abusers shiver with your eternal power.

Your faith in Hanuman will save and is a sacred saviour to you. When your intuition says that you are in danger immediately escape and seek help. You also have to brave very tough situations ahead. But nothng will happen to you once you escape and brave tough situations.

You will not look back in life, you will be transformed into a Beautiful Warrior Princess. You braved suffering, and injustice that could easily kill 8 women in a row. You will never ever Commit Suicide, because I know that the Goddess will save you. She will repay all your tears and triple your credibility. I don't advertise myself as a Astrologer, This temple is from Centuries, women like you have battles in their life. Your beautiful life starts from 2016. Being good and braving hurdles will pay you good.

BINDU AND SUDHIR PLAN MRS SUNANDHA'S RETIREMENT FUNCTION – DEC 2013

Shivani rings Mrs Sunandha and says, we don't have visa for Ameya, my P.R is about to expire. He is beating me and not eating food. What can we do?? She first acts like I don't know all this he is such a secretive person. I thought you guys are doing well. And don't tell him you called me. Shivani feels like asking, don't you have any freedom to speak to others and live with Respect. But she feels like she has get out of this hell. So, she says if you have sympathy on me and Empathy on Ameya, you will ask him to send to India when you are retiring.

Sudhir and bindu discuss about the gift they are going to give it Mrs Sunanadha. Sudhir says bindu want to talk to you about the gift. Shivani says, what do I know, I am not that good at selecting anything. Sudhir says, I will let you know by evening. Sudhir says now here is the deal, you will speak to bindu and then to my Vani aunty. Then I will allow you to speak to your parents and also to go to their home.

Mrs Sunandha though she plans everything according to her wish and will says "I am not having any celebration". When you guys are fighting with each other, but I want to advise you that it's not good to tell your family problems to anyone. Shivani says, then why does he beat me so much and doesn't allow me to speak to my parents. Already you lost your intelligence, what will you do except taking care of Ameya.

Mrs Sunandha says there are millions like you, who are enduring this what's the big deal, men have several issues,

wife should endure all their anger. For this time I will ask him to eat what you have cooked.

Shivani thinks, yes this is a power game and she knows all, even when I didn't say, anyways these people love Negative drama. Sudhir acts as though his mom is the only Anchor shivani has in the world. Her blood keeps boiling inside, but she doesn't speak a word. Common you abusers weave and act more drama, her inner voice says.

Shivani looses all respect for Sudhir and his family. She feels that they are the worst people behind their good masks outside home. She applies for her P.R renewal and Sudhir calls her and abuses her so much, if yours is finished is done right. Why would you bother about Ameya, even a step-mother doesn't behave so rude to her. Even a psychotic woman feeds her baby properly. Look at her she doesn't eat at all, you don't know you raise a child, he says I don't know what a curse you are to me and my family.

Shivani applies Ameya's visa and she gets in few days Visa to India. Then she renewals her visa too. Mrs Sunandha rings her and says bindu is coming, bring all of your jewellery. Shivani feels what a big deal has let this woman take all my jewellery and its control.

Now with this bruises and scars I am tired. Shivani gets very tanned as Olanzapine makes her skin very sensitive to Sun, even when she applies Sunscreen. Whenever Shivani goes to any party, Sindhu always asks Shivani, why are you wearing all old dresses, Shivani says it's been 3 years I have been to India. I didn't get any new ones. She doesn't speak to anyone, because her motive is to brave this anxiety and get back on her feet.

Sudhir asks Shivani to apply only 3 months Visit visa to Ameya as she has her school re-opened in February. Shivani collects all Ameyas' yearly reports and both attend the Parents and Teachers Meeting.

Ameya is doing well and she is very intuitive says her teacher. She doesn't eat her lunch, she always skips it.

Shivani says that is what my major concern is, she doesn't eat at home too. Sudhir doesn't say anything about it. Shivani on their way back to home says, you and your family say I have not raised Ameya up to the mark and don't give her food. Now the teacher says the same, only up to Year1, teachers monitor whether kids are eating their lunch. Sudhir says now don't start it again, and spoil my mood.

Sudhir invites his friends for dinner, Shivani cooks all items according to his list. Sunitha also comes to their home with her husband and family. She asks if she needs any help, shivani says no I can manage, please monitor whether Ameya is eating. Shivani and sunitha don't give a clue to other friends as what pain shivani is enduring with weaving Violence from Dublin and India.

Ameya's eating habits and also her bowel syndrome makes her tired always; she doesn't know how to tell her to drink more water. She tries all means, looks in the internet. Sometimes she even prepares Pizza at home. Sudhir doesn't like it, he makes a big deal out of everything. Shivani still tries to make Ameya love food she makes at home. She gives her flavoured drinks, by adding Oranges to her water.

Sudhir asks Shivani to book tickets for all three of them. He says he will come in January. Shivani does accordingly, she packs basic items and she feels good that she is going to India with Ameya. Sudhir finally gives permission to speak

to her parents and he says if my mom doesn't come to the airport, your dad can come and pick you and Ameya.

Shivani rings her Dad and says I don't have any good clothes to wear, Can you bring some cash to the airport, if I have to go with Sudhir's mom. Shivani's dad says it's ok, don't worry I will get you money. Shivani's mom says, I will bring dresses to you and even cash, if you don't like some of them, as you say you have gained weight.

SHIVANI COMES TO INDIA WITH AMEYA TO ATTEND MRS SUNANDHA'S RETIREMNET CEREMONY – 25TH DEC 2013

Shivani thinks that since it will be late in the night, Sudhir's mom won't come to pick her from the airport. But, to her ill fate she comes at late night and she has to wait for her for hours in the Airport. Mr Girish and his friend Rahman arrange a Welcome Note to Shivani and Ameya. As soon as she clears customs, Rahim and Girish come to her and help her with Ameya and her luggage. Looking at Shivani, her mom and paternal aunt shed tears, the way she has become so tanned and vulnerable.

She lands at the airport and Ameya starts crying that she has cramps in her stomach. Shivani's paternal aunt says, let's go to our home, it's closely. Suddenly Sunandha rings shivani's mom and says I am coming to pick them from the airport. They have to come to my home, bindu and jagan have come.

Shivani says Mom manage somehow I don't want to go with her and stay with that abusive bindu and jagan. Shivani

takes the clothes parcel and the money. Ameya doesn't go close to shivani's mom and dad though they have raised her. Shivani says to her dad let's go to our home.

Shivani's dad who is a Stereotype says "Wait she is coming", don't get into new trouble. I did speak to her brother Srinivas and he said this time, he will talk to the entire family as what have they achieved abusing you so much. Why is bindu and jagan again involving and weaving violence from Dublin. Mrs Sunandha comes to the car park and she starts grumbling at Girish and his wife. Saying where is shivani and ameya. Girish's sister says, shivani took ameya to the bathroom she was crying so much.

Mrs Sunandha rings Sudhir and says, your wife doesn't want to come to our house I guess her whole family is here to take her. Shivani's aunt says why are you jumping into conclusion, we didn't say we have come to take shivani and ameya. They are your family Sunandha says I'm dying with this shivani, she has no time management and doesn't know to manage ameya.

Shivani brings ameya from the bathroom, she gives a nice clean to her and gets her dressed in new clothes which shivani's mom has got for her. Mr Girish, says it's too late in the night. Let us all stay at my sister's home tonight since both of them are sick, they have jet lag.

Sudhir's mom says I will ask Sudhir what he says. She doesn't allow shivani to speak to him and says Sudhir is on rage, he is saying if she goes to Warangal, she need not come to Sydney. After a while, Mr Girish brings Ameya some fruit drink and gives her a teddy bear. Suddenly Ameya says Nana, shivani's aunty says ameya is just like our little shivani. When Shivani's mom makes her drink some juice,

she says Nani. Both of them hug Ameya and she says I want to come to your home. I don't want to go with her, she is so rude.

Shivani says I want to explain him, the stomach cramps shivani is having and my panic attacks too. She speaks to him, but he screams at her and says, my sister and her family have come to India. Just do as my mom says. Shivani's mom requests her that its 2:00am and both of them are sick, why don't you stay at your sisters' house close to the city?.

Sudhir's mom says ok, I will come with them, you guys carry on. In the middle of their journey, she says to the driver common divert the road. Shivani consoles Ameya who says "Mom this car is bad". We should not have come with her, she is very rude. Mrs Sunandha tries to touch Ameya, she shouts and screams, you are so rude. Nana and Nani are good they don't shout like you.

Sunandha gets fumed up and says if you shout once again, I will drop you and your mom on the road. Ameya starts crying, she says I want to go to Nana. Shivani whispers in her ears, that if she doesn't listen to what she says "We will be in trouble with dad". Ameya likes Sudhir but she is scared of him too. She knows that he smacks her sometimes with a comb too. And can stop talking to her for a day. So, being a innocent child she always gets perplexed as how to keep a big secret that her mom is abused and silenced.

They reach Sudhir's home town at 4:00 am and Ameya cries a lot with stomach cramps. Shivani says "Namasthe to Sudhir'dad who becomes with Parkinsons. She observes that he is losing his cognition by the day as Mrs Sunandha even confuses him too.

But, Sudhir's dad doesn't support shivani even he knows she is getting abused and silenced. He is the one who raised his hand against her and gave licence to sudhir from Silence to Violence and the Cycle is taking a nasty turn by the day.

Shivani feels very tired and she throws up as she couldn't attend Ameya's bathroom needs each hour. Mrs Sunandha says, she is asking you and is not letting me in. Ameya shouts Granny is rude, I want to go to Nani.

Mrs Sunandha threatens Ameya, if you shout more this is my home and your dad is my son. I will tell your dad to put you in a hostel. Ameya gets scared by the word hostel, because she can't sleep without Shivani by her side and also she is very dependent on her for everything. Shivani whispers, ameya let me tell you a story of a Princess. Ameya loves Shivani's creative stories.

But she asks her will we go to Nana, shivani says yes, we will ask Dad and go, now princess shouldn't scream in the toilet. When do good kids scream? "Ameya says I scream you Scream for an Ice-cream."Right answer, see then this is not the right place to scream. It is bad manners, to wake up everyone at this early hour by screaming in the toilet.

She weaves a story in her mind and she tells her a new one each day. Ameya says to Sunandha, my mom is so nice and kind. Why does Dad beat Mom? You are his parents why don't you say to stop beating mom. My teacher told me that beating is bad, we need to tell her if someone does that to her.

But, mom is not a kid, she even worked her cousin said, why does Dad beat Mom?. Sunandha gets very angry and says who is teaching you all this, is your mom. Ameya says no, Mom says Dad is good and we should understand that

he is tired from work. My teacher told us about abuse. I am now in a big school.

Mom says we shouldn't speak about Nana, Nani and Chinnu mama to dad. But, why should she speak to you all and Bindu aunty and uncle? Sunandha gives a angry look at shivani, she says to Ameya, let's go to sleep. Ameya, says I want you to sleep, she doesn't allow Sunandha to touch her. Sudhir's dad comes and tries to squeeze ameya's cheeks. She doesn't like it and Sunandha pushes him like a servant, keep away from my son's daughter. Shivani gets scared by the way Sunandha treats Sudhir's dad. Yet she can't forget the way he abused her so much. He is very selfish and shed crocodile tears.

Shivani and Ameya go to sleep and shivani wakes up at 8:00 am. Sudhir rings his mom and even when shivani wants to speak to him. She says, don't need to, are you so irresistible to speak to your husband. Shivani feels very embarrassed, she just wants Sudhir to send Ameya'slatest Eye Screening test reports. Shivani doesn't bring the box of her anxiety medication. Because she knows what Mrs Sunandha will do?

She keeps saying to Sudhir that Ameya is scared of Shivani. Why doesn't she have patience with the child? Shivani gets shocked; Sudhir says you know right these days she is on some stupid medicine. I keep telling her not to take it, she says I have to.

After a while Sudihr says give the phone to shivani, she speaks to him in a private room. She says I am not being rude to ameya, your mom was threatening her, how can she say such bitter lies. Sudhir says, don't ever dare to speak about my mom, whatever she does you have to accept it.

Now, see the real feast for you is when my sister and her husband come. Shivani says, I am used to it and braved it, I have been taught to be civilized not vandalized.

MRS SUNANDHA USES BIGOTRY TO CREATE AND WEAVE RUMOURS ON SHIVANI'S ANXIETY –

They have a party among Sudhir's relatives; she says to shivani that she bought a sari for her. Then again she says, I don't know where I lost it. Now let me check whether you have some good stuff. Shivani opens her suitcase, she brings all her old saris to give it to her mom or anyone and buy new ones.

Mrs Sunandha says you don't have any new stuff. All relatives there will ask so many questions. Shivani says I don't want to come. Ameya and I will stay at home as she is still having Jet lag. Ameya always has problem with her stomach cramps. She gets tired and sleeps in the evening. Mrs Sunandha puts party clothes to Ameya and she takes her to the party. Shivani gets so tensed as what if she wakes up and cries in the middle of their journey.

Sudhir rings shivani and says, my mom might be ashamed to introduce you to my relatives, that is why she took ameya with them. Anyways you say, you don't like family parties so good for you. Shivani says, I know how much you are enjoying by giving me such trouble and anxiety.

Yet, I am younger than you, so I do respect your age but not your callous attitude. This is not sense of humour. It is

killing hope of a Mother too who was once called NLC of HCF. Whenever Sudhir says something assertive, Sudhir says I don't want to hear your daily soap dialogues.

Shivani says I don't watch daily soaps. You and your family in collaboration with Jagan and his Paranoid family have made an NLC fail and God will prove it one day. Even J.K Rowling suffered a catastrophic Marriage, and was even clinically depressed. But when she healed and bounced back she became a "BILLONAIRE". And to me she is my inspiration.

Psychological disorder is not Psychotic, I worked in the Neuro-Science Project, and I know even the chemical composition of my medicine. No big deal even doctors have endured this and bounced back, I have seen many patients of my Dr. Mama gone through the worse and even healed.

His good deeds will be re-paid by God. I will heal and brave all this once nobody in my kith and kin will be ashamed of me. I braved and I am braving ugly violence for their reputation. Had this been a marriage of my choice, I wouldn't have been this patient with you and your family.

But I am not Clincally depressed. Dr. Helen told you that its inhuman stressors created and I couldn't fit into your archaic rules, where I am a free spirit person. Each day and moment I took this life as a challenge, yet I don't regret because I come from a School of Courage. I already braved half of the dosage.

Ameya doesn't wake up in the party too, as Ameya has no good sleep for about 2 days with jet lag and also with stomach cramps. Sunandha comes home, shivani makes some less spicy curry for Ameya to eat. The very next day

one of Sudhir's cousin rings to Sunandha and he says my wife lavanya wants to speak to shivani.

Shivani calls her sissy because she is quite older than and they hairom the same home town. She is also related to shivani even through her Paternal Family. Lavanya asks shivani if her fever is down., shivani says I had jet lag sissy not fever. Susheel wants to speak. Susheel calls her Sis-in –law though shivani is even younger than his own sister. Shivani with due respect says, I am younger than your sister Nischitha.

You can call me shivani, and please do consider me as one more sister too. Susheel says ok Shivani I have mentioned that way because Sudhir bro is elder to me. Anyways it's been ages we haven't met and even your parents too. Shivani says yes time flies and family obligations. Susheel says now that we are here settled in India for good, you have to come to visit us. Shivani says, yes with pleasure, when sudhir comes too.

The very next day Bindu and Jagan come with their family, shivani speaks to them very well as she knows that they fuel more violence. Mr Jagan says in a saracsatic way, you have made a fool of yourself by not being in goodt terms with us. Now, you are suffering with anxiety, this is what God does when you don't listen to Powerful people. Shivani feels like giving one tight slap on his face and call the cops to arrest him.

Shivani struggles a lot with Ameya's health and they enjoy their suffering. Bindu, says I am a doctor, I know how to fix your problem. Ameya in an assertive tone says you are a dentist not a doctor. My friend Sofia's mom is a doctor. She told me and mom what to do. You only check people's

teeth. Suddenly Jagan shouts on Shivani saying, Shut your Ameya's mouth. How dare she speak to bindu like that?

Ameya comes crying to shivani, she says to her "Momma they are rude", we will go to Nana. Bindu says hey Ameya, your jagan uncle was joking. Come and play with Sakhi. Ameya feels bad when they treat shivani bad. Mrs Sunandha sees shivani crying and instead of consoling her she says I will tell sudhir to keep you away from our family. You don't even need to go to Sydney too.

The next day shivani hears bindu and sunandha speaking to her cousin in U.S saying shivani lost her cognition. Shivani feels very bad about it, and she comes to sunandha and says why don't you all kill me at once, than to spread rumours about my cognition. Suddenly Jagan intervenes and says shivani we are all good, we are saying everything to your wellbeing.

What's a big deal if your dad is saying to Mr Srinivias that we are giving trouble to you and you are suffering each day? So bindu and her mom are revealing the reason behind the chaos. Shivani in an assertive tone says Prove that I'm incognitive and then weave rumours about my Cognition. So, pathetic you all are, I will ask Sudhir how far is it good to speak about a young mother this way. Sunandha says you want to create rift between bro and sister once again. I will not spare you thistime if you create any scene in my function. I am already having tough time with Sudhir's dad ailing health, because he thinks toomuch about Sudhir and his future.

Rjeshwari calls Sunandha and wishes her on her retirement. Then only she invites them, she is such a controlling woman who doesn't want shivani to heal and be

happy. She just wants her bindu to shine. Shivani's mom says Shivani did put on some weight, I was just thinking what dress have you purchased for her. Sunandha says bindu and shivani will wear sari. Shivani has plenty here, with her it's a small get-together we don't need to be a show off. Rajeshwari who always wants the best to shivani and sharth's wife still purchases some new dresses for Shivani.

Sunandha brings icecreams and toffies to ameya to attract her towards her, so that she has control over shivani and sudhir. Shivani always warns her not to give ameya somany junk foods. Yet, she says you are jealous of ameya, Shivani says me and jealous of ameya. I had a wonderful childhood very privileged than Ameya. My dad and his family is not abusive like you all are.

Ameya slowly gets attracted to Sunandha and bindu as one gives ice creams and the other gives video games to play. Mrs Sunandha on purpose asks Shivani to serve food to Jagan. Shivani feels so bad, when he shows his weird looks on her. Shivani starts to suspect Jagan's behaviour as he speaks of vulgarism on T.V so open to everyone. His questions always involve sharath and his properties and then Dr. Rama Krishna and his super speciality hospital. Shivani tries to avoid his presence and takes ameya out for shopping.

When she goes to out, she calls Rajeshwari and says I want to come out of this hell. Do take me to home after this silly function. This woman is celebrating as though she has won President's award. Mom I don't want to stay here, that Jagan's attitude is very vulgar. Rajeshwari says, don't panick shivani you just need to spend few days with them, just do meditation when you feel stress.

Sunandha says you didn't bring the parcel your mom gave. Shivani's dresses are in the parcel, she feels that what sunandha is saying is wrong. She might have hidden them as she hates me wearing new dresses and wants to see me in her shoes. She said she bought some new saris to both bindu and her. But, she then says she lost them.

On the day of her retirement Sunandha asks shivani to wear a sari and she gives a new dress to bindu. Shivani feels I will not complain now let my parents see what mind games she has played and my dad hates to see me in old clothes. This attitude of theirs will trigger my dad's anger and will be good to him and his stereotype attitude.

Ameya says mom you look old and bindu aunty looks good. Sunandha says, your dad is unlucky to have a ugly woman as his wife. Ameya says mom looks beautiful in her marriage picture. Dad says mom was beautiful, that is why he married her. My teacher says we shouldn't say to anyone they are not beautiful.

Krishna aunty who is a doctor said to me that mom is sick as dad beats mom, so she lost her charm. Jagan says you are very beautiful Ameya, I love your eyes, come and sit beside me. Ameya says you yelled at my mom I will not speak to you. I will complain to my dad about you when we go to Nana. My Nana is very nice and he bought so many dresses to me and mom. This is my special teddy from U.S my sharath mama sent me and I keep it with me always, Nana gave me this in the airport.

Shivani will be forced to say good words about Mrs Sunandha, she just says, she is a good teacher. Shivani feels like she is walking on thorns and doesn't want to stay at their place. She often feels that its not her real brave and assertive

behaviour. She feels like she is enslaved in Marriage. She writes in her book all her feelings which are bottled up deep inside her heart.

I can't imagine what my life is bringing day to day walking on these thorns each single day.

Is there any ray of hope in this swamp of despair and family violence each day?

I was born as a saviour child and raised as a princess with all privileges given by a famous doctor and an Entrepreneur.

I think my dad made a bad deal one business day with an engineer and I became the target of Money, Power and Control grilled each day?

God I know you are seeing this negative drama each day aren't you bored to see my tears, bruises and scars every day.

Your saviour child who is a young mom is getting diced and sliced, by abuse every single day.

Show me the way and take me to the healing land I know that you are not offline today.

Shivani's dad says to Sunandha that he wants Ameya and Shivani to come to their home. He says it's been three years they have come and we want them to come with us. Sunandha asks Shivani and Ameya packs all her stuff to leave to their home.

Shivani says, I don't know mom, again Sudhir will start his silence and violence if I don't tell him. Sunandha takes shivani to another side of the hall and threatens her that you can't leave bindu came to spend time with you. You know temperament of Sudhir and rest is in your hands. Shivani says to her dad she will come after two days. Just send the car you don't need to cancel your business trips because of me.

Shivani's dad always shows empathy to Sudhir's dad and when he is about to stumble down he says Shivani hold your father-in-law. Shivani looks at her dad and says, these people are spilling venom in my life and I have to be a devoted daughter-in-law. I wish my dad has some intuitive outlook like all his cousins have. Shivani holds him, suddenly Sunandha screams at her when shivani's mom is watching. Shivani just leaves the palce and says to Sunandha I am not your servant.

Shivani says see this is what I get to take care of him as a devoted wife of Sudhir. Dad is gone too dramatic after few words of sugar coated venom. He forgets my pain and believes all people are so honest and gentle like him. I feel like locking dad in one room and teach him what gullibility looks like in real world. Bindu comes and says mom is tired that is why shouted at shivani. Shivani says I got used to this cold attitude didn't your husband shout at me and Ameya. All her relatives think shivani is in trouble. Because, they know how aggressive and manipulative both bindu and sunandha are.

SHIVANI REVEALS HER PAIN, SUFFERING TO HER KITH AND KIN—jan2014

Shivani's parents invite sudhir to come to attend a holy rtual for their marital bliss and for Ameya's health at a temple. Sudhir controls shivani's every move and all her kith and kin observe how much he is using his "Power and Control". When her family asks him to stay for a night with

his family, Mrs sunandha plays her mind game and asks him not to stay for the night.

He does the same as his mom; he says we are going to meet Dr. Rama Krishna and then once they start off, he tells the driver to divert the route to his home town. Shivani gets reminded of sudhir's mom impromptu manipulation. She gets a clear idea, that he is so tough like his mom and this is her feedback.

After few days MrGirish comes to take Shivani and Ameya for a new land registration. Sunandha and bindu play mind games with shivani's stuff. They refuse to give Ameya's Eye test reports. Dr. Rama Krishna asks shivani to get Ameya's eye test reports. Sudhir goes to Hyderabad and shivani comes to Warangal. All of her kith and kin gather and they shed tears to see their lovely princess all worn out with abuse

She reveals to her family how they have abused and silenced her and says that her label is "Incognitive Mother". Dr. Rama Krishna hugs shivani and he cries tears of blood. I raised you with my hands; these people are after your life.

Shivani doesn't cry as much as her family does, she says Mama when violence takes an ugly shape, God will intervene. You have given me the best and now you people are adding one more property to my inheritance. But, they are playing a very dangerous game with your high profile status they have abused and silenced your princess.

I am going to sign and give this letter to you, if anything happens to me, all my belongings and also these properties will be given to Ameya only when she is 18 years old. Since they have a abusive record in NSW medicare, they will not have Ameya with them. I am not a fool dad, I have recorded

even bindu and jagan fuelling violence. Simple if ameya has to suffer so does bindu and her family too.

Everybody in her maternal and paternal family says Princess you don't need to stay with that guy who is a mooma's boy of a Manipulative Parents and very conniving Sister and brother-in-law. Shivani says to her dad that jagan's attitude is very vulgar.

He has very bad eyes on us and some mantras he keeps chanting when we are around. He yelled at ameya and me too. Her grand ma and her mama cry so much.

Mr Girish says that Sudhir's maternal uncle is not aware of everything, shivani says dad you are so ignorant. They all are a team and I was a good catch that Mr Srinivas cant utter a single word before my inalws and sudhir. And his favourite is bindu and jagan. They all say that Marriage is just a label, you are abused and enslaved.

You don't need to stay with this guy and family shivani. We won't force you anymore we know how much you have sacrificed for Ameya and our reputation. Shivani says "Dad I don't believe you". Within days you will be stringed by social stigma and start chaos at home. You only said even if I were to die, it's at my marital home. Now, I am doing the same, I don't believe you. Now if I back off, they will bombard all of you that they are so good people to let an in cognitive woman as their family member. You don't know this game I understood it, but one day I will break it too.

I can see that my father-in-law is getting for all that he has done to me. Shivani's paternal aunties say we are afraid that you might end up like him. Shivani says, no aunty don't ever think that way, he is very scornful and paranoid that is why he is the stage of delusion and slowly he will get

into psychosis too. My mom-in-law plays mind games with him too. Yet, I don't empathize with him as he is one with crocodile heart and tears.

Shivani says I am suffering like" Mother India "during the regime of British Colonization. Same archaic procedures are being used against me. I just pity them now, I don't even hate them. I know that one day God will show me the way and heal me. I saw miracles happen to me and ameya.

I was in deep sleep and the wind blew so strong the balcony door smashed, I was sleeping on the couch, after taking my medicine. Ameya was at school and Sudhir at work. The door slashed down and broke into pieces, yet nothing happened to me, even there were glass piece on the floor underneath the couch I was sleeping.

Ameya hurt her head, stitches on her head and nothing happened to her skull too. I was drowned in water, and swallowed a lot, thought I will end my life. Yet the life saviour came and saved me. I saw that god was sending his messengers to save me when I was about to meet death. One in four women experience Domestic Violence in Australia and some even die too.

I can put him behind the bars and do you why I didn't do it, because his mom wants him to be her slave in her retirement days. She says, he doesn't need any work to do there and if I complain to the cops, he will lose his job. Such a pathetic idiotic approach his parents have towards him. She says ring the cops and you guys can come over and live on my money or my daughter's money. His family's intentions are worse than him mama. He is a scapegoat; I have read al lot about this kind of phenomenon. He cries after he beats me and then again does the same.

Shivani's mama takes her to the Nuero Physician, Dr. Samuel, says except inhuman stressors our princess cognition is perfect. I am unable to believe how she can be so brave and courageous even when they are abusing her beyond human threshold. I can bet you buddy she doesn't need any medication, if she heals her emotional and physical wounds and stays here with us.

He says that fellow her husband needs Counselling, he doesn't know that he is abusing another Xerox brain, phantom intellect of Dr. Rama Krishna. Dr. Ram Krishna says shivani doesn't want to give up, she doesn't want the taboo of social stigma on her.

She would have been a doctor like you, look at her intuition and her knowledge about her medication. She is even telling you that she changed from dosage to dosage with CBT and also telling you that she is using generic brand, because of low chemical composition. She knows each bit of her medication and she has read a lot about CBT and about anxiety disorders.

I will tell you, that her intellect is far more than they ever imagine and her courage is far more than we can ever expect and anticipate. She is a rare combo of beauty, brains and courage. I respect you shivani for great sacrifice you have made for ameya and to your family's reputation. you have such commitment to marriage and he is behaving inhuman to you. This guy is the most unlucky one to abuse a Beautiful Princess with high intellect and warrior Courage.

The problem with her suicidal thoughts is because of inhuman stressors and weaving violence. These people should be behind the bars, because this guy has hurt shivani's head, there are injuries on her skull too.

Dr. Rama Krishna cries a lot, and says because of some stupid drama in that Jagan family, he hurt her onto the washing machine.

Shivani tells uncle he hurt me on my head several times. Yes princess your skull has injuries, but hypothalamus is perfect. Keep this report with you and don't ever show it to them. When we need to punish them, they will not have a word to say about your cognition. It was my mistake by not being assertive to that family in 2008. My princess is being abused and beaten black and blue.

Shivani says something is very fishy about this mantras and rings. I need to get a clear understanding exactly what are their cruel intentions. Shivani says to her grandma "I want to know what my Star sign is". My in-laws blame my zodiac sign for chaos. There is something going on very bad at Mr Jagan's home on us. I don't say it's Occult worship, yet I can say Evil Eye black magic.

I know mama that you won't believe in this stuff, but there is negative energy and negative vibes used in that home in Ongole. She Visits the temple and tells him what has happened to her ever since Ameya is born She shows him the stone anywhere in the bin. These people know that you are beyond perfection.

She asks him Shasthri uncle is my Zodaic sign a havoc to marital bliss? The priest says shivani what is the meaning of your name—SHIVANI (GODESS OF ETERNAL POWER) – DURGA DEVI. Yes Shivani I can bet on my life and say your star is similar to the Warrior Princess of the Kakatiya Dynasty, RUDRAMA DEVI – SAME STARS SAME INTELLECT, SAME COURAGE, SAME MORALS. SAME PREVILEGES.

You will get healed one day in such a way that the WORLD WILL KNOW WHO YOU ARE. I know your birth history you are a saviour child born with blessings of this SHAKTHI GODESS. You are very charming. You are a beauty with brains and courage. Your husband will one day repent so much for his flaws that he will fall on your feet.

From that day onwards, their downfall starts and your Credibility begins. He says you are blessed by the Eternal Power of Shakthi, the goddess has saved you and she will save you, you have a long life Shivani.

You are born to rewrite and to heal mental disorders in women suffered by adversity. Don't cry anymore, walk with confidence and remember to recite "DURGA CHALISA". And be careful with your honesty. Just play Gulliblity with gullible people. Your credibility will make your abusers shiver with tremor by your eternal power.

Your faith in Hanuman will save and is a sacred saviour to you. When your intuition says that you are in danger immediately escape and seek help. You also have to brave very tough situations ahead. But nothing will happen to you once you escape and brave tough situations.

You will not look back in life, you will be transformed into a Beautiful Warrior Princess. You braved suffering, and injustice that could easily kill 8 women in a row. You will never ever commit Suicide, because I know that the Goddess will save you. She will repay all your tears and triple your credibility. I don't advertise myself as an Astrologer, This temple is from Centuries, women like you have battles in their life. Your beautiful life starts from 2016. Being good and braving hurdles will pay you good.

NEW HOME BRINGS HOPE TO HEAL AND TO RELIVE MARITAL BLISS– OCT 2014

Shivani, Sudhir and Ameya, enter into the new house on 24th cot 2014, which is Durga Dashami. The day when Goddess of Eternal Power has killed deamons. Shivani steps into the home with many dreams. She likes the house even it is simple and small. She infact wants a small house. She believes in simple living, high thinking.

Yet his mom rings, her everyday and inquire about everything. Shivani feels that she will be controlled all her life. She always says I do not understand why you are not searching for a job. Shivani says Ameya has to adjust to the new school. Sunandha always wants shivani to struggle for her existence and be abused and silenced.

Sudhir makes shivani run on egg shells to unpack and settle down everything. Ameya has to go to new school, she has to pack his lunch and then unpack everything.

Sunandha keeps dauntimg her that she is too slow. Her entire body becomes fragile with abuse since 9 yrs and also because of his controlling and weaving violence tendency.

TEJAS CRADLE CEREMONY SHIVANI GETS ABUSED --- NOV 2014

Sunandha wants every tiny bit of information in Shivani's maternal home. Shivani's uncle who knows her crisis from the scratch sends referral to Shivani. Shivani is selected on the phone interview. Ever before the interview, sudhir informs bindu and sunandha. Shivani says slow down I did not even go to the interview. He completes her sentence saying shivani wants to buy a nice dress for you with her hard earnings.

Shivani feels why he impresses them so much. She is reminded of his parents' abuse for an E- Spirit shirt. Moreover, how much did Sudhir beat her for being assertive to them? He says now once shivani gets a job, I will apply PR for mom and dad. Hearing this shivani gets startled because his parents are a weaving violence and rumours network.

However, she has no experience with SAP and she is always anxious about her life day in and day out controlled by sudhir and his folks. Shivani prepares well for the interview.

However, she forgets to take her homeo destressor pills. Her hands tremble a lot in fear when the HR manager gives her a shake hand. She still gathers confidence and answers their questions. After the interview, she feels very restless and she faints in the cabin. That is when the HR manager asks her what is the problem. Shivani explains she is in a Family Violence situation.

Showing much Empathy, the manager says I will speak to your uncle, about your fragile situation. You need to heal shivani, you have a sharp intellect. You can easily get back on your feet with much Credibility.

Shivani remembers the words the Manager has said, Sudhir has his own plans, as his Weaving violence network will now stay at home. Next phase would be expensive holidays to his family and corporate slavery to her. He does not know what Shivani had in her mind. When she comes home, Sudhir says my mom and sister want to talk to you.

Shivani says I do not think I will get this job. Sudhir says it is ok for a while and then says you have spoiled your competency with your bad relations with my family.

Shivani says I didn't spoil any relations, they enjoy Power and Control and you do so. I am not in a mood to discuss about all this. She cooks all stuff for the day and just concentrates on what the HR manager has told her.

Sharath's wife Shwetha gives information about online courses. Sudhir feels very agitated inside, because he thought shivani would add more to his family holiday treats.

After days ask shivani, to post a letter and then says do not get confused as you messed up an interview. Shivani gets fumed up and says "I am not suffering with delusion or hallucination thoughts", like your dad who lost his Cognition. Sudhir calls her from his work and says, who said to you that my dad had lost his Cognition?

Shivani says who should tell me I saw partly in India and my dad asked me to be aware of him. He has been very restless in Tejas Cradle Ceremony. Therefore, I said it to you when you triggered my self-esteem of my anxiety. This is in the last, stage of healing, with homeopathy. He was making fun of your maternal uncle and making himself a Showstopper in the party, speaking gibberish.

In the evening, he comes home, rings his maternal uncle, and asks him "Did my dad speak gibberish? He does not say anything; he just says he is not in a good health condition.

Sudhir starts weaving Violence, he shares the same with his mom and his sister. Then Sunandha rings her and bombards her with war of words. Never ever, any teacher would say such kind of words she speaks to Shivani.

You are almost in the last stage of your Cognition

You have lost your sanity; I will show you what I am when I come to Sydney. You are not even worth of a nanny.

You cannot maintain a house, handle ameya and then says you are fit only to eat well and sleep. Sudhkar sheds crocodile tears saying, I thought we could spend some time in Warangal. However, we did not know that your folks who are rich have such opinion on me. Sudhir takes revenge like a serpent. Until, she says "Sorry". He does not stop weaving violence; this is his entire family's attitude.

He cannot hear a small word against him and his family. Yet, keeps silent and remains as a bystander when his family bombards her and even beats her black and blue.

Shivani feels broken, she gets so freeze for the callous attitude of Sudhir. She rings her cousin's wife Usha and shares her pain. Usha comforts her saying that they are abusive and sudhir is a master in abusing you and weaving violence. You do not cry to live with dignity and respect is your divine right.

The very next day bindu calls her and says, shivani you might have lost your sanity,

Why don't you see a Psychiatrist? Shivani says bindu, I am doing good, I know you all are powerful and I am vulnerable. I am on Destressors and you are a dentist not a Nuero Physician or a surgeon.

Sudhir does not let shivani eat food that night and asks her to prepare Chapati. She says there is no flour left.

He then shows the flour packet. Shivani says there was a Cockroach in the packet. Sudhir says now show me where was the cockroach. Shivani feels so silly and she thinks, "This guy is gone out of his mind".

He truly needs Psychotherapy. Shivani says, "Cockroach doesn't stay at one place, it flies". Sudhir disconnects her call and does not come, untill midnight.

The next day when he comes home she says, "I wouldn't have stopped my family". They wanted to discuss this weaving violence and abuse beyond human threshold with you. Sudhir picks his phone and starts weaving violence once again. He says, to his mom that he has planned to come to India.

She rings shivani and bombards her saying, my co-sisters are enjoying life, and one of them is going to South Africa. And I have this in my life, You don't even have a job and be so strong in your speech. Shivani gets fumed and says if you all can prove I don't have Cognition, and succeed in it.

I will leave ameya and sudhir and leave this world or go back to my maternal home. If you cannot prove and if you fail to do so. You will ask Sudhir to stop calling me insane and this weaving violence network and abuse.

Now I have surpassed the so-called stage of happiness, I want respect and my human rights and my dignity in motherhood.

Sunandha gets a clear understanding that now shivani will do whatever she likes, because she is not afraid of social stigma than her Cognition and Credibilty.

She has this kind of exploitation of human resources capability too. She then rings her and says; now you do not say a word. I have told him not to come to India.

Shivani says Ameya has no Indian Visa her visa expired otherwise I would have come to India ages ago. She feels as though she is doing a favour to shivani, wherein she encourages sudhir to weave violence and beat her black and blue.

Sudhir hears shivani speaking to her mom and shwetha takes the phone. She says sis-in-law you do not need to put up with this abuse. They will be behind bars if you give a complaint on them to the Cops.

Now, do not get scared of anything, this is beyond human threshold. Your in-laws have no shame or guilt. They are so self-centred and want all luxuries at the expense of your sacrifice. Sudhir then again calls his mom and says now ring his sharath's wife parents and tell what his sister is up to.

Shivani texts shwetha about this. She says I do not bother, neither, my family and your brother. Let them call sissy, I want you and we all want you to standup for yourself and give them a shut up call.

They do not know how much my dad adores you as a daughter. He knows each bit, do not get scared. Be alert and prepare a safety back up plan.

Your vulnerable situation has, been explained to a great leader of B.J.P. Sharath, Girish meet him and explain her vulnerable situation. He assures them that they will her in emergency. Sharath says sissy ask them to ring my in-laws and tell them that they can reveal whatever they want to reveal. Now even my wife is a new mom and how is she treated, how were you abused, they also know bit by bit.

Sudhir looks at those messages from sharath and he becomes alert. He now tries to blackmail shivani saying he will drink a BOTTLE OF VODKA, and become sick.

I am going to resign my job, this is what he says. He makes shivani sit it one corner in the bedroom and says, now you can't move from here.

Shivani doesn't know what to do, and she just texts sharath, in any emergency I will ring you.

He is not abusing me and if he does so, I will ring the cops as you have been saying to me ages.

Sudhir's mom rings Girish and says that she does not know what is happening to sudhir.

She tells that whatever may be the issues between them their relation should not get, affected. Because, she is very tired with, Sudhakar.

Sudhir makes shivani believe that she has lost her cognition. He behaves in the most, mean way and says, "I will send you to mental asylum, and if you give back answers to my folks and me".

Sudhir explodes with anger when it comes to any assertive issue about his folks. He loses his temper, and abuses her verbally and does not allow her to live at peace. He tries to hit her that is when she says now doing even think about it. I am going to ring the cops

In a much grandiose way, he says I will tell them you are seeing someone. Shivani feels like she is broken, yet remembers the words her family Nuero Physician has said to her. You are perfect, he is the one who needs Psychotherapy. Shivani says I am as pious as a flower at the feet of the Eternal Power who saved my life.

SHIVANI SEEKS PROFESSIONAL HELP – DOMESTIC VIOLENCE COUNSELLOR – NOV 2014

Shivani feels that now she has to seek professional help. She goes to the nearby Medical Centre. She explains her fragile and vulnerable condition. Dr. Asar who is a G.P there refers her to a Domestic Violence Counsellor and Therapist the next day. Shivani drops Ameya at school and reaches the centre.

She explains how Sudhir being doing this and how much violence is weaved. She asks her is there any problem with her cognition. Dr. Fea checks her Cognition and she asks her to check her Psychopathology too.

She reveals to them that she has been a Quality Assurance Analyst in HCF, and worked as B.A in North Sydney too. Moreover, because of weaving violence, from, Dublin to the office too.

She had to quit her job with bullying, violence and divorce threats even when she is at work.

Dr Fea says shivani this person has Pyschopathy and you are beyond perfection. Your cognition is, called NLC, yes, they were right at HCF. You are gifted and talented.

However, you are abused and silenced. With these inhuman stressors, you have developed these racing thoughts of suicide. You are depressed by situations and not clinically depressed. If you reach a safe place without any abuse, you will and can prove your credibility.

Shivani says doctor my intuition says that I might be in great risk for my life. Are these weird thoughts or paranoia.

Dr. Fea says because of the violent history, Power, and Control these people have used on you.

It is quite common to have these thoughts. Remember be safe and have our numbers and make a safety backup plan.

Now that you do not want to take any medications other than, the plant extracts for your Post Traumatic Stress and OCD.

I suggest you to make a good safety back up plan and beat Gullibilty with Credibilty. He and his family is using Weaving violence, and using Ameya to enslave you and make you look like a Bad mother.

Women in abusive situations, find it very difficult to mentor and raise the kids. To them parenting becomes a walk on thorns and eggshells, as the other abusive partner turns the kids against the victim parent.

Calling her names, showing she is worthless and so on. This makes the victim mother vulnerable and she struggles each day to raise her children who call her by the same labels given by the abuser.

This kind of parenting is called Narcisstic- Parenting. Where the, Perpetrator of Violence uses the child against the victimized mother.

Start your work at Schools when they come, keep yourself busy and make sure you and your baby girl are safe. Do not hesitate to call the cops if they abuse you once again. Violence against Women Australia says no. Yet, there are women who never raise their voice and seek help. Once kids are involved these abusers take you for granted in Indian society.

Shivani this is not Hinduism this is nothing but "Narcissism". Remember this person and his attitude is the reason for your stressors, you are his cure and he is abusing you. In short, he is a SPOILED BRAT OF A PARANOID WOMAN.

I appreciate your courage in volumes to brave this and feel your parents are truly lucky to have a beautiful, courageous girl. You can stand on your feet in a much higher position. World is Global and you can study many courses Online.

Your Credibility can only come out when you unveil their Gullibility of abusing you and then making you vulnerable.

SUDHIR'S DAD GOES MISSING; SHIVANI BRINGS HIM FROM THE POLICE STATION --- NOV 2014

Sunandha is always curious about shivani and her clothes and jewels. She does not even bother about her husband while showing her packet to sudhir saying her parents have stapled everything in order. She says may be these plant extracts will make you gain weight. Shivani says it is a proven experiment by a famous doctor in California. That plant extracts and the medication made from them is very good for anxiety disorders, and if they work well, you do not need medicine again.

Sunandha speaks about bindu and her medical knowledge shivani says bindu has no idea about neuroscience.

My friend is a nuero surgeon and my family doctor in India Dr. Samuel is a Nuero Physician from ages.

He knows each bit by bit and can study about all neurons and their transmition. Anxiety disorder he says is all because of being abused and silenced.

Sudhakar says I have to see the neighbourhood and he needs to take a walk. Therefore, he walks away while she is busy with ameya and both sudhir and his mom discussing about sharath and his wife.

Sudhahar doesn turn up even after15 minutes, shivanis says sudhir your dad is missing. Sunandha runs in another direction. Shivani drops ameya to school and starts searching him everywhere. Sudhir makes shivani walk on eggshells and yells at her.

She says all this is chaotic and in the scorching sun she feels dizzy and feels like she is about to faint.

Hetal, Vyshali and all see her and say shivani why are you walking so fast and what is that you are searching for. Shivani says both my inalws are missing and we are in chaos.

Hetal says hey I saw a lady going into the woods of Farham road, she wore a brown sari. She looked all new to me and she is perplexed. Shivani says yes she is ameya's granny. They say friend she went in the opposite direction.

Shivani says sudhir I am tired, your mom is at Farnham road. Sudhir says these both people they have made my life hell. Shivani finds sunandha and tells her to stay at home. Shivani drinks some water, starts searching him on every road, and asks every vehicle that is stopped by. Whether they have seen, an old man.

Shivani finds that a vehicle that is stopped at the entrance of the community and a woman calls her. She asks them if they saw an old man in his 70 is walking towards the church. Her husband says are you looking for an old man of Indian origin.

The woman says, do you mean an old man who looks like he has lost his mind and is speaking gibberish.

Shivani says yes, hey he came to our home and was saying he knows some MrSudhir, and he is into politics.

Shivani says yes he was speaking about my husband. Oh my god where is he now. The woman says, we dropped him at the police station.

He sounds crazy and he is not in a good condition too. They say come with us we will take you to meet him. Shivani never ever trusts any strangers; she says I will inform my husband and we can go together.

Shivani rings Sudhir and informs him that he is at the police station. Sudhir says come lets go, when they reach the station. He says now they will ask me hundred questions. Go show your Id and bring him. Shivani says ok and goes to the station. She looks at sudhir's dad and he becomes a showstopper at the station. She signs the paper and says, "He is having trouble with his cognition". He is my husband's dad. They tell her that he is asking, them all weird questions and was making big fuss there.

He needs a care taker and should be in a Rehab if has trouble with cognition. Shivani says I am thankful to your empathy, and this won't repeat, he has not taken his medication and is having cycles of positive and negative thoughts.

Sudhir daunts his dad on the road and says you will wreck my job. Who asked you to come out of the house, luckily shivani's friends saw you. If not I would have been in trouble. Shivani who has empathy and is not prejudiced like them says, now if you daunt more his cognition will get affected more and more.

Yet, nobody thank her and sunandha proclaims that she found him. Shivani takes the phone and tells Vani, what happened, as she knows these kind of patients while working in HCF.

Sunandha does not acknowledge shivani's empathy and she lives in her own fantasyland of travelling Europe and Thailand. Shivani does not bother and then they start their daunting repeatedly.

Shivani thinks she has never seen any opportunists like them in her life. They san empathy and they just want "Power and Control".

SUDHIR'S PARENTS ABUSE SHIVANI – IN SYDNEY IN HIS ABSENCE EACH DAY

Shivani speaks to her friend Dr. Mythilli quite a senior to her and is from her hometown. She also says you did a good thing to seek professional help. Shivani says mythilli I have browed in the internet and only way to beat narcissism is to just "Outsmart with Kindness". You will have to observe their style of game from the scratch as it is weaving violence.

Moreover, perfectly it is Imperialism. Our rules our wishes, you are our corporate slave and we will extort you and weave rumours on your cognition.

Moreover, outsmart them and beat them on their own game, act exactly like them. Her school friends and college friends become alert and call shivani each one on Roster basis.

Girish is a very stereotype person, he just want shivani to be a obedient daughter inlaw, even at the cost of her own wellbeing. Sharath and Rajeshwari bring some stuff to shivani and they give gifted amount of 250 US dollars.

Sudhir and his parents feel like they have conquered the world by abusing shivani and making her walk on eggshells. Sunandha and Sudhakar feel very superior when Girish and his wife, come and meet them to give shivani her House Warming Ceremony clothes.

It is a tradition in Hindus, that the Girl's parents send their blessings to her and her family by gifts. The girl and her family have to wear the clothes given or sent by Sudhir's dad who has a kind of a scorn in mind yet very sarcastic in speech.

You are now in good position in politics. I want my reimbursement money back as soon as I come from Sydney. This is like a wedding gift to your daughter and to ameya too. Girish who knows what is happening to shivani says ok, I will try my best.

Rajeshwari request Sunandha that shivani is healing and she is very fragile child of their family. Now that all of you will be together, I hope you will not make her feel outcast and make her more vulnerable.

Her emotional situation is very fragile; she says, I am living like a corpse and forgot to smile.

Allow her to wear the outfits she like, shivani has been privileged and we never made her feel short of any thing.

She is like princess of our two families. Sunandha in a much superior tone says, Shivani does not understand sudhir and his temperament.

He is very stubborn and is very, much attached to his sister and us. I have never caused any trouble to her, and women have to go through this, she is not a new bride.

That is when sharath intervenes and says, yes. We know that our sissy is not a new bride, but her motherhood is very vulnerable and you all have abused, her and silenced her beyond human threshold.

My sissy who always used to smile, forgot to smile, she is just surviving. We have given you the land paper and we have registered another land on her name.

Even I am married I have an infant son; we do not behave like this to my wife.

It has been 8 years, she is suffering with inhuman stressors, and I hope you understand the affects of Cognitive instability now that his dad is also suffering.

We cannot afford to lose our sissy to Maternity Suicide and Maternity death. Girish tries to stop him, but he doesn't, he just says, this is age of drones and how long will she endure such pain.

I have seen her pain in the emails she writes to my wife who is three years younger than she is. She quit her job, and could not tolerate abuse and then you all multiplied it, what is that she is expecting from you.

Sudhakar sheds crocodile tears and says sudhir is very stubborn and we will try to tell them. By the way, we have heard that you people have good valuable lands close to the Warangal Airport. Sharath, who is very generous says, Dad and I have decided to give the fruitful part to sissy.

Sudhir does not allow shivani to speak to her family. Shivani feels very agitated, yet she maintains her poise. She cooks a special dinner to them and arranges everything in an order.

Because she has her own plan on her, mind. It is to outsmart their covert narcisstic traits by Killing with kindness.

Now truth will come out, whether they are venomous and dangerous or they are just cowards and using Power and Control, to enslave her for their convenience.

Shivani plans to stay, all day at the school. Sunandha starts her daunting, as usual. She says you do not have a job and your parents are being so mean to us. Your brother did not even bother to come and see when Sudhir's dad is sick. His wife does not even speak to us when we went to the cradle ceremony.

Shivani remembers the words the therapist, and the priest said, "Don't succumb to their abuse". She gives assertive answers this time. When I am dying here with abuse, how my folks can be happy. Of course, they will ask you the reasons.

What will happen if Sudhir hits me hard and, something tragic happens to me?

Infact one of my mama's friend Dr. Samuel said that it is only your abuse that made, me to take these tablets or even distressors. Now, I am on homeopathy and it is working too. My anxiety has come down too. Moreover, my cognition is good; I know this process of healing through CBT (Cognitive Behaviour Therapy).

I just do not understand why you should agree to get me married to your son, when you do not want him to marry me. I was not desperate to marry him; I was just 23 and finished my graduation. Shivani just gives very assertive answers to them. I had planned to complete my Masters in U.S. I got my I-20 too.

I am not a dumbo student, I was good at studies and I did get my job very soon in IT. I did not even study computers, I am an electronics graduate. Yet, I got the job by my own competency. I worked with all Fortune Five hundreds as clients.

Abuse, Power and Control has failed me on epic scale. I did not even breathe happiness one day after Ameya was born. Is it a plan to enslave me after I have a kid? My motherhood is an epic saga of pain, suffering and grief beyond human threshold.

Sunandha says my bindu worked so hard, that is why she bought a home. Shivani in an assertive tone says, may be your bindu has got a chance to work

I had to quit my NLC job at HCF, where I got it only by my competency and talent.

You all weaved violence and made me lose my wonderful career. I quit my job and that day I can never forget how my team felt for me.

I am still living, with a hope that one day, things will fall in place.

In addition, you all can see how much close I am to death with such abuse. She then says I am going to school. I have arranged everything on the table, you can have breakfast, lunch too. I have a special class with differently abled kids. Shivani takes up the responsibility to work with Autistic kids.

Some of them can remember some things and lest they forget. They do not listen to anyone in the class they become hyperactive. Yet they are embraced, and given a chance to compete with the other kids.

Shivani helps the kids and ameya feels better. Sunandha starts her control over ameya. She says I teach bindu's son and he scores well. Shivani says that it's a different syllabus in India and Auz. It is not easy for you whose medium of instruction is not English.

The next day sudhir's dad makes a weird comment, how can you eat your food, which my son is bringing home without a job. Shivani says to sudhir while pressing his clothes, why does your dad pass such comments on me?

You know how fragile my situation is, and my physical and emotional health too. Didn't my dad tell you that they have registered another land on my name?

Sudhir shouts in a very loud tone, she is saying you people are abusing her.

Shivani gets fumed and she leaves home, she spends all day in the scorching sun.

A noble and young mom of a 7 year old looks at shivani. She is very sad and is unable to control her tears.

Hetal comes to her and says what's wrong shivani, you were so happy with the new house and all. She says I am going through a terrible marital crisis.

His parents and sister made my life terrible and now they daunt me for even eating food. Hetal invites shivani with empathy, she explains her family status, and how vulnerable she is.

My folks never gave an assertive answer to my husband and his family. They don't even have a clue as what is that I am experiencing. She understands her problem and consoles her, asks her to eat food. Shivani eats once slice of toast and she goes back to school.

After a while, she goes home, and she does not speak to anyone. She just plays the Durga Mantra, and closes her door. She writes her painful experiences. Moreover, feels very intimidated and vulnerable.

I never thought I would become such an object of consumerism and a mere corporate slave at home.

I was in the scorching sun, god can you hear me, because I never heard you in these eight years.

Is motherhood a boon or bane you should decide as I am losing my anchor in life that is because I do not see any hope?

She plays the song "Durgamantra" eternal chants of the goddess of Creativity "Shakthi". Sunandha says in sarcastic way, oh you think she will solve your problems.

Shivani does not say a word and she says if she cannot solve then there will be a debacle. She is goddess who makes "Miracles happen in Adversity".

Sudhakar says I am sorry shivani, I shouldn't have said that to you. For the first time shivani hears the word sorry from him.

Sunandha says none of had lunch, Sudhir did not eat anything. Sudhir says, look at my dad his condition is bad because of you. Shivani says, can you allow me to speak, your dad had Parkinson's ever before we got married. Tell me who is responsible for my anxiety, back pain, and nervous tension. He does not say a word.

Shivani says I had enough of this abuse and torture I feel like ending my life each day. I am just living to do my duty towards ameya. My heart is broken ages ago by abuse and weaving rumours.

I feel it is a life of a curse and would be, better if I cannot get on my feet to end this horrible slavery life. Shivani goes inside the laundary to wash ameya's clothes. She slips on the wet floor and she falls down with her head also hurting the tiles.

Sudhir comes from backyard and finds her on the floor. She will not be able to stand on her feet. She cries at lot in pain, he comes and says to his mom may be she is acting.

When shivani says I am not a coward to act, I have got nothing to lose as I am on the edge of sacrificing my life And praying god for my natural death, because I don't break promise I gave to my Dr. Mama. He told me a Global Institution is running on Infertility, because I am his inspiration and his first saviour child.

Sudhir says, I didn't think it really hurt you, his mom says what a man will do to help you. I will use a Painkiller Spray. Shivani says I do not need your help, I am better off with this. I am a wounded soldier.

Sudhir comes and looks at shivani at night; he says what you have made out of yourself. You do not know any tricks and behave like a man in courage. I don't know what you are upto. He thinks shivani is asleep, but shivani listens to what he says. She thinks he is not bad always; he is being spoiled by venom.

Things become normal next day and sudhir says go see a doctor. He drops her at the station, and she reveals to the doctor how she fell down.

He says shivani, you need complete rest, and this body is all wounded. Shivani looks at him and says, I cannot now, as my in-laws will weave rumours that I am lazing in bed.

He gives her prescription for painkillers and checks her nerves too. He asks her if she can bend, she says doctor I am unable to bend any further than this.

Sudhir comes late in the night and shivani waits until he returns from work. Sunandha does not allow shivani to speak to her family. She keeps grmbing and tries to scare her about her marital bond. Shivani says I'm studying and I love to see my nephew Tejas, he is my first nephew.

She weaves rumours to sudhir that shivani is neglecting them and is busy with her ipad. Shivani says sudhir, your parents are here and I won't even ask my parents to come But I have every right to see my nephew and moreover even when doctor asked me to take rest I am still doing all chores in the house.

SUDHIR'S PARENTS INSULT SHIVANI AT HIS FRIENDS HOME, YET SUDHIR DOESN'T SAY A WORD--- DEC 2014

A day before bindu comes to Sydney. Sindhu and Jay invite sudhir's family to lunch. Shivani gets well dressed and even she makes ameya wear a good outfit. Sunandha who is always jealous of shivani, says you have all these from your parents. They are just spoiling you with privileges.

Shivani says I used to wear the best in my college days. This is not even half of what I wore during my student life. Moreover, I love trendy colourful dresses. Sudhir's mom gets a clear understanding that shivani is being very assertive and different to them. Yet she does not speak a word.

When they reach jay's home, they start daunting shivani. Sudhakar says shivani and her family are rich but they do not have competency only bindu is intelligent. He then says, that shivani is lazing around without a job and even not having a heir to their family. Her brother has a baby boy, but she is reluctant to have any more kids.

Sudhir who sees tears rolling in shivani's eyes does not say a word. Sunandha adds saying sudhir changed entirely after his engineer and was so adamant about marrying her. Shivani just doesn't walks away from their goes to the kids ameya and his friends child, Tanmay. She does not turn up until sindhu calls her to have lunch.

Her parents add more to her pain saying, shivani serve food to your father-in-law. Shivani does not say a word and says he does not keep well and all his welfare is in hands of sudhir and his mother.

Shivani with tears in her eyes, she eats her lunch. Sunandha keeps daunting her saying she eats only curd. She turns dark whenever she goes to her hometown Warangal. Shivani feels like giving them a shut up call immediately. Yet she knows how manipulative they are.

Therefore, she maintains her poise, and does not speak a word about anything. Sindhi enjoys this drama with her stereotype mom and they leave the place.

Shivani doesn't speak word in the car and when sudhir's dad asks her about hotel food, she says do as per your wish. This is your world and you set the rules, I am just a punching bag.

Sudhir's parents explode in anger saying why your dad spoke about my cognition. Shivani gives an assertive answer, you should have called my dad. Why did you make me vulnerable in front of sindhu and her family.

After coming home, sunandha shouts on the top of the voice. Who is going to cook now? I want you to listen to us, or else leave the house. Shivani asks sudhir is this your anwer too. Sudhir doesn't speak a word, ameya starts crying. Shivani tells her don't cry ameya I wont go anywhere without you. I know you cannot stay without me, even if they force you to stay.

Ameya wakes up in the night, and she cries a loud momma don't go to india. Sunandha comes into the room where shivani is studying and shouts at her. Shivani says she is studying and cannot hear when the door is closed. Shivani goes and sleeps with ameya. She says to ameya that she is shifting into her room. Ameya who always looks at shivani like a friend.

Shivani feels very dejected and she cries a lot with pain in silence. She decides to break their game with their own hands. Because, bindu and sudhir when clash with their ego's then, this time she will not succumb.

BINDU AND JAGAN GET BEST HOSPITALITY – DEC 25TH 2014

On Christmas day, sudhir goes to the airport to bring bindu and jagan. Shivani tries to prepare some stuff, as they will be going on a visit to BLUE MOUNTAINS.

Sudhir stops speaking to shivani even when she does not say inspite of his mom asking her to get out of the house.

Shivani smiles at them when they ask how they are doing. Yet, she finds something weird about jagan. He asks all financial status of sharath. He then says your dad might have got the acquisition of the land close to WARANGAL AIRPORT. This strikes shivani as why is he so interested in her dad's ancestral property.

Shivani gets a clear idea as what they all might have planned. He then behaves so grandiose, now shivani gets an idea, I will have to find out what is the face behind this fake masks, He always says to shivani, your brother's wife is very beautiful and rich. Your in-laws have told me. Shivani says I don't know, how rich they are, but shwetha is very empathetic and not conniving. She is highly intellectual and they have a good upraisal.

They get the best of all the house facilities; shivani splits all her belongings and keep it in ameya's room. Bindu behaves as though it is her own home. Shivani gets to eat only after all have eaten. When shivani tries to speak to her parents and, shwetha. Sudhir's mom starts grumbling, we all are here and you are speaking to your parents.

SHIVANI SAVES AMEYA FROM A FALL OFF THE BLUE MOUNTAINS – 26TH DEC 2014

Shivani has to prepare all the list of guests who are coming. And then arrange everything. Sudhakar starts making fun of shivani infront of jagan. She gives an assertive answer to jagan. My maternal grandpa is the advocate of high court in hyderabd and he has solved the famous high profile mystery of Ex-Union Minister Jaipal reddy's niece. He is quite aware of my vulnerable situation.

He says with much grandiosity, yes they had some family problems and property issues. Shivani then cooks all before hand and she wants to know, jagan and his family rapport with bindu. To beat bindu and sunandha at their own game she speaks to jagan's sister.

Sudhir does not speak well with shivani and she still manages to come along and takes care of Ameya.

Wherever they go, they make shivani feel outcast and sudhakar does not even speak with respect. He is one of his own somewhat most arrogant person who when confronted sheds crocodile tears.

They go to the Blue Mountains strip after a tour. Shivani keeps calling AMEYA, COME DOWN, THERE IS NO FENCE AHEAD. Sudhir says why you are shouting, my parents are getting irritated. Shivani says go run after ameya she is climbing the stairs where there is no fence.

She will have a fall, yet sunandha does not allow him to move. Shivani runs leaving all the tickets and her bags and holds ameya. She bites shivani, yet she doesn't say a word. When shivani hugs her and explains what was the reason she smacked her, and brought her down. Ameya says I am sorry momma.

Sunandha and sudhir always encourage ameya to call shivani crazy and all weird names. Shivani confronts her many times, how can you allow my daughter to call such names when my cognition is perfect? May be you all do not know what neuroscience is and what stressors are.

Bindu and Jagan say we did not see. Shivani in an assertive tone says, why would you is she is your responsibilty. I know the value of motherhood and the price of violence I paid to save it and to endure the pain. After few days shivani finds that jagan is taking very weird pics of her and Ameya.

She does not know what to do and she shares the information with her friend Dr. Mythilli. She says keep a watch on this person as shivani; remember a picture speaks more than thousand words.

When she sends ameya with them alone on the beach he takes her topless pictures. Even when the laws in any country doesn't allow to take such weird pics of a 8 year old studying in Australia.

Shivani shares the same with her friends' vamshitha and haritha. They say common friend go see a therapist and inform what is happening. Now that you do not have visa for ameya you cannot take ameya with you.

Shivani calls the doctor the very nextday and she takes an appointment. Shivani informs the doctor about her situation, and tells her that they are going on a round trip of the country visit.

She is perplexed about her ameya and her safety. She says I want you to know that if anything happens to me, these are the perpetators of violence and they have come from Dublin. Her husband is very controlling and he is abusive too. Her inalws have made her life hell, she informs to doctor Asar. The therapist Dr fea is on holiday, yet you can ring me on this number says the doctor.

Sunandha and bindu ask her to bring somany groceries and ask her to ring after she finished shopping, to get picked up by Jagan. Shivani rings them yet nobody picks the call.

She knows that they will do something weird, so she carries all alone.

Shivani is all tired and she looks at the phone somebody has purposefully placed it away from the handset. She asks bindu that the last call on the phone is from her. Sunandha says in assertive voice, why are you asking bindu? I myself did it, what is the big deal; I used to walk a lot carrying so many groceries.

Shivani says, yes nothing is a big deal until I leave this world. Sudhir comes from work and sunandha does not even allow shivani to eat food. She grabs a fruit and goes along with Sudhir.

She is fumed up, and shows her anger in silence. With this sudhir gets irritated and his violent angle is triggered. I am going to drop you here on the road. Shivani tries to be normal amidst his violent behaviour.

AMYEA JUST ESCPAES A TRAIN ACCIDENT ON THE DAY OF FIRE WORKS – SYDNEY – 31ST DEC 2014

Shivani forgets to get the Fireworks tickets from the car she goes to get them. While going she asks jagana nd bindu to keep a watch at Ameya. Sudhir goes to buy some snacks to the kids.

By the time shivani returns, ameya will be caught by a gujarathi man who confronts both jagan and bindu. Don't you people see this girl is running very close to the platform and the train is coming so fast?

Shivani cries a lot when she hears from them. She says thank you very much uncle, I just went to get the tickets. I have asked them to keep a watch; I know my child is very restless.

Sudhir who comes there doesn't say a word to jagan or bindu. Shivani hugs ameya tightly and she sheds tears.

Shivani says their negligence would have costed my angel's life. Sudhir says keep quiet do not say a word to them they are my family. Shivani trusts the elderly man's words, who refuses to sit next to jagan when he offers a seat. He says to shivani, don't trust these people and never leave your baby girl alone.

He scolds jagan in the train too. You are busy taking pictures, what pictures are you taking on the railway platform. I never saw a stupid person like you. Can you bring back the child to her mom, what you know Motherhood is? Jagan smiles at him, but does not say a single word.

Shivani feels the elderly man is teaching good morals to these grandiose people. It strikes her mind when he says what pictures you are taking on the platform. Because she saw weird single pics, he took of her and ameya on the Blue Mountains trip day too.

Shivani thinks logically and since they did not bring their laptop, let me check all the pics he is taking. Uncle is right and elders with morals do confront with empathy.

SHIVANI FEELS MY COGNITION IS ALL BACK –NOW THIS NEEDS A SERIOUS PLANNING

Shivani feels that she needs a serious planning, to expose his dangerous peadeophile, instincts. She knows how those people are and their instincts too. Because she reads each day about these warnings in the school. Keep an eye on who is having dangerous and dirty instincts on your kidos.

She saw such people being warned in Haberfield and Hambeldon schools. She knows the rules and regulations the schools follow even if they were to publish the school pics of the kids taken in the school.

RAHUL COMES TO SYDNEY WITH HIS WIFE – 2nd Jan 2014

Rahul and his wife come to Sydney for the house warming ceremony. Shivani is very good with both of them and they get along well with each other.

Shivani who reads a lot about Narcissim understands that she has to do exactly as how Sunndha and bindu behave. Moreover, she likes rahul and his wife. She and amweya have more comfort with them. Sunandha says to adjust all the curries and serve rahul and his wife. Shivani knows that rahul does not like silly stuff. Shwetha likes her cuisnes, so she prepares everything according to their taste and for sudhir.

Bindu and sunandha go to their friends home, shivani does all the cooking alone. Sudhir rahul and swetha all have dinner together.

Ameya likes their company and shivani always says the unborn baby boy will be her brother. Rahul adores ameya as he likes baby girls so much.

SWETHA AND RAHUL SUPPORT SHIVANI TO PERPARE FOR THE HOUSE WARMING RITUAL

Bindu and Sunandha who grind grudges look at sudhir and shivani having good rapoort with rahul and his wife. They start grumbing at shivani, saying why should you have to overcook when we have done it. Shivani says I know them more than you, rahul is like my brother and they gave us best hospitality when we went to Melbourne.

The next day sudhir sends shivani and rahul to get some important utensils from an Elderly family. Rahul looks at shivani and says sisinlaw you have become weak. Shivani says it is their home and their rules bro, I do not have a voice they blame me as a bad daughter in-law. Rahul says just be assertive that is your family home.

She gives a hint that she is taking medication for destressors and they weaved rumours. Yet, shivani does not reveal that sudhir does abuse her physically too.

SHIVANI CHANGES THE PARAMETERS– OF THE GAME ---NARCISSTS HATE FAVOURTISM WHEN PLAYED AGAINST THEM. ⁻2ⁿᵈ Jan 2015

Rahul and swetha comfort her "It's your family sissy". Never say I will leave. Shivani says how her in-laws daunted her and asked her to leave to India. Rahul and his wife say "It's your marital right, and it's the childhood home for ameya.

Bindu who is a master of the game, doesn't like when things go out of her control. She wants to create chaos in aggressive sudhir who is supporting and appreciating shivani.

She says to her parents common let us leave, how she will manage everything alone we will see. She even takes ameya with her to the city. Rahul says its ok, do not panick all we need is some groceries and the Puja list is here. Let them enjoy sightseeing and if ameya is also not, there we can do more work in less time.

If they are so rude just let us outsmart them with our teamwork. Swetha who is very good in aligning things does all in detail. Shivani without any prejudice says swetha you are very good in aligning things.

They shop for all the necessary items ever before Sudhir returns home. Teamwork success says Sudhir. Rahul says it is all sis-in-law who planned everything we just supported her. Sudhir says she is good when she puts her intrest in it. Swetha adds to it saying she is all the time with ameya, who is so fussy in eating.

Shivani appreciates Sudhir's other friends and says you people have arranged everything in a short time. Everyone in his peer group knows that shivani is very honest and speaks her heart.

They have their dinner before bindu and sunandha return home. Shivani and swetha ask them to have dinner, but they refuse to do so. Shivani finds ameya is having terrible stomach cramps. Therefore, she just spends time to comfort her as she cries a lot.

Shivani feels very emotional for swetha who is 5 months pregannat and has worked so hard to make the home reeady for the next day puja. This triggers bind and sunandha, they start grumbling saying that she has done all her work to impress brother and others.

HOUSE WARMING CEREMONY – BINDU AND SUDHIR FIGHT WITH EACH OTHER --- 3RD JAN 2015

Bindu who is always with super ego denies eating her breakfast. Shivani prepares it for the kids and she doesn't know their game of ambiguity. Sunandha brings the most low quality sari for shivani and a good quality for bindu. However her parents send her a designer piece which is much expensive. But sunandha doesn't allow her to wear it and she gives a evil eye even when swetha is there.

Bindu screams at shivani when she says, if she wants to join for the breakfast. Shivani still obliges with her choice and she wears the sari even when she doesn't like it Shivani gets fumed up when sunandha starts grumbling and doesn't allow her to tie up ameya's hair and make her ready. Shivani takes help of swetha and she makes sure that the puja is according to the hindu ritual.

Shivani who finds that everyone are giving her an evil eye, finds that sudhir friends should have a glimpse of how much pain she is enduring.

She reveals to the Priest, about her maternal and paternal families when he asks her the details.

Bindu gets fumed up, since shivani did not introduce her to sudhir's friends. Shivani shows good hospitality and all of sudhir's peers understand her vulenerabilty when they ask her that did your parents send some gifts to your family. She becomes emotional and she does not feel like bowing to sudhir's parents who look up to her nothing less than a slave. Her close friends give her a sign to be careful with jagan.

Rahul and swetha leave the place in the evening. Shivani goes into the garage and she speaks to her school friends about jagan and his dirty pictures and his way of exploding without any respect.

Sharath's wife says sissy you have to be very careful and we are happy that the plant extracts have brought back your cognition. But, make a safety back up plan for you and ameya.

Shivani's friends vamshitha and haritha take her number and say, we will call you everyday. You do not need to worry and be confident if that stupid fellow jagan says, anything be assertive to all of them.

Shivani's cousin aravind also comes who has common friends in sudhir's peers group.

He knows shivani's vulnerability and gives his blessing as a sister when shivani feels burdened with work and by power and control of entire family.

Sudhir walks away when shivani does all the packing and she distributes all things to her friends. She doesn't feel like leaving the house the very next day because she has to offer pryers to the GOD SATYNARAYANA – LORD VISHNU (LORD OF CREATION AND WHO PROTECTS ALL PIOUS PEOPLE).

She prays to god saying "OM JAI JAGADISH HARE SWAMI JAYA JAGADISH HARE, -- Maat pita tum ho sab swami – BHAKT JANOKE SANKAT DAAS JANOKE SANKAT – KSHAN MEIN DUUR KARIEN – OM JAI JAGADISH HARE –

The lord of nine planets and, who saves the entire universe
Please do accept my prayers and bless me like my parents
Today I am in a most vulnerable situation; I know you will save the pious and those who are enslaved.
I do not need to tell you what I endured, now please save me and my baby from negative forces.
Who are suffering since ages and being treated nothing less than as slaves.

Shivani offers her prayers and she feels very fumed up when everybody is hostile, nobody wants to reveal the reason why there is such a hostile environment.

Sudhir says to shivani we are not going, bindu is going with her family. Shivani feels sad for ameya because they have been to Surfers Paradise, but ameya didn't see it.

Ameya starts crying and jagan starts lauging, shivani doesn't say a word. Sunandha says if you people are not going I will not leave the place. I am sick and tired of your dad and I need you people to care of him. She says its all because shivani went into the garage and spoke to her parents. Sudhir got fumed up.

That's when shivani for the first time raises her voice and says don't try to fool me. I know the reason, your bindu screamed at sudhir and me when we asked her to change into the puja clothes.

It is her ego clashes and do not ever bring my parents into the picture who are not there. I was speaking to my brother's wife; my mom was busy with my nephew.

Enough did you all play a game with me with your power; now do not put ameya in these shoes. She tells ameya, if you deserve something you don't need to plead for it.

Moreover, this holiday you deserve it like bindu's kids. You are not a scapegoat and I will not make you one. Sudhir says I gave every priority to you and bindu. Shivani has nothing to do with this, what she says is right. You people are just diverting the issue. Bindu then shouts saying see how he is supporting his wife.

Sunandha says these days it's all about his wife and ameya. We do not even come to him in his family picture. Shivani says sudhir I have endured pain beyond human threshold by all this bullying. You decide whether we are going or not I will pack accordingly. Negative drama is not new to your family.

Sudhir asks her to pack all their clothes. All of his family behave very hostile to her and ameya. Shivani says that she has to put all her jewellery in the locker and she cannot carry it all the way everywhere. Shivani tells sudhir that if he fails to put it in the locker, he has to take the responsibility, as she is very tired with this chaos all the time.

CHAPTER 4

CRIME CAN HIDE UNDER THE CARPET- BUT EVIDENCE WILL NAIL ITS CONSPIRACY. NARCISTS WEAVE VIOLENCE AND SILENCE THE VICTIMS.

bindu who comes to the hotel does not speak to Sudhir and her parents. Jagan starts to shout at ameya when she wants to play with bindu's kids. Shivani does not avoid ameya until she cries coming to her dad. Sudhir says be away from them, they are not in a good mood.

On 4th jan 2015 – at Surfers Paradise hotel, bindu finds her keys missing. She has a habit of missing somany things. Shivani gets busy with ameya who has travel sickness. Shivani forgets even to bring the new house keys too. She does not bother much when they were searching. Sudhir comes and asks her if she has seen the keys.

Shivani who is all the time with ameya says I didn't even unpack and I am all day with ameya. She is having terrible stomach cramps. Ask your dad may be might have taken by mistake as our neighbours complained that he was misplacing their shoes when kept outside.

NARCISSTS USE EVEN THEIR KIDS TO INTIMIDATE THE VICTIMS --

Shivani says I do not even know about any keys. I myself forgot to bring our home keys. Now we have to call the locksmith to open the door. That is what I was about to tell you when we go to home after the trip.

Bindu accuses shivani saying, "Some people can't digest others happiness and families don't teach them ethics". Sunandha comes to shivani and asks her to open the bag. She checks all her belongings and even tries to check her trousers.

Bindu's eleven years son keeps grumbling that he has checked everywhere and they all suspect shivani for the missing keys. Sudhir gets angry and says to his mom now this is getting out of control, how can her son blame my wife for stupid keys? She forgot to bring her own keys of the house.

Shivani is fumed up and says, "Now it's more than enough". You people are accusing me of taking some stupid keys, which are not even quarter worth of a ruby ring I wear on my hand. What do you all think of yourself talking about, my family upraise and manners.

Have you any idea where my maternal and paternal family's contacts are up to. Living with humility is their attitude that is why they are being so empathetic to you.

Jagan yells at shivani "I am gonna kill you tonight". Shivani gets scared and feels that if sudhir does not defend her nobody will be her anchor. She remembers the weird pics he took and his unpredictable wild attitude towards ameya and her.

SHIVANI TAKES A STERN STEP TO STAND FOR HER SELF -ESTEEM AND DIGNITY.

She says sudhir I did not come here without any Preparation. I have all the Passport numbers and details, including their Dublin address.

Sudhir says, "I already told you I will divorce her in 2008 only, you people have mended the relation". Shivani says mind your words sudhir, you did not do any charity by reconciling with me. Do not forget the fact that you yourself admitted that this marriage is of your choice and not your parents and sister choice.

She starts crying for the noble status she enjoys at her hometown and her vulnerability at marital home. Sunandha says "Jagan forgive shivani she is the youngest of the family". Shivani closes the door and she gets scared and even intimidated too.

Shivani says in an assertive tone with broken heart and tears in eyes. Except sudhir nobody will enter my room or even touch my ameya.

If you people think of causing any harm to ameya or me none of you will cross Australian borders.

The doctor is none other than my family friend who knows my crisis from ages. In addition, each hour I need to report them how is my health and my nervous tension with your violence and abuse. I have even given details to Dr Asar a G.P close to our new house too.

Sudhir is alerted I will manage and jagan has to feel sorry to threaten you. Sudhir shouts at jagan saying who are you to threaten to kill my wife. Jagan says even if bindu is wrong, sudhir you have to support her because she is your sister. Shivani is manipulating you and she wants chaos in the family. Shivani says manipulation, and me, just look at you and your pattern of abuse. Mind your words learn empathy and humanity.

My childhood friends will call me every day and they should know my welfare. I told my dad and maternal uncle even if you give your entire property, these people would not keep me safe and happy.

This game is called Power and Control and Narcissism. You can never ever satisfy a narcisst and they lack remorse guilt and shame. They are so self-centred and manipulative they can make anybody a victim.

They abuse the victims and silence them with threats of separation. Empaths are their targets and they prey on Empaths. Sudhir's parents say send her to India and we will speak to her parents about her behaviour.

Sudhir says shivani let us go for a walk and you will feel better. He takes her out and says to her be calm and do as I say. Shivani says your family lack empathy and you have abused me from ever since ameya is born. I have lost desire to live, I am living like a corpse and as a soldier to ameya who should not lose her mom at such tender age. Sudhir offers her to eat something; she does not eat all of it and says I am scared of your jagan.

NARCISSTIS TRY TO MANIPULATE THE VICTIMS – THEY DON'T WANT OTHERS TO KNOW THEIR ABUSE

The next morning, bindu jagan come to counsel her. Shivani just wants to hear "Apology". She sits there and jagan starts his own self – praise. He says I should not have threatened to kill you. However, you should not have given back answers to bindu. Do not discuss about these matters to rahul and his wife.

Shivani says may be high time bindu should learn to respect her elder brother's wife. Bindu says we will start over again. Shivani says some relations cannot be mended because this is narcissim. I do not want to get hurt any further better you consider that I am no longer related you. Bindu says you are always in my parents and my good books, just they always think that someday you will know how to behave with in-laws.

Shivani says I do not want to be in any of your good books. I am commited to sudhir by hindu marriage and ameya I adore and love her more than my life.

NARCISSTS NEVER EVER APLOGISE FOR THEIR VIOLENT ACTIONS – THEY ARE SELF CENTRED

Sunandha behaves as though its shivani's mistake to be threatened by jagan. She just wants shivani to succumb and get her work done. She often tries to intimidate her and make her feel guilt that something bad will happen if shivani does not be in good terms with them.

Sudhir is fumed up for the first time ever in his life, because he can see it crystal clear as how much his parents support bindu and her husband.

NARCISSTS TERRORIZE THE VICTIMS TO COVER THEIR MISTAKES – IT IS ALWAYS THE VICTIMS FAULT.

Shivani gets tired with ameya and her stomach cramps the little one feels anxious because of the chaos. Sudhir says both of them are tired and they need a break. You can go on with your holiday. Shivani says why your parents should miss the fun. "Let them go with bindu and jagan". Sunandha however does not agree to go, because she does not like to trouble bindu and she knows that jagan will not even take any responsibility too.

She says to sudhir let us go back to Sydney. Ameya starts crying, I want to see Surfers Paradise like them. Shivani never tells ameya not to speak to bindu and jagan. Yet bindu teaches the vice versa to her kids.

SHIVANI SAVES SUDHIR'S DAD FROM AN ACCIDENT AT SURFERS PARADISE --.

They all startgrumbling about their family history and fight with each other with burning cgos. Sunandha tries to make shivani'life impossible by making sudhakar sick and beating him at night. She does not bother about him even when he loses his cognition.

He does not look at the traffic lights and starts to head on to the otherside of the road. Shivani quickly runs after him, when a car stops on her request on the street. She just says to them that he has problem with his cognition.

Shivani knows that its sunandha's plan to act to be sad and get her things done. She has seen this attitude before. She confronts sudhir saying do you have any idea if something would have happened to your dad.

She explains sudhir that even resentment needs some valid logic and it should be in limits. I never asked you to create barriers, build boundaries.

Sunandha is fumed because sudhir gets so amazed by shivani's moral attitude and he says they don't deserve you. Bindu shows her cold attitude and doesn't even bother to speak to her parents or sudhir. Shivani says to ameya, "Momma is not that weak to make you lose your holiday". Common lets go and have fun.

Shivani learns from her maternal grandmother to teach and mentor husband with ethics values and morals. Their success is our success and we should be a pillar of our house. Tolerance and Forgiveness is a sign of strength and not weakness that is what she is taught from her childhood.

Treat your husband equal to your child and love them unconditionally even when you are angry with them. That is what shivani does all the time and her enture family is very proud of her tolerance.

She creates ambiguity to jagan and leaves impromptu with her phone. Whenever sudhir asks her where she went, she says I went to complain the cops that ameya is not drinking water and wasting her time in the toilet.

Shivani feels happy when Ameya goes to the duck tour and plays with the Jellyfish. Sudhir says she is just like you. Remember when we came for, the first time and you were collecting all these shells.

Sudhir's parents never like it when sudhir says ameya is shivani's Xerox copy. She makes a close look at it, as her aim is to bombard shivani with bindu and sudhir together.

Shivani says yes the best times of my life on the seashores.

The waters are same and so is the seashore and the coastline too

Yet everything changed like a storm hit our ship

Marriage and my Maternity.

It hurts you a lot when your dreams are shattered and you do not get what you deserve

I believe in hope, faith and never did I give up, I know god will weave good fortune to my endeavour one day.

Because god accepts, my challenge when I was shedding tears in scorching sun.

Time and tide waits for none, I am not the one who writes my life and my family's future on sand.

I will rewrite my book of life; it should be worth reading for my ameya.

JAGAN TERROZES AMEYA IN CAIRNS –SHIVANI GIVES HIM A SHUT UP CALL.

Jagan wants to create terror in shivani, so that she doesn't expose his evil deeds and also his dirty instincts on her and ameya. He sends bindu to bring ameya to take her to snorkelling, even when ameya has thrown up very badly because of seasickness.

Sudhir behaves neutral and says it's all up to you shivani. Shivani tells bindu, that she is not ready, bindu still says "Common ameya you got to be sportive".Ameya refuses and hugs shivani tight. Jagan looks at bindu and gives her a hint, shivani who has all her cognition back trusts her intuition. God Ameya will be in danger with this predator.

She tells bindu your son is 11 yrs he can go for snorkelling because he can swim well. Ameya is close to her Eight Birthday, she did not even complete half of her swimming sessions and is trembling with fear. Bindu leaves the place and shivani feels relaxed that ameya is out of danger from jagan.

Sudhir's dad says while ameya is about to run after the car. If you get struck by a car then your dad will save a fortune in life. Shivani gets agitated and says, "You are the end stage of your life and she just started her primary school. Is this what you curse your own son's daughter.

Sudhir does not say a word, when he speaks about ameya being struck by an accident. That is when shivani gets a clear understanding that they all are a team and sudhir is just acting to be good.

NARCISSTS NEVER STOP THEIR MIND GAMES – SUDHIR'S ULCER TABLETS GO MISSING

Sudhir's behaviour also looks unpredictable yet he behaves as though he is against his sister and even his family. Suddenly he screams at shivani expecting her to go along with bindu.

However, Shivani who understood the game and determines to be non-cooperative so that she can be safe and save her self -esteem.

She does not even walk closer to them even when he screams she comes by his side.

Therefore, their game of terror is bindu? Neutralized and she does not need to succumb to them. Sudhir's dad says in an aggressive tone why are you being so hostile to Shivani says even when your bindu accused me of stealing some stupid keys, should I smile and laugh with her. After coming to the resort, jagan starts reciting some mantras, shivani finds it very silly. Who will recite and chant mantras in a Tree House. She makes friends with the natives close to the tree house.

Bindu and Sunandha cook some silly stuff, but shivani does not eat any of it. She feels now sudhir should also feel the pain she felt when he stopped eating for 3 months and gave her pain beyond human threshold. Sunandha shows her angry looks, yet shivani does not give up. Sudhir says he is having terrible cramps in his stomach.

He asks shivani to bring his tablets from his wallet. Shivani gives him one and by the next morning, she finds the tablets missing when he needs another. Shivani remembers very firmly that she placed the tablets on the kitchen platform.

She just tells to ameya be careful ameya things are missing, even your dad's tablets too. This is like a Haunted house in movies.

Sunandha says jagan is very angry on her and better she start being nice and friendly. Shivani says this not India or Dublin. This is not even sydney.

This is Cairns and we are just like on a group holiday. I am no more related to him and better he keeps his voice low. Otherwise cops can come anytime here as I am scared of this monster like person jagan. They all get alerted that shivani might have reported to cops.

She just repeats my friend Dr. Mythilli has to know my wellbeing and also Dr Fea has to see me in sound health by the end of this trip. They have their plans if something goes wrong with Ameya or me. Sudhir feels tensed and says I am there do not worry.

Shivani says high time hubby learn to show empathy to wife and child unprejudiced by such an abusive and self-centred family.

TRUE FREINDSHIP CAN BREAK BARRIERS AND GUARD A VICTIM ACROSS THE SEAS --

Vamshitha rings shivani everydays from California. To know how she is doing. Sunandha keeps daunting her about her friends, yet she does not succumb at all.

Bindu starts to feel dejected as her super ego is hurt and she sheds crocodile tears.

Yet shivani does not succumb and she says, "No false tears can bring back my health, career and self-esteem". I am not a punching bag to your family. Already you have crossed your boundaries in 2008 while I was working in HCF. Breaking barriers, I have learnt because I know the value of sacrifice.

Jagan gets perplexed and each time he asks bindu to bring shivani's phone. He gets confused when she says I had enough and my wellbeing is monitored.

Sunandha sheds tears every day and night that made shivani a doormat and a punching bag ever since marriage. She explodes when they say, "what if we complain to the cops that you are giving trouble to my aged parents".

Shivani says go ahead I want you to do it let them come on your request. Because I am, still following Hindu traditions that is why I did not ring them even when jagan said he is going to kill me.

Shivani's inution tells her that sudhir is just acting to be good, but even that is better because if she loses this pawn then abusers become more powerful.

NARCISSTS NEVER LIKE THEIR ABUSE TO BE REVELAED TO OTHERS – JUST OUTCAST THEM, THEIR EGO TRIGGERS AND THEY EXPLODE.

The entire family goes to Melbourne, where Rahul and his wife have arranged their stay. Jagan acts too modest and to rip his mask, shivani tries to be very normal.

Shivani is very tired and she feels much stressed out. She decides to take rest. Even when sudhir's parents and bindu try to give her angry looks, she does not bother.

She tells to rahul and sudhir "I am going to take rest; you can take ameya also with you to the city tour".

Shivani explains swetha, how much they have been giving her pain and what kind of cold attitude bindu has. She asks her to be aware of such people and their covert masks. My life is an epic saga of pain and suffering but do not trust them as they can intrude into your lives too.

Rahul's wife who saw sudhir's hostile attitude before says Sissy now that he is changing just be calm and positive. Shivani says I am being positive and infact forgiven him like a mother, but seeds of venom are very strong and manipulative.

NARCISSTS ACT TO BE GOOD – BUT THEY OFFEND INNOCENT PEOPLE –THEY ARE COVERT MANIPULATORS

Shivani helps shwetha after a while and she rejuvenates her senses to be feel better. She has one percent hope as sudhir never ever stood for her. Yet, she knows how manipulative his parents and sister is.

She does not give a clue that she has told everything to swetha. Shivani does not sit next to bindu and she avoids her like an outcast.

Jagan takes them out to his cousin's house. Jagan does not even bother to see that a pregnant woman almost 15 yrs younger than him swetha is sleeping on floor. He is very grandiose and thinks he should be given all privileges of the world. Shivani feels very bad for swetha and she tries to help her as much as possible.

NARCISSTS SHEDS FALSE TEARS OF SYMPTAHY – THEIR MOTIVE IS POWER AND CONTROL.

Shivani gets a call on her mobile that sudhir's cousin who had an impromptu caridiac arrest is dead. She doesn't know how to tell the news to sudhir. Yet she whispers in his ears that your cousin is serious. I got call from your other cousin in U.S. Sudhir, Rahul wake up, and shivani does not wake up Shwetha who already had no good sleep. Sudhir shows his true emotions and he cannot believe that a lad who is 22 yrs old is no more.

Shivani reminds him the innocence of the lad who adored her as a sister when she gifted him a customized key chain on his name. Yet she says it was a medical adversity as his weight was increasing exponentially and none bothered to show him to a Gastrentologist.

Shivani is fumed up inside about bindu who all think she is the master of any medical health issues.

My goodness what does she knows she already wrecked her dad's health by relocating him up and down to Dublin. Anyways these people san empathy its better I keep quiet.

Empaths always empathize with humanity and do not mix their personal resentment in situation of family bereavement. Shivani goes to sunandha who has been very cold to her and reveals the news. She sheds tears and yet doesn't allow shivani to speak to the lad's family and say that sudhir got the call from his cousin Raghu.

Shivani feels it is hopeless to rebound with such conniving people who san empathy and cover the truth for no reason. It brings a lot of surprise to her, as jagan never even comes out of the room when all are discussing loud about the unfortunate demise of a young lad.

The next day they start their trip to Apostles. Shivani says ameya and I have been to the place. Moreover, I had terrible time with those roller coaster roads. Rahul says yes both were throwing up very badly.

They are very sensitive to that route and infact I have some important task at my work place.

Shivani feels worried about sudhir as he was crying inside out for his cousin and he did not sleep for an hour. She says to him why can't you rest too. Jagan is driving with his licence send your parents in the big car they can have nice time.

Jagan says why you and ameya do not come with us too. That is when shivani gets her intuition Apsotles is very steep and high and the trip will give her nausea. She feels what if this monster pushes me off the cliffs as his dirty instincts are only known to me. Moreover, sunandha is so good at manipulation she will say that was an Accident.

She reminds herself of the Priest at the Shakti Temple that jagan, his people have created health havoc, and they want to destroy you. He told her that her intuition is very sharp like her maternal uncle. So, trust your intuition and escape when it says its danger road ahead.

Sudhir asks bindu is that ok, they can have nice time and since Apostles is a very famous place, they can easily locate it too.

Sunandha gives a very angry look and says sudhir has to come even when he is tired and with no sleep.

Shivani feels relaxed and after a long time she makes good food for ameya and she sleeps well.

Rahul and Swetha listen to shivani and they just say to her maintain your poise sissy they are playing mind games and this is the right time for you to be in bro's good books forever.

Shivani cooks for all of them but she does not tell rahul that sudhir is physically abusive. When he is at work she tells swetha about it, yet I am enduring this pain because of social stigma and ameya's functional childhood.

NARCISSTS NEVER EMPATHIZE WITH VICTIMS–

Ameya is good at art just like how shivani was at school. She even attends Art lessons at her school. When sudhir and his family return, Shivani cooks everything which shwetha is not good at taking help from rahul.

She tells Rahul to make sure that shwetha who is carrying his baby needs good sleep. What is wrong if jagan sleeps on the couch? Rahul says yes sissy you are right they san empathy, I need to take a stern step today. Cannot trouble my wife for some extended family.

After their dinner, rahul says it has been very difficult for his wife to sleep on the floor. Sunandha asks rahul the phone card number and rings his parents. They tell him that they have to give much importance to bindu and jagan as they are guests.

Shivani and sudhir understand their vulnerability and maintain their poise. Shivani has two cousins living in Melbourne and she has never been to their place.

When they call her and shivani speaks to them, bindu gets irritated, because she considers herself as the most important person of the family and shivani stopped talking to her.

Yet shivani does not succumb to her evil looks and manipulative traits. She has seen the worse and she knows how she failed her career at HCF as an NLC on epic scale.

They leave Melbourne and head towards Sydney, Rahul and Shwetha say bye to all. They invite shivani and ameya in her school holidays to spend quality time with the little to be born baby boy.

NARCISSTS ARE SCORNFUL. THEY WANT TO WIN THEIR GAME EVEN AT THE COST OF INNOCENT LIVES –JAN 2015

Bindu and Jagan leave to Dublin, Shivani still follows hindu tradition and gives blessing to bindu as her elder brother's wife. She gives chocolates to her kids too.

Sunandha feels she is losing control of the house and starts to break things. She starts to beat her husband and says, "Its better you die soon than become a fuss to me and my life".

She does not even move a glass from her table and wants shivani to serve them each day. Shivani's back pain starts to trigger. However, she does not have any time to see the doctor as she takes his dad to the park and says he is missing. She wants to show every minute that she is having tough time with him.

Shivani still manages to cook all savouries and she starts to prepare Ameya for her NAPLAN exam. Bindu who reaches Dublin starts to weave violence an teach ameya that shivani is bad. That is when shivani takes a stern step and says that nobody can do any help to her other than her mom.

No good aunt and grandparents say that Mom is bad. If they say so, you should not speak to them as you are like mom this is what all your friends and teachers say right. Yes, says ameya momma is my best friend and my teachers like her so much. She helped Lizie, and now she is helping Mason and Jason who are differently abled and special with Autisim.

Sunandha explodes on ameya saying, yes your mom is only great and now we are nothing to you. She breaks all the glasses in the shelves. She then hides ameya's gold earrings so that ameya gets wrong impression on shivani. Shivani who understands the game, calls sudhir and says it's just a matter of 50 auz $, you can get them here in the closest Suburb.

That is when she brings them to shivani saying may be she forgot to take her anxiety medication that is why she could not see the earrings. Shivani says those are plant extracts and they have no side effects they only help to distress and to avoid suicidal thoughts.

Bindu gives advice to her parents to leave to India and give one week of tough time to her. Sudhir makes her cook three different recipies a day. Moreover, shivani does not even know when they wake up.

Sunandha starts breaking all the glasses in the house. Ameya gets scared and she says they all are momma's friends gifts to us. Sunandha explodes and says your momma is everything to you. I am nothing, ameya says my teacher says I have got the best mom in the world.

Shivani warns ameya no don't speak against them, let's go to the park to play and go to Hetal home. All this is chaotic and you do not need to take all this at this tender age. That is all it makes them explode more they break the door and even a plate too. Shivani says ameya let us go, we already have such kind of wild behaviour with your dad sometimes.

Ameya says dad got all this anger from them. He has very angry parents, who like when he beats you.

They say that they are going back to India, ameya says to her mom when they go to play. I am so happy momma they are leaving, I want us to be happy.

Shivani does not say a word when they decide to go back to India. Sudhir does not like it because sunandha starts balming sudhir for being nice to shivani and even calling sudhir a henpecked husband.

They just decide to leave and threaten shivani that they are going to put her to guilt and shame of mistreating them and bindu. Shivani then decides to alert her dad who is very stereotype and can't hear a single complaint on his flawless upraise of his daughter shivani.

Sunandha curses shivani to the worst, which she never heard. She says that she can never have marital bliss and the house where she builds a nest for ameya will not be there. She warns her that God will curse her and she will soon come to India in tears and coming to her rescue.

She tells Sudhir that same happned to Srinivas and he had trouble in his work because of being assertive to his grandmom.

Shivani thinks god will never curse her at any time. If she is cursing me then she is curisng sudhr and ameya as they are her family. Shivani yet does not mind and goes to the airport and seeks their blessings.

Empaths never trouble the sick, sudhir does not book any wheel chair assistance to sudhir's sick dad. Shivani with her negotiation skills goes to the counter and asks them if they can help them as they are going on a family emergency.

The airlines crew say they can help them and she need to fill a form for formalities. Shivani does everuthing and she wants them to reach safe without chaos as her upraise is what they are going to question now and scream at her dad too.

After a week, Shivani's mom flies with little Tejas and his mom to Phenoix to help them with the infant. Shivani does not speak daily to her parents or her brother too. She just want to study something new and regain her credibility to get back on her feet.

NARCISSTS NEVER CAN SEE VICTIMS HAPPY
AND ALSO THEY WANT TO HIDE TRUTH –

Shivani tells the same to her mom and dad as how bindu accused her of stealing some silly keys. How jagan threatened to kill her.

She says that she is with Sudhir as sunandha has mistreated him by not serving him food in his own house. Yes, I know that Sudhir has been very rude to me all these years but today other than me, he has nobody.

Moreover, their entire motive was to exploit him and remain the winners of this game Wheel of Power and Control. Shivani's mom says I will tell dad to ask them your flaws. Now you do not worry at all. Start to rebuild your marriage and your health.

Shivani decides that its high time that her dad has to go and speak to Sudhir's parents. Sudhir rings shivani's dad and says that Yes Jagan threatened to kill her and my parents supported them and not us. Shivani warns her dad that he should not use any coercive language against rude and arrogant people. Shivani's dad always listens to her when she is assertive.

Girish says I am going to ask his brother who is a MLA – Mr Ashok from the YS Jagan Congress Party as is this what he taught his younger brother. I will not keep quiet this time, yet I need to speak to your maternal uncle Srinivas about this issue.

Now Sudhir do not trouble my gem like daughter you have no clue as how we raised her nothing less than a princess. She used to draft my entire official letter and with good precision. All my engineers at site used to say she is very intelleigent and everybody has her in their good books.

Sudhir says yes I know how innocent shivani is and she has served my parents and sister to her best inspite of her back pain. I am going to your cousins Death Ceremony and after things get to a balance, I will speak to him.

Loss of a young lad at 22 yrs is a big havoc to the family. Shivani calls them and comforts his mom that god takes angels to his house very quickly and she has to be strong.

Sunandha wants to pretend that she is in good terms with shivani, yet shivani doesn't speak to her as she remembers her curse.

EMPATHS ALWAYS FORGET PAINFUL PAST AND LOOK FOR BUILDING A BRIGHT FUTURE.

Sudhir says that he is unable to withstand work pressure and is very difficult to cope with family chaos.

Sunandha keeps saying to all that she does not have a good son and he is a henpecked one. Sudhir who believes a lot in astrology says that my mom parys every day.

Her curses will come true now. Shivani says do you know what the in-laws who curse their son and his family god will never make their curse come true. If you are so worried about all this evil eye and all.

Let me confirm with Shasthri Uncle who is a lecturer at Kakatiya University and is a good priest too. She reveals all her situation as Rajeshwari goes everyday to the temple and prays for shivani. Shasthri says pray to God Vishnu, if you want success in career and to protect yourself from evil eye.

He says shivani I do not know whether you know or not but do not trust your husband his attitude and even his zodiac sign is of a Serpent.

There is a very big danger to your life in 2015, but once you overcome this, you will rewrite your life in 2016 and stand unique in your family.

You are born at the same star constellations of a Warrior Princess" Rudrama Devi "who ruled Kaktiya Dynasty.

I know you from your childhood and I was the priest of your marriage too. Shivani says Uncle that stupid tailor Vicky who reads astrology also says I am Rudramdevi' s incarnation and I shouldn't recite "Shakthi Mantra". As they will be havoc to ameya from me. He asked me to wear the Sapphire stone too. Shasthri says No you will ever wear such wrong gem to your Strong Personality. Shivani says uncle long back in December 2013 I lost that ring on the road and never even found it. Then only the next week, my college friend said that Plant extracts are doing marvellous healing for Stress Disorders.

You will wear nothing or wear a Coral ring, which you had before you got married when you met with an accident.

Wear nothing, but don't wear wrong stones, that has created a havoc in your mind.

you are suffering with irrational thoughts because of abuse and the opposite gems of which sudhir is wearing. This is all negative energy. We cannot stop him so just remove yours and if you have your coral ring wear it. Otherwise, do not even bother wearing any of them.

Shasthri says first remove all their gifts they bought and look if they have taken any of your clothing.

My predictions of evil eye and black magic can never go wrong. Shivani calls him after few days and finds that Sudhir's new shirt and even her new red dress is missing along with a Perfume bottle. Ameya had danger from water, he says but somehow she was saved. Shivani says uncle I stopped jagan from taking Ameya to snorkelling.

Shasthri says Yes Shivani they are attempting to do some evil magic against you, but they cannot destroy you once godess of Shakthi will bless you with long life. Even if they plan to do, you will become so powerful that sudhir will fall on your feet. Because your intellect and courage is of 8 women. You are blessed by GODESS SHAKTHI.

You both have similar courageous attitude and even beauty with brains. However, she was backstabbed and died in Nalgonda, which is your in-laws native place too.

Moreover, her enemies were from the same place where Jagan native place is.

Look at the coincidence your dad has now his lands fallen near vicinity of "Warangal Airport "which has to renamed as "RUDRAMA DEVI AIRPORT".

Bifurcation of the states benefited him. He has started "Mission Kakatiya", to help farmers with irrigation. Your maternal uncle is a World Renowned Doctor. You are a Princess of two families who adore you so much.

Shivani you are going to rewrite your life if you can cross all the hurdles. You will become a healer and will heal victimized women and children.

The stars show that you will become a Creative Writer too. As she was good at Creative Arts and Management.

Shivani this is sheer pure coincidence though I do not say Incarnation. However, yes, the courage is same and the sacrifice at heart and creative intellect and empathetic attitude is same.

Only your health and life chart is alarming and there is potential danger from backstabbing. Your intuition can show you gullibility.

Chant the Mantra of Goddess of Eternal Power Shakthi. Shivani who trusts her true love to sudhir says uncle don't you think he will change now atleast. Shasthri says I am not only a Priest but also a teacher too. We are looking at his pattern of abuse and weaving violence tendency.

So just, I am asking you to be alert and your health needs healing. Shivani trusts his astrological predictions, she starts her Vishnu Mantra reciting it for 21 days.

She calls a neighbour Rajeshwari who has given her food at her home. She gives her a house-warming gift of Silver Ganesha and seeks her blessings. She is a good and pious innocent woman; shivani says I am seeing my Mom's reflection in you. Had she been here she would have got this return gift too. Shivani seeks her blessings on the last day.

She prepares Sudhir like a schoolchild on his day of De-briefing. She even combs his hair, shows him how to dress, and gives him compassion as a wife. So that he should know that, his wife loves him unconditionally.

Sudhir says even my mom did not care so much for me as much as you do.

Shivani says its ok, do not always reminds yourself of your painful childhood I am there for you even a better combo pack than your mom.

Sudhir says he has passed the Debriefing too. However, says I think my mom will return to Sydney if your dad does not go and confront them.

Shivani asks her dad to go and ask them as why is she taken for granted to the extent of even serving food in a servant's plate.

For not being in regular, touch with bindu. Moreover, when bindu came over she always claimed it is her house and even sunandha has asked her to get out of the house too. Girish says leave it shivani do not worry too much and plan to go to U.S.

You settle down there very well as all our kith and kin are there. Shivani knows that if she goes to U.S she knows core attitude of sudhir. He could not tolerate when she got her job as Quality Analyst in HCF at age of 26 yrs when he was 33 yrs old.

Shivani thinks it will be a wild goose chase for her and even her school friends who know shivani say the same. This will be a big hurdle to sharath as these kind of scornful people do anything to destroy successful people with one sensitive issue.

Shivani comes to know that her dad's best friend Madhav Rao's daughter is no more. She has ended her life with marital suicide within a year of marriage.

Shivani writes a blog to show her credibility to her parents and kith and kin who fear she might have lost her potential. With such inhuman stressors in the long run of her roller coaster ride.

She reminds of Anusha who was working in IBM India as a Project lead and a gifted and talented student too. She feels very dejected and agitated too. Her Moms says Shivani

I have been hearing your abusive life ever since ameya is born. Moreover, why you lost so much weight. What is wrong with you, you lost a smile on your face too.

Do not do like Anusha, we can still have you as our children. She says Aunty I am very sorry for the loss of Anusha, she was a gem of a girl and she was such a beautiful bride.

I do not have that thought I braved those thoughts even when all of them said I have become in cognitive too. Incognitive and you my child, I think those who think you are incognitive they need a psychiatric assessment. She says we did hide this from you since 4 yrs because you are on Antisuicidal. There was no much physical abuse like you, but you know how sensitive she is, and she could not succumb to marital conflicts too.

For all the wealth, they have troubled her for we got all we gave her in detail. Shivani says "Madhu Uncle" gave her more than a fortune and she earned a good amount too. However, she was very sensitive unlike you and social stigma was killing her from inside.

She left the world at the tender age of 26. She decides to write a Blog on her name "Brides are Not Hostages". She sends the open link of the blog to Srinivas too.

Sunandha who comes to know that shivani is sending her dad to ask them what her fault is becomes very cold and wild. She calls sudhir and says what kind of nonsense is this, if you do so I will not eat food anyday.

She is immature don't you have any sense. Shivani says now that she called me and labelled me one more name, my dad has to know what my fault is.

Girish who is a public person and who is a stereotype says they have become old now leave it. Shivani says she is not leaving a single word to label me as she want and you want to leave such a matter.

I am telling you like a wounded soldier that unless you promise me that you will go and ask him or her. I will not talk to anyone of you especially with mommy. \

Girish who knows the will power of shivani says ok, shivani call Srinivas and tell him in detail. Rajeshwari has all her life rest in wounded shivani and she can't stay without talking to her even a week. Girish knows that his wife is very sensitive and shivani has become numb.

She tells to her mom I will not wear a single gold ornament in my life. If dad doesn't ask them about this cruel violence ever since ameya is born from Jagan and his family too.

As shivani is born to her after, almost all doctors gave up hope that she will never be a mom with so many miscarriages. Shivani is considered as the saviour child of two families and Dr. Rama Krishna named her after Godess of Eternal Power so that she will have all blessings of Godess Shakthi.

Shivani calls Srinivas and tells him as how much bindu, sunandha and even jagan have troubled her.

She says that qualified students are leaving the world because of these archaic procedures.

Do you want me to end up like Anusha who is no more? I have no energy left in me to handle them. She is weaving rumours about my cognition since ameya is one year old and the abuse has started.

I do not want anything from Sudhir or from Dad. I want justice for my pain and suffering and losing my career on epic scale.

Srinivas warns shivani that what if sudhir records all your calls. Shivani says if he does so, he will be accused of Phone Tampering to terrorize a victim.

Finally, they all conclude that shivani is standing for her self-esteem. They decide to go to Sudhir's parents and ask them the reason why Jagan had been so cruel to Shivani.

She says your Silence on their Violence is killing me inside and my heart is being sliced and diced each day.

Moreover, why did she give her food in a servant's plate after Shaarth wedding? Why did they trouble her for her gifted money given to her in sharath's wedding?

NARCISSTS TURN THEIR PAWNS INTO SCAPEGOATS WHEN THEIR GAME IS REVEALED IN LIMELIGHT. --- MARCH 2015

Shivani who expects that since Mr Sudhakar will ask Dr. Rama Krishna to stop this family meeting by shedding crocodile tears. She calls him and explains all in detail.

Dr. Mama if you want to see me happy I want your cousin Keshav uncle to represent you, as you are very busy.

Dr. Rama Krishna tries to convince shivani but he knows that she is deeply hurt and is fighting for her self-esteem.

Ok. Princess I will send him but do not hesitate to ring us if Sudhir turns his side and becomes abusive to you. As we do not trust sudhir anymore.

Only you are having that trust in him. She says mama you will have to divide the abusers so that they stop weaving violence.

Strike the rod when the iron is hot – Divide the Abusers when they have clashes among themselves.

Moreover, this is the only way to break the game of Narcissim. This is reducing weaving Violence and volume of abusc too. As they easily can team, up and become monsters threatening with divorce. Bindu rings Sharath, but he doesn't pick the call.

Shivani sends an e-mail to his wife saying to bash bindu if she calls her.

However, bindu is so egoistic that she does not ring once you have neglected her unlike sunandha who is very cruel and will see the dead end of the victims.

Sunandha explodes and asks Sriivas not come with them. Girish goes with Kushalov who has arranged the match. Sunanadha explodes all at once and ask Mr Srinivas not to come with them.

Before they even step into the house sunandha starts crying loud that their son has left them nowhere in the world. Kushalov is very smart and he says we didn't come to hear your life story, we came for shivani.

Why did your bindu accuse her of stealing some silly keys and why was her husband so cruel to her. We are not being aggressive to you. So, do not create a dramatic scene here it is about a intelligent smart honest girl's sad life of maternity. Sunandha says we apologize for their behaviour towards your shivani. Shivani texts to keshav that this I want from them who insulted my upraise.

I told shivani that this family is very close to my wife and her nephew. That is when that innocent smart girl accepted to marry Sudhir. You all made her to live on antisuicidal.

Now when she found a solution to her never-ending problem with some plant extracts you are weaving rumours on her cognition.

Sunandha says we all are sorry for our Son inlaw jagan's rude behaviour towards shivani. But shivani was not happy with bindu.

Keshav then says with all the words shivani is texting to them listening to their meeting on Viber. Is this what in-laws do to every pious daughter in-law and how could you say to our Princess of golden heart that she is immature.

We have seen many people like your son and you. Because of people like you today we are witnessing so many Maternity Suicides. She is very smart and has a brave heart that is why she is alive. All of us call her Warrior Princess with weapon as morality and truth in our kith and kin.

Even today, she is trying to study and work hard to neutralize all your rumours. Sudhakar cries saying that they do not have anyone to take care of him or her. Sudhir is very rude and has become dangerous too.

Your daughter is in trouble and his attitude was like this ever before he went to Sydney.

Shivani only requested Wheel Chair assistance to him on a last call notice. He says Girish you have a gem as your daughter. She is more intelligent and smart than Sudhir.

See your daughter will come in one month or so, because he has become very controlling. She is in deep trouble save your daughter from him.

His way or highway is his attitude, he is controlling her every nerve with his eyes. Girish gets perplexed, and he cannot speak a word about it. Sunandha however does not say anything good about shivani. She just says that we do not have issues with your daughter, only she does not speak to bindu properly.

We do not have a son now, he is changed completely. We want you to take all belongings of your Sudhir who has sent you against us. Girish says we didn't come to be aggressive to you, it's about your daughter's husband jagan who was cruel to my shivani. Sudhakar says he doesn't deserve a smart girl like shivani in his life.

Sudhir comes from work and he asks shivani what happened at the family meeting. Shivani shows him the recording, he becomes agitated against his parents.

He says, they want us to fight with each other since they know bindu and jagan are wrong.

Kushalov, Keshav call shivani and say if you have any trouble or danger to your life shivani come to India.

We will arrange everything for you; we do not want a sportive and smart girl like you losing life with abuse.

Kushalov says to sudhir except shivani nobody is supporting you. She is a divine blessing to you as a wife and do not trouble her. She has good wisdom and she is much matured. She is very courageous; such girls bring glory to maternal and marital families.

Girls are sensitive; she has braved your abuse and your family's abuse too. He then says to shivani not to repeat anything about his family.

Shivani once commits to anyone she does not give up her word. She says uncle I do not want about past that is gone I want to rewrite my life. I know that these people will change the parameters of the game. This is called Narcissim.

It is a chain of abusers weaving violence with one another and then hides the truth to play a Sympathy card.

They have made bindu as a trophy child and sudhir as a victim. Now after ameya is born sudhir is giving same pain as his parents have given to him.

To him ameya is the trophy child and now I am his target. The after effect of this Narcisstic Parenting is that the victimized child becomes scapegoat and they become very stubborn and rigid.

Girish who is ignorant of the game unlike kushalov becomes emotional and says my shivani is my pride.

Having such a wonderful girl as your wife is your blessing, so even when your parents disown you, I will consider you as the the older son of my family.

SUDHIR BECOMES ABUSIVE AGAIN ON THE VERY NEXT DAY OF AMEYA'S BIRTHDAY CELEBRATIONS –

CONTROL FREAKS DO NOT LIKE INDEPENDENT THOUGHTS.

Shivani inspite of her severe back pain wants to plan ameya's birthday. She gets freedom to wear the outfits of her choice. She feels good, but sudhir drains her energy by completely monitoring her every arrangement.

Shivani says I will do my best but don't call me each minute it is very disturbing to my friends. Vyshali, Hetal,

Sarabjit help her to drive. She asks each one of them to help her with each diiffrent thing.

They all like shivani and even the school selects shivani as the new Parent Teacher with good intellect and anlystical writing and reasoning.

Sukanya know her vulnerability and she always says nobody judges you with your homeo medicine for stress. She often says shivani you are so beautiful, golden hearted woman and with privileges why do you take abuse. Shivani says I have to endure this for a functional childhood of my child and I have seen my worse.

She spots a bruise on her neck and says what is this, all red shivani says hey its very personal, like a love bite sort. Sukanya says this guy is a serpent he is hurting in you in intimacy too.

Oh, my God I can say even Jesus cannot see this pattern of abuse. Shivani says now things might be good as he is out of negative influence of his folks and specially that jagan. Rajeswhari says I suspect some negative energy on you.

I will double check it with my husband's uncle who is very good with hindu astrology.

Shivani invites her cousin Aravind and his family to Ameya's bday. Aravind and Ajay who look at her and who has no siblings look at her like a sister. Their wifes Usha and Swati empathize with shivani's weakness. Usha says you have been drained out of energy shivani.

I could not come to the house warming ceremony. Shivani celebrates ameya's bday with her new friends who like them.

They help her so much as shivani teaches all their kids Analytical writing which is very important subject.

She feels better as Ameya's bday is celebrated with cheers and joys. Sudhir comes late at night after work and he is drenched in rain. Shivani looks at aravanind like an elder brother and finds the reflection of her maternal uncle wisdom in him.

He says to shivani just like Dr. Rama Krishna your blog is very good sissy and you are very good at analytical writing.

Shivani looks at sudhir who gives her an angry look and then suddenly changes when ajay looks at him.

Shivani says to them, please go on with your drinks we will feed the kids and eat our dinner too. Usha and Swati help her so much with cooking and build her confidence that they are there like her own brothers wives.

Swati who is quite younger than shivani says always ajay says you were smiling doll of the neighbourhood.

Now, we all empathize with you and salute your courage to endure with such a person for Ameya.

She does not even say that to sudhir she says to her cousin, because sudhir drains her out of energy even when he knew that hairline fracture needs only rest.

SUNANDHA PLAYS HER TRICK ON AMEYA'S BDAY AND SHE IS ANGRY WITH SHIVANI --- April 2015

Sunandha is a very egocentric woman who thinks being a social teacher is like winning a gold medal in the world. She is unaware that she has failed her son's wife who is a credible Quality Analyst and made her prone to "**Maternity Suicide** "with archaic procedures.

Yet, she does not want to admit the fact that shivani is beyond perfection.

She rings Sudhir to greet ameya, yet speaks in a sarcastic way about her birthday celebrations. Sudhakar who sheds crocodile tears and always worried about bindu says she is all alone in Dublin.

Sudhir does not speak well to them as before as they have demeaned him in front of shivani's family.

He just says I do not even deserve a good wife that is what you all said nevertheless she did not outcast me. Sunandha sugar coats her words saying we all are a family do not feel like that. Shivani tries to speak to her but she daunts her again saying you will never be happy.

Shivani is fumed and says its better I do not even try to empathize with your parents. She just comforts him saying I do not feel that you do not deserve a good life and wife. Why should you bother so much now, you have a beautiful ameya and I can rebuild my career.

NARCISSTS MANIPULATE YOU TO GET THEIR WORK DONE

Sudhir says go to U.S and you earn more than bindu and can be a right competitor. Shivani says I do not want to give ameya tough time with schooling and all stuff. Shivani knows that sudhir can turn his side easily as they are the branches of a same tree Narcissism.

Yet, maintains her poise because it is a fragile time to him as a man who his own family has hurt him so much. Girish who has sent all good clothes and jewellery wishes Ameya.

She speaks in a cheeky way and girish who is very strict with discipline says you only look like my daughter. But you do not have sportive attitude like her. Sudhir gets angry and says Ameya Momma's family are rich but they do not have kindness. Shivani gets scared as he kicks the bin and says we do not even have food now.

Shivani thinks sudhir will eat the leftover of the party. But he gets fumed up when one of his friends say that shivani forgot to call his wife. Sudhir pulls her hair and drags her down while she is in the bedroom.

He says now I will show you and your dad what sportive attitude is. You woman you want me to get outcast from my friends too.

Shivani who becomes weak says I did not do anything wrong look at the number and check the call records.

Why would I have scorn on anyone, but life is very fragile and you do not even give me a break. You do not even know that I am on destressors and she gets panick attack.

SHIVANI IS ABUSED CONSECUTIVELY THREE TIMES AFTER SUDHIR PARENTS LEAVE

Sudhir gets conscious when ameya says what happened to momma, he says she is tired and she is sleeping.

He wakes her after a while she feels very scared to look at him. She texts her dad that she needs a break and wants to go to her mom as she has no energy.

Girish who is a stereotype says no shivani sudhir needs you and your affection. This is the time where a wife mends a broken heart.

Shivani rings Dr. Rama Krishna's wife and she says shivani go and see the doctor for your panic attacks.

These people are stupid ignorant ones I know how fragile you are and sudhir is the most stupid person in the world who has abused you so much.

He lost everything, which you could have multiplied with your intellect and courage.

Shivani still endures the pain, but one day when Shivani tries to study a new course. He hits her hard and says that she has not cleaned the tiles of the bathroom.

She remembers story of BHAGAT SINGH who has revealed to the WORLD, the Colonial Rule and British Conspiracy.

Now this is the same, it is all "Wheel of Power and Control". She says to sudhir that I am not the baby sitter who your mom has abused and silenced.

I have seen your mom beating your dad to terrorize ameya and me. When a mother is so aggressive, what can a son be like? I just do not even know why you are abusing me verbally and physically too.

Narcissists Speak Rubbish when they become Aggressive

Sudhir says that I have recorded what intimate moments we have shared as husband and wife. Shivani says go ahead, I am as pure as ameya.

Now I need to behave the same, as physical wounds cannot deter my ideology of independent thoughts.

I own my cognition and my freedom. I am not a bounded or bonded slave; maternity should not make you one too.

He hits her hard and when she tries to defend herself. Shivani collapses on the bed and he gets conscious whether she is alive or not.

She once again has a panick attack. He becomes so rude that when she wakes up after 10 mins that she has to come to Ameya's eye clinic.

Shivani doesn't know what to do, she just maintains her poise. If she does not speak after violence. Sudhir drops her anywhere he wishes to. He drops ameya and shivani immediately. She cries all the way on the train and they come at 7:30 p.m on a cold winter dark night.

Hetal looks at them and she says shivani what are these bruises and what is this black eye too. Now until she rings him and says that she will not trigger his anger.

He will not return home. Shivani to maintain her family balance always texts him that she will not ask him that she wants to go to India.

Shivani writes her NLC assignment on the Indian Governance web page on Congress.

Gandhi's eroding credibility of Gandhi, are these Gandhi's Truly Gandhi's. Gandhi was a simple man.

He used his intellect to empower nation and to free India without Violence. However, these Gandhi's are making a fortune using his name and without any credible education or any Policy making strategies.

BJP has replaced their incompetency by their good effective policies and strategies too.

She feels better after she gets a message that she is selected now. To be an official blogger of BJP. She reveals her Credibility to her maternal Uncle who grieves in silence about her fragile situation.

He says I have no words to congratulate you shivani. However, remember when you think abuse has taken a toll

DR FEA REVEALS SHIVANI THAT SUDHIR IS PYSCHOPATH –BEHIND CLOSED DOORS

She says to sudhir that either she needs break to INDIA or she has to go to for therapy.

Sudhir says ok go and see a therapist. Shivani gets to meet Dr. Fea who is a double doctorate in Psychology. She reveals her epic saga of pain and suffering. She says that her cognition is disturbed because of this abuse.

She says I have worked as a Quality Analyst and NLC is my expertise. Sudhir's mom send congrats messages that it is good that she is being beaten black and blue. She even tries calling her, but shivani does not reply a single word.

She shows the messages to Dr. Fea. She tells shivani your life and even Credibility is at stake.

She shows her blog content and says that does she need any therapy. Dr. Fea says shivani what you write is called Ideation Thoughts and Creative Writing.

You have reverted your pain into writing. This is a talent and no abuse can kill this inborn talent.

I can refer you to Ideas at the house. It is a gifted and talented programme and you can prove what you are.

Shivani says I have been labelled as a bad mother. Yes because you have been abused and silenced.

Your honest personality is being maligned by his conspiracy and his weaving violence tendency. I know these kind of men are like serpents inside home.

Dr. Fea says normally people who have extramarital affairs do these kinds of mind games tricks.

There are somany bruises on your body and he is controlling you each day and each minute.

They just want the offspring or use the offspring against the vulnerable mom and label the victim as "BAD MOM".

Bad mothers do not endure abuse, but be careful do not smack ameya who is having Kaka Syndrome. This is all lazing in and around.

Moreover, even kids in abusive environment feel extreme anxiety where mom is vulnerable and dad is controlling her with silence and violence.

She says that she has reverted her OCD – Obsessive Compulsive Disorder into Obsession, Passion and Creation.

This person and his family have played mind games with you but do not tolerate it, these wounds are very bad.

You need to plan a rescue, for you and your daughter to prove your Credibility. So, beat gullibility with credibility and plan your rescue. You do not need any medication if you are not in such a violent environment.

This is wheel of Power Control and he is spoiled brat of a Paranoid Narcissist Family. Shivani says to her dad that she needs a break and what Dr.fea has told her too.

TEJAS 1ST BDAY –SHIVANI OPENS THE PRISON DOORS WHERE SHE WAS ENSLAVED AND ABUSED FOR EIGHT LONG YEARS.

Shivani comes home with shock about Psychopathic Traits of Sudhir and his weaving violence tendency.

Sudhir says now my mom wants to come back as she is getting tired with my Dad. Why can't I come she is saying because your Dad is going to your nephew's bday they have come to know. She is saying she will speak to your dad and she will come.

Shivani gets fumed up and says, she has sent me congrats messages while I was in Dr. Fea's therapy session.

Moreover, you have said that now you are on your parent's side, as they are being good to you. Where will she come, she said to all that she will never come back to Sydney in her lifetime.

Shivani calls her dad and says that in Ameya's School holidays that start in June, she wants to come to India.

She asks her dad to speak to Sudhir and arrange a Visa to Ameya. She says to Sudhir on her bday that she wants to apply for Ameya's visa for school holidays.

Sudhir does not like Shivani to go to India when she cannot go to Sunandha's home. Sunandha would even say that Sudhir is a henpecked person too.

Sudhir goes to enjoy with his friends when shivani has planned a small bday to him.

Moreover, he does not like shivani to have freedom. He has no clue that her health is declining because of this abuse ever since ameya is born. He starts his game again, shivani gets tired calling him for almost 200 times.

His answer is why did you say to your dad to please me for Visa of Ameya. Now ask your dad to make me come home.

Shivani says I was asking you to send me once in lifetime in good terms. I am tired of this chaos and my health is not good too.

He makes a mountain out of a mole and threatens her again with violence and divorce threat. Shivani criesso much. He says he is going to some other state and is not coming home.

Shivani rings her dad Girish and he sends her cousin aravind to bring shivani and ameya home.

Shivani says my cousin is coming now do whatever you want to do. Victims like me have an option to fly with kids as Indian government has established Visa on Arrival for everyone who wants to visit India.

Sudhir gets alert and he comes home, he looks at shivani and she is collapsed on the floor. Ameya is crying, momma wake up. Shivani says ameya bring some water I am unable to walk now.

Sudhir comes into the balcony and says I cannot touch you now as your dad might have called the cops. You need to stand on your own and let us go the court; you might lose custody of Ameya.

Shivani gets fumed up and says Custody of Ameya, you coward abuser, you are full of venom. I do not even need custody battle take her and live with her.

Alternatively, even give her to someone who have more money and kill me now. Ameya says no "Daddy I can't live without mummy". She needs help; she collapsed on the floor.

Moreover I want to leave the world now tired of being like a Warrior Princess "Rudrama Devi".

Who died in the same Nalgonda by Gullibilty. She was backstabbed, like me. She was a tough competition to backstabbers and Male Chauvinism.

I fought a battle alone for a functional childhood of my girl child as I know how wicked you people are. Do not forget that I have a sample pic of what your Jagan took of saanvi and me too. He has dirty instincts on me and ameya. He is a Paranoid Paedophile and I know what those instincts are as I was a part of STANGER DANGER in ameya's Schol. I am almost 12 years younger than him and this is what he grinds on me and ameya.

Sudhir says to ameya now if your uncle comes, I will not be able to see you again. Your grandfather will not spare me I will go to Prison for 8 months. He comes and hugs ameya.

Shivani wakes up when Usha comes home and she lifts her, she hugs usha and cries so much. She says to her cousin brother I do not want to live anymore.

Sudhir tries to manipulate Aditya saying a small issue, she is making a mountain.

These days she is on some Plant extracts and she is behaving somewhat different.

I told her we would go and see a doctor for her anxiety issues.

Shivani gets angry and reveals what happened to her brain with abuse. I worked in a Health Care Fund and I know even the names of the medicines used for mental disorders.

She says bro one of best school buddy advised me to take such medication, as it will not have any side effects.

I was never on such medication before. These plant extracts only have reignited my cognition, which was diminished by abuse and even sudhir hitting me against a washing machine.

Reason my dad did not attend Death Ceremony of Jagan's Dad. After that injury on my head, I started to live on Anti suicidal Olanzapine. He called me names as the chemical pill had given side effects. This pain is beyond human threshold brother.

Her cousin says shivani sissy don't worry things will settle down. Go to India for few months you need rest.

Shivani says that is what I wanted brother and he says no I cannot go without his permission. It is all his way or high way. Usha tries to convince her, but she says I am dying inside out Usha bruises and scars inside out.

Aditya says Uncle is saying you are even withholding both of their passports. What is this sudhir what is wrong we even have common friends? Women and kids are like flowers who will protect them if we do such things.

Sudhir says no nothing much about passports and all she can go and take ameya too.

Aditya says Uncle is saying Ameya wants to have a safe home she is crying too. Ameya says Mom is sick aunty.

Aditya who has no sisters of his own says ok let us go to my home. Sudhir says hey things will settle down easily. He says to shivani you need rest I will take day off. Shivani says I want empathy not sympathy.

ABUSERS TERRORIZE THE VICTIMS WHEN THEIR TRUTH COMES IN LIMELIGHT – AND EVEN PEOPLE WHO RESCUE THEM WILL FALL IN TROUBLE—

Shivani goes to Usha's home and she has her dinner. She feels safe and usha gives her assurance when she cries a lot. However, Sudhir who is very adamant about his way of thinking, starts to threaten her that Aravind is not her own brother.

Shivani is fumed up and says that she has chosen to come here instead of going to a Shelter home. He starts threatening her that he will come to the airport to stop Ameya. Shivani says go ahead, if you want to make yourself and me a public spectacle.

They decide to liase with him on the next day. When aravind and shivani come, sudhir keeps her luggage outside. Shivani says that she did not come to take the luggage and leave to heal in bad terms.

Sudhir says the day you have stepped out of the house itself I do not consider we are in good terms. Aditya says that she needs break sudhir, but he doesn't agree and says that he is also alone without anyone.

Shivani then reveals aditya and even shows him the place where he said that he would put her in a mental asylum. She even tells him how Jagan was so cruel to her inspite of giving a good hospitality even with a broken back. Sudhir says my sister would have been in trouble if her husband would have killed or caused any harm to her.

Shivani says see brother he is not worried about my health, he is just worried about his sister's credibility and career.

Sudhir's threats make even Usha very scared, as she never has such negative problems in her life. Aditya now says shivani it is high time sissy you have to decide now. I can even pay for both of your tickets do not worry as usha is getting scared.

Shivani does not like to trouble anyone and she looks in the website where she finds that, you need permission from both parents to get Visa on Arrival.

Sudhir threatens her again that he is selling the house and even noody will know his whereabouts. Shivani knows that one of his friend whose parents call him each time his where abouts nobody knows. Shivani even feels that she should not go like refugee.

She says now I give you a choice, I know you are quite capable of terrorizing innocent ones. However, I am not such scornful; neither have I trouble the people who saved me.

Now just make your choice, whether it is you who will come first to my brother's home or do not even bother and leave us to none as you did to me in 2008.

Your wish there will be agent who is coming from Indian high commission as I wrote my NLC exam in Official Indian page. Now I am selected as official blogger of Indian governance. They say that they are going to help me in such adversity.

Those days ameya was not there, now she is also getting affected. You can go the extremes of your terror, destroy my life at wish, and will. Sudhir always likes shvani's intellect but he wants all to be under his control. Shivani who looks at the tensed face of usha, doesn't like to give such innocent warm-hearted people even a single trouble.

Sudhir comes home, yet shivani's mom warns her that there is danger ahead, this person will kill you shivani. Shivani says I have seen worse in 2008, he will change says his friend. Now I cannot come to India like a refugee, I deserve respect for child and me. Look at sharath he is not even bothered to speak to me; such stereotypes need not get a chance to see that I am in the loop of infinity.

CONTROL FREAKS NEVER CHANGE THEIR ATTITUDE – TERROR IS WHAT THEY LIKE TO CREATE

Shivani packs all stuff and she gives usha a warm hug and gets her homeo medicine too. aditya and even his brother come because they get scared of how much sudhir can create chaos at their home. Shivani says I will never come again to your home with negative vibes.

She bows to Aditya she respects her maternal uncle. He says to sudhir you are blessed to have a pious wife like shivani even when all of us and even her dad stopped talking to her for her choice.

Still she is coming to you with hope, her health is not good even my wife usha says she has lot of injuries too. Sudhir says I will take care of her and thank you to them. Shivani says thank you and sorry to Usha and says that I have always wished to have a elder brother and god sent you today.

VICTIMS HAVE HOPE, BUT ABUSERS FEEL SO DEJECTED WHEN THEIR BEHAVIOUR IS QUESTIONED

Sudhir brings his car and ameya hugs both Usha and Aditya. They say that Ameya is very intelligent and she is just like shivani.

On the way home sudhir starts his verbal abuse saying what you will do if I drop you in the middle of the night.

Shivani keeps her calm and she does not utter a word. She comes home cleans all the stuff and doesn't even utter a word, gives ameya a good shower. Both of them go to sleep. Shivani has severe vomiting and she gets scared that she might have got high fever too.

Shivani does not speak a word and she has a good shower as her friends say that a warm hot shower can relieve stress. After two days, she feels that her back is not supporting her and she is unable to walk.

Sudhir examines her that her vomiting increases. Shivani takes the thermometer and she finds her temperature is high. Sudhir makes food for her and later after few days, Aditya calls shivani. He says shivani I was very assertive to you, as you should know how to overcome hurdles in marital life. Shivani says I have endured worse than this brother and it became like a whirlpool. He says usha was also very sad to see you braving all this.

Sudhir is also saying you are very innocent and he likes you too. He was saying she is very talented, but only problem is with the plant extract medicines you are using Shivani says these are like destressors and I do not even need after one month.

Aditya says try meditation and you will come out of this. He still says I am so proud of you, who endured so much but looks at the positive side of life. Shivani says I have even asked him to be very gentle to you.

POSITIVE PEOPLE NEVER FOCUS ON NEGATIVE ASPECTS IN LIFE –

Shivani helps ameya to get third prize in the Public Speaking Competition. She speaks about Harmony day. Usha applauds shivani and she speaks to ameya. Usha is such a pious woman who has shown utmost empathy to shivani.

Shivani gets an idea, how about I ask one of sudhir's friends in U.S to start an E-3 visa consultancy. Now this is the best way to prove my intellect.

She writes a write up to his consultancy and says that she wants to grow with it. She posts it in the facebook page to get some clients interested.

Sudhir does not like her credibility to be known when she says she wants to go to India. He says now I do not have anyone, that words make her confused. His mom, sister and all speak to him each day.

Shivani doesn't know what do, her back pain increases and she cannot walk. Shivani yet manages to make ameya get to her Public speaking competition.

Girish speaks to sudhir and says if you beat her, once again she will come back. You have destroyed my beautiful daughter and her intellect too.

Shivani who knows sudhir's scornful mind says, his mom beats his dad. That is what they do to each other, and she terrorizes all. He says he cannot live without both of them and she is very intelligent.

He says she has started her own franchise of consultancy with his friend. Girish says I know what my daughter is she is very courageous and even intelligent too.

She is not scornful like your mom who rejoices when you beat my daughter black and blue.

With shivani's write up and her online volunteer workshop, everyone start appreciate her.

NARCISSTS NEVER LET VICTIMS BECOME SURVIVORS –

Sudhir says now my mom wants to come as she is finding difficult with my dad. Shivani says your dad lost all of his cognition. He already went missing; the day one he came here and it became a cycle. Now what do you want more, I have no energy at all. If she wants to come, let her come I will take a break and let her handle alone. Shivani slips in the bathroom again and she becomes bed sick.

Sudhir does not know what to do and he thinks that her health is in very bad condition. He takes day off, and yet she finds difficult to manage.

Shivani feels dejected with abuse and even when she gets some clients questions, she feels she needs rest.

GOD HAS NO COLOUR AND SENDS HIS MESSENGERS ---

Ruth is shivani's neighbour and she invites shivani to a movie night out. Sudhir makes her walk on eggshells when they come to take her. Shivani goes to the movie their Ruth asks her if she can tell her what happened to her all these days. She says that Church has a shelter facility if she needs any help.

Shivani thanks Ruth and she shares her pain. Ruth who likes shivani's young charm and her creative writing skills say she can have a bright future.

MOMMY'S DAY OUT – Movie makes her laugh so much. Sudhir still intervenes to know what shivani is sharing with Ruth.

Sudhir wants to find out whether she has shared about abuse to Ruth. Shivani maintains her poise and says the movie was good.

She just wants to have a break and she needs core healing of her body and mind, which is stressed.

TEACHERS PLAY THE ROLE OF MOTHERHOOD IN UNDERSTANDING THE INTELLECT—

Shivani posts about her school go viral with her friends. She says friends I am living like bhagat singh trapped. However, my credibility should reach India before I reach to heal from the core.

Shivani's favourite regional language teacher reads her posts on social media on Motherhood. She says hey shivani you write so well. Shivani says teacher you have taught me Creative Writing and even translation too.

Her Nirmala teacher then says I can see some pain in your eyes shivani. You are not happy; shivani says do I look like that. Nirmala teacher yes you do shivani, I know my students and I can never forget a leader with bilingual expertise, your vocabulary in English is too good.

Shivani then asks her number and rings her, she burst with tears and says I have lost my career and my bliss with abuse after maternity. How much Sudhir's mom used her rage to enslave and target her.

She says teacher he is such a chauvinist, does not understand the word empathy.

I am enslaved and swallowing venom for both Ameya and for the reputation of my family.

They have kept me as a hostage for making my paternal and maternal families dance on their tunes.

I never was sent in good terms to Warangal ever since ameya is born. I have endured pain beyond human threshold and lost bliss because of women with venom.

I feel like ending my life. Nirmala says no princess don't cry my child, I know you well. You never carry the baggage of the princess. Now listen to what I say, you are healing slowly, and it would be good if you come to India. Even with a slightest of hope

PLAY THE SAME GAME OF GULLIBILTY TO GET CREDIBILTY – ESCAPE WHEN HELP IS AVALIABLE –

Shivani does not know what to do when she finds herself sinking the bed. She feels all negative aura in the house; sudhir does not even speak to her properly. Shivani does not get to speak to anyone when she is around.

Shivani speaks to her cousin Ravi in U.S and he knows the pain she endured.

He says shivani you need to go to India. Mom will also come and we are thinking about your wellbeing as how much abuse you have taken.

He tells sharath to see something, but sharath does not know the solution as how to bring her out.

Sudhir starts to act as he has become sick too when she says that she needs healing.

Shivani decides to scare his Parnoid God Fearing mind to make him feel that Godess of Eternal Power has entered into her and she has become the incarnation of WARRIOR PRINCEESS—RUDRAMA DEVI – who was a Great Queen and she hailed from WARANAGL. The capital of KAKATIYA DYNASTY. She died in Nalgonda, the native place of SUDHIR.

He then beats himself with shoes when she says, "THIS IS A SOUL OF A LEGEND". Shivani will reach the land of KAKATIYA DYNASTY. Now she is reborn with all the power, as the newly formed Telanaga state has endured so much pain. She is going to save women and kids with her PEN. She was a Creative ARTS AND SCIENCE GENIUS. She mastered even Marshall Arts too.

Shivani says that nobody and no force can stop her now. She collapses but remains in her conscious. Sudhir gets scared now and he decides to take her to the doctor.

The doctor says she is fully stressed out and her test reports and going to take time. Sudhir says why you do not give some antidepressants to her. That is when shivani reveals to the doctor that she has her Psychopathology reports.

First, do some psychometric tests and then give me the antidepressants. I need a break it has been two years I have never been to my maternal home. I have to get one to one consultation with my Therapist in India.

He does not give up and says that she has to take antidepressants. Shivani is fumed up when he says he will leave the house when she collapses on the floor.

Her health has declined and she is unable to meet even ameya's basic needs.

She tells her teacher about the wounds to her brain and skull, she shows her bruises and scars.

She says teacher mom is in U.S, but I can even come to your home that is my situation.

I want empathy someone who can understand my pain where my credibility is at stake and I can heal from the core. I prayed to Jesus here the same.

Her teacher says shivani when innocent girls like you with intellect and courage, empathy are poisoned. God changes his colours my child, yes god will heal you come to India.

They are convincing my dad that I need antidepressants. Where plant extracts liquid is healing my nueral wounds with distresses. This is attack against my cognition. Her teacher says shivani my child, god is never absent to the tears of Princess with a golden heart.

I know you very well you might have lived without life. As you are a rainbow child and with vibrant colours as I know your family and its inheritance too.

SHIVANI DECIDES TO COME TO INDIA FOR HEALING—SHE WRITES TO DNA INDIA

Shivani says that she wants to go to India. Sudhir doesn't like when shivani makes her own decision. He says I do not have money to book the tickets.

Shivani feels so awkward, when she knows his malicious behaviour where she gave her pocket money, her blessings money to him when he went to India.

Nevertheless, now it is not about money, I have my jewellery I can sell it and get my tickets booked. Her dad says shivani if sudhir doesn't like and is ready to take leave why don't you stay there.

Shivani says his leave doesn't change my situation, I need freedom to breathe life. My cognition, which has been ignited with such a great research of my friends in Nueroscience, is at stake.

I need to have to one to one consultation from the homeo doctor who has sent me plant extracts. Her dad says now ok I will arrange the tickets.

That is when she calls her dad who says to call sharath's friend shammanth. Shivani feels very bad and dejected because she hates the way she is being treated even when she is privileged enough. She wanted a life of dignity and empathy not sympathy even from her maternal family.

Sharath becomes so rude to her inspite of being her younger brother. He says I will arrange the money but get sign on the Visa statement of Ameya.

Sudhir starts to act weird when she says she needs Visa on Arrival papers to be signed by him to take Ameya.

Ameya says I want to have holidays like my friends Alisha at their nana's home. Moreover, I like nana's home since my toddler age I never get to stay there for long.

Sudhir tries to become very weird saying I am not feeling good. I do not have anyone to stay with me. Shivani becomes more scared as she knows these are the mind games of abusers.

This is all to control the way to core healing of shivani. She texts hers friends and vamshitha says shivani you became very weak, you need to plan to your rescue now as soon as possible.

Common I want you to go to India right away. Your mama is right; you have so many health issues to be cleared off too from the core. Do not even worry about sudhir who has brought you to this stage his acts are very malicious.

Shivani decides to take minimum stuff and she does not like to carry anything which sunandha has brought to kill her happiness.

She puts all few party clothes, as she knows that these are very important because her dad will be angry if she did not pack good clothes he sent her.

ABUSERS NEVER GIVE UP ON THEIR MIND GAMES – Narcissist have scorn in their mind --

Shivani wakes up very early at 5:00am as the flight is at 9:30am. She has a quick shower and prays to the God Hanuman that she has to reach India safe with Ameya.

Sudhir wakes up late and starts playing with ameya. She says ameya if you want to come with me common get ready quickly.

She makes ameya pack all her stuff very quickly. Sudhir asks her in a sarcastic way is your dad going to even send someone of your hometown to drop you at the airport.

Shivani doesn't say a word, my temperature is very high and this is a call from my DrMama who has saved my life and my saviour since my birth.

Have concern do not judge me as a wife look at me as an Indian Daughter suffering so much across the seas.

She knows sudhir will play some mind games to make her miss her flight.

Because he once missed, the flight and he had hidden the truth and created more chaos in shivani's mind. The airlines agent reveals the fact why sudhir had missed his flight.

Shivani who does not observe that sudhir is in the house says ok this was the reason to the agent.

She does not focus much on the aspect, as she knows if she repeats it, sudhir will not drop her in the airport. Sudhir keep saying to ameya that she has to see her granny and he will tell which dates is available for her.

Shivani does not utter a word, as her focus is to heal and rewrite her life with Cognition she lost because of abuse and control.

Sudhir goes to the petrol pump even when the tank is full. Shivani gets very fumed when she looks at the watch. She looks at ameya and says ameya I am going to sell my favourite expensive necklace and book the tickets for tomorrow.

Sudhir gets a clear understanding that shivani can take even her cousins help to get away. He knows that all like shivani her friends, cousins and neighbours.

Sudhir asks shivani to ring Sindhu who does not know what is happening to shivani and a sugar coater to sudhir. She rings sindhu and tells her that she is bed sick and she is going to India.

She looks at sudhir and says is now the purpose served, can you take us on time. Sudhir instead of admitting his mistake, says you woke up late to shivani. Shivani does not utter a word, because he will terrorize her even in the car too. She says to ameya to eat the sandwich she made her in the morning.

They reach the airport at 8:45 am and sudhir says to wait until he returns after parking his car. The airlines crew ask shvani to check in her luggage. With much pain in her lower back she does check in the luggage.

The crew ask her to move on with the Express Card, as she cannot board the flight on a wheel chair, since she arrived late at the airport. Shivani knows sudhir's mind games and she asks ameya to walk with her fast.

Sudhir then rings shivani when she is about to get into the Customs check. He says he has got some snacks for ameya and comes from behind and takes ameya.

Shivani loses her Expresss card in the chaos. Yet she trusts God and Air India. She calls him, screams at him saying even if this flight is missed I will sit at the airport sell all my jewellery here itself, and book another one.

He then comes with ameya and then says now common both of you make it faster. Shivani feels dejected to see sudhir having such scorn in his mind.

EMPATHY HAS NO REGIONAL BOUNDARIES

Shivani request all the Japanese and Vietnamese, Korean and Canadians who have their flights scheduled after 2 hours of her flight. They all help her and give her the way, to jump the queue they even say to her to hold her passport and I important belongings safe as they can see her very sick.

Shivani reaches the entry to the gates after the Customs check at 9:15 am. She has to walk more to reach the her gate, all the airlines crew come along with her running to make her and ameya board the flight.

One of them says now both of you run. Shivani tells ameya run like we are getting late to the school.

At 9: 25 am, shivani reaches the gate where she and ameya are the last passengers to board the flight.

She shows their passports and as soon as she enters the flight, she has a panick attack, with lot of trouble with breathing.

She cannot speak a word; the crew gets perplexed with her condition. As the flight is a nonstop 12-hour flight to Delhi. They wait until she calms down and starts to speak after coughing uninterruptedly for 10 minutes.

They ask her to give a call to Sudhir, sudhir comes to know that shivani is in a vulnerable situation. He says I am coming with the airport first aid team to bring her back. Shivani gets shocked, all her endeavour to breathe without abuse and heal from the core will be vanished.

She says he is the one who is responsible for my present chronic health condition. She pulls her jacket sleeves and shows the bruises to an elderly Airhostess. I am going even when my mom is not in India.

I need this break no doctor here can heal me from the core.

A doctor onboard who resides in Sydney comes to examine shivani and says yes she is broken inside out we have to fly her as its emotional and physical wounds. She will be ok with the destressors she has with her it is all abuse and terror.

The airhostess, Manisha Malhotra understands shivani and her abusive situation. She says do not worry we will outsmart your husband, you can relax.

She says that DNA India has sent us your details – Indian Daughter in terrible Crisis fly her without fail and noise.

Shivani says yes I did write to DNA India, as my husband monitors every email of my phone and mine.

I am selected to write as an Official blogger of Shanaknaddh too with acrostic lines. Sudhir keeps calling and when the flight is about to take off Manisha takes the call and says she is fine, she took the medicine also we have a doctor onboard. Shivani says the same when he tries to be nice to her before the crew.

Shivani calls her dad that she has boarded the flight. She feels happy; a fellow passenger gives her a comfortableseat to relax.

The crew treat her with empathy, they say now you are safe don't worry relax and eat something.

Shivani feels better as they are in the air and she eats the Indian breakfast and feels happy. The airhostess and her team keep a keen look on ameya and her needs.

Ameya asks her"Mom are you ok, Shivani says ameya thank you very much that you did not throw a tantrum and made it to catch the flight. You have no clue as how much I need this holiday.

AIR INDIA CARRYING A WOUNDED DAUGHTER

Manisha comes to her and says shivani you are very young and look even younger with a charm of a teenager. Why have you put up all this, shivani shows ameya and says we are from India and we believe in one marriage and one life once we have kids it's a lifetime project.

I know I have been foolish, but I was never selfish so God gave me the power to endure any pain.

When I said and prayed to him, he changed his colours and sent his messengers and said now it is high time, you need to heal from the core.

Manisha tells shivani about her sister who escaped with her two kids from Dubai with a husband who is a psychopath behind closed doors. You are well-educated shivani you should have left this abusive relationship ages ago. You do not deserve this kind of inhuman pain.

Shivani tells her that she quit her career and did her best and will do the best for ameya and because she is a girl child. She says that there are bunch of stereotypes who question a child each minute, who comes from a dysfunctional family.

Shivani shows her writing work and her contribution to a school in New South Wales who have recognized her inborn talent. Manisha says shivani I do not know why but I can tell you once you heal your wounds you will fly very high.

You are very intelligent, patient and very generous. We take pride to have such a young creative writer onboard and taking our help.

She hugs shivani, shivani says I feel like I'm seeing my mom in you, who can't even come even when I reach INDIA.

She reaches Delhi and the airport authorities arrange a wheel chair to help her.

She feels very happy to give Ameya's passport to the Customs, and they grant Visa on Arrival to Ameya. Shivani says ameya this is the Capital city of My India, New Delhi. Ameya says India is very beautiful momma.

After two hours of stopover, she catches the connecting Flight to Hyderabad. Shivani feels so happy that she is reaching her hometown as soon as possible and she feels better too. The air of freedom in itself has a healing power she says to ameya.

Girish comes to the airport after she collects her luggage and the porters help her so much to get her luggage with empathy. Girish asks shivani to stay in their friend's home and then travel next day to Warangal.

Shivani says no dad Im not feeling good and if ameya has stomach cramps as she has them usually, I cannot handle alone without help.

The very night they start to Warangal and shivani tells her dad as how much sudhir has given her pain.

Ameya starts to have stomach cramps and she starts to cry a lot. Shivani somehow manges her and puts her off to sleep. Girish friend who is an ex-millitary man says you are coming like a wounded soldier from the war.

We are very proud of you shivani that you have endured so much pain and brought ameya safe your offspring.

EMPATHS ALWAYS HAVE HOPE –ABUSERS SHOW NO CONCERN

Shivani comes to her hometown Warangal, the air in itself looks very fresh, and her eyes feel so better.

She says to her maternal grandmother and her paternal aunt not to cry so much.

I have endured much worse days than these, now I am happy that I am with good cognition than on some generic drugs, which cannot, bring back my intellect. To me my Credibility is very important than my physical health.

Shivani's paternal aunt says you did a good thing to come for your healing even when your mom is overseas.

Shivani says unknown people have helped me a lot and I even took shelter at a cousin's cousin when abuse made me ver sick.

Dad only feels the pain for a minute or two I was the one who was being sandwiched with his ignorance.

There were days where I did not even have food to eat, they all ate stomach his family attitude is evil. They all are paranoid anything goes wrong they do chant some mantras. I have never seen such people in my entire life in our entire kith and kin.

Shivani's dad says now you don't ring him, he should have concern that his wife and child have come alone when she is bed sick. This person is very money minded, his entire family is very paranoid, and they are good manipulators too.

LOVED ONES SHED TEARS WHEN THEIR PERFECT PRINCESS IS BED SICK WITH ABUSE-

Shivani goes to her Dr. Mama's hospital, with her grand mom. She takes all her reports; he comes out of the surgery room. He looks at her and starts crying. He does not stop crying for 15 minutes to see all the bruises and scars on her hands.

Shivani stands there without a tear and both Dr. Rama Krishna and his mom cry tears of blood.

Shivani says mama don't cry now show the way to heal all these wounds.

I have suffered worse than this, never told anyone about this. I have become like water now.

I do not even feel any pain it became a usual thing now. He refers her to a Nuero Physician.

Shivani goes there and he examines her throat and finds out through an X- Ray and keen observation that she is having chronic Respiratory tract infection.

He even arranges a defibrillator and says shivani breathe life, you can make this. Shivani finds very difficult but her determination is to prove her credibility with exuberance.

Shivani finds the medication very sour, yet she follows the dose. Shivani's dad doesn't know how to console shivani, when she is continuously coughing.

Her paternal aunt and grandma get perplexed that what if shivani will not be alive until her mom turns up.

Dr. Rama Krishna becomes lifeless and shivani decides to stay strong. Ameya becomes sick and she doesn't allow anyone to touch her except shivani.

None of them except shivani get to understand what ameya is saying as she is very fluent in her aussie accent.

Shivani tells ameya that she has to understand that "Momma is sick and she has to take help of anyone". Ameya" starts crying.

Momma what will happen to me if anything happens to you. Will you be alive, why are all crying?

Shivani says ameya Momma is not a Coward, she is a rainbow child of Dr. Grandpa's intellect in medical adversity. She will try her best to heal, I have to be alive for you ameya. Shivani gets nightmares of her ill health condition and sudhir and jagan coming to kill her. She starts to say in her sleep, "Don't kill me sudhir, ameya will become a motherless child.

Mr Girish doesn't know what to do, he starts to break down in tears whenever ameya says nana will momma be ok. Who will take care of me if anything worse happens to momma?

Mom always falls sick after dad beats her and then goes out of the home. This is how he is doing from so many days.

Shivani becomes very sick as the tablets become very harsh on her stomach where she did not eat food for days. Shivani's stress levels increase and she feels short of sleep too.

All the neighbours come and say that shivani might have been poisoned, she does not look even sick.

She might have been food poisoned; never did we see this girl like this. Shivani breaks down when she looks at her cousin Kiran's mom, both of them cry a lot. Shivani what have you made out of yourself, these people planned your death and you did not even know it. How will you recover, what is this adversity, your dad is unable to control himself, your mom is coming next week.

HOPE IS WHAT NEEDED IN ADVERSITY:

Shivani wakes up in the midnight and says to her granny and aunt that she has to go to the temple of Eternal godess. I am seeing her in my dreams and that powerful soul says I am Rudrama devi reborn and will Rewrite. Those paranoid Jagan and his tailor used to say I'm the incarnation of a soul of a legend "Rudrama devi".

They all did something weird to me, I am unable to sleep and I am getting nightmares of war, and godess of eternal power shakthi. She takes a shower on a Pious Friday, takes ameya with her, goes to the temple, and offers the godess a Sari and some other Puja items as per the shakthi temple Priest says.

She offers her prayers and says uncle, that immoral jagan had bad instincts on ameya and me. I had a intuition that he was about to drown ameya in the water, where she doesn't even know snorkelling. The priest says shivani, ameya is this godess blessing, nothing will happen to her, she also has phantom power.

She then asks him, what is the mystical relation of Rudrama Devi, and my life. Why did those paranoid people say that I am incarnation of her?. Where I just played the same game and escaped to be on antidepressants?

The priest who knows the kith and kin of shivani and her external family says, you are born with good intellect and beauty. Shivani you are a Perfect combo of both Ram and Sita to your family.

These are the attributes of Rudrama devi, there is a coincidence which they might have mapped too. The airport land where the WARANGAL AIRPORT is going to be constructed is a part of your ancestral property.

These people, jagan is a very greedy and immoral person shivani. The intuition you had is right, yes that jagan planned death attacks to both you and ameya.

None of your kith and kin knows what tough life you have endured behind closed doors. However, you did suffer for your ameya and her functional childhood for the reputation of your family.

Therefore, you are now as wealthy as a princess is and fought a battle alone with morals and courage. You have both of their inheritance too. Yet you never were treated good and respected as a wife.

We all know how many death protocols you have crossed. Shivani you are blessed by the goddess of shakthi, and when evil people try to kill a blessing of goddess, that is when they see Souls of Legend.

This violence could easily kill eight sensitive women in a row. You lived like a warrior shivani. Your attacks where on your cognition as well as on body.

Yes, Rudramadevi was also a very generous and with never give up attitude. Do not have any negative thoughts, you can Rewrite your life Shivani. You are a brave girl with phantom intellect. There is no incarnation and all this is some stupid people's evil magic.

You go and study and you have a healing touch in your hands. You are a born Creative Science Genius with an inheritance of your maternal uncle and courage of your Dad and his brothers.

You are fragile by innocence, yet you will rewrite. Don't worry no negative energy can destroy you shivani.

I already told you, the day you become assertive, you will win all, and see how you got back your credibility with herbs. Your intellect is what they wanted to attack and they did it too.

Your husband is very jealous of you and he has shown his male chauvinism by either violence or by divorce threat.

However, he will soon realise that he cannot give divorce to you. Shivani says uncle; I went to a school and showed my writing which was my childhood hobby, poetry. They say it is Creative Writing.

I do not call it incarnation myself too, but when a beautiful girl with good intellect and morals suffer so much. Then goddess of eternal power comes to save you. Shivani says aunty, now even if I die I do not regret, as ameya is in safe hands, you all will raise her. I am not dearth of money, but yes, I do not have a marital bliss and they wanted to kill me.

After few days Susheela comes and says shivani, nothing will happen to you, you came here by the grace of goddess Shakti and you will be ok. We all prayed for you each day and we know that you crossed many broken bridges to come for healing in India.

SHIVANI MEETS HER NEPHEW – HER GOLDEN PRINCE WITH LUCKY CHARM

Shivani starts to heal with her medications and she feels better when Jaya comes to her house.

She says shivani, you are not eating well; you cannot heal with these medications. Shivani says aunty my tongue is all-sour and I do not like to eat anything.

Jaya goes to her home and prepares all favourite dishes of shivani in her childhood. Shivani is favourite of all. Only aspect that was a limitation was her assertive tone. Which she has reverted into words than yelling and shouting, exploding anger.

SELF CENTRED PEOPLE DO NOT RESPECT VICTIMS

Shivani gets to meet her nephew Tejas, to her he looks like a golden prince. Shivani likes tejas so much and the cute kido becomes very close to her and Ameya. Inspite of sunandha's all attempts to keep shivani isolated from her kith and kin, she gets to spend good time with Tejas.

Shivani decides to stay for few more days in India to heal from sicknesss. She asks sudhir to send the visa extension papers for Ameya. On the day of Festival of flowers, sunandha rings shivani and accuses her for coming to India without informing her.

He doesn't even bother to inform shivani or ameya that he has come for a short stay. For the very first time shivani becomes very assertive to her mother in-law for treating her very bad. Sunandha who is a self-centred callous woman feels very jealous of her for having good time during festive season.

Sunandha after a month spreads propaganda that shivani has trouble with her psychological delusions and sudhir is having tough time with her. She spreads all false rumours on her intellect among her relatives and sudhir's childhood friends.

FESTIVAL OF FLOWERS –BLISS AND BLESSINGS TO SHIVANI AND AMEYA

Shivani loves the festival of flowers. It is her favourite festival and she loves the ambience of it, which reminds of good golden moments with her grandmother in the village. Ameya loves the arrangement of flowers and it is a new experience to her who loves colours and designs.

Ameya and shivani's mom arrange the garland with holy flowers. This festival of flowers is very pious to all the people of Telangana.

The flowers are all placed following a pattern. Then they are worshipped with prayers, songs and dances too. The festival is very colourful where all women and girls deck themselves with ornaments and dressed in colourful outfits. Shivani gets to wear beautiful clothes of her choice. Shivani loves the arrangement made by ameya with her fragile beautiful hands and her enthusiasm with colourful flowers. Shivani feels so happy even when she is not sent in good terms to her maternal home.

The mystical relation between flowers and water makes her feel better, where she was always beaten black and blue and humiliated by her in-laws and husband. The colourful flowers and their patterns, show integrity in diversity.

EMPATHS STRIVE TO PROVE THEIR POTENTIAL AMIDSTS ALL RUMOURS AND ODDS

After few months, shivani decides to pass a course in psychology and criminology. She then joins as a CBT therapist in a hospital as a therapist.

Sudhir and his parents do not acknowledge any of shivani's accomplishments. She finds that mental health is not treated as physical health.

It is almost like taboo if women and girls have premarital, postnatal mental disorders because of domestic violence. She doesn't like the way patients are only given medication but not advised to have a brain diet and brain excercises like in Australia.

Shivani studies online course "Successful ageing and Brain Health "in Trinity College of Dublin. She finds very suprsing when a medico and engineering graduates come as an inpatient and refuses to acknowledge that he can be cured. She introduces CBT (Cognitive Behaviour techniques) which is quite new in Warangal.

However, research has proven that medication along with CBT can make patients recover quickly and without any relapse of the symptoms.

She learns that CBT enables the patients to get back to their feet and continue to pursue their career.

DOMESTIC VIOLENCE AND SEPERATION LEAVES KIDS IN DESPAIR

Sudhir comes to India but does not even visit ameya in her school. Ameya feels very sad and gloomy, as she does not like a dysfunctional childhood experience away from Sudhir.

Shivani even when stinged by social stigma by stereotypes tries her level best to get empowered on own. Sudhir and his mom only want to see her gloomy and sad because of social stigma. He leaves to Sydney without even meeting ameya. Shivani feels very agitated as even when she has texted him about ameya's well being and also her pictures, he does not respond at all. She feels cheated by him even after enduring so much pain and humiliations.

PERSERVANCE LEADS TO PEACE- EMPATHS KNOW WHAT TO OVERLOOK

Shivani finally decides to send emails to Sudhir about his escaping attitude instead of focussing on reconcialtion. Sudhir uses narcisstic traits to hide his flaws of violence. He then reveals that he has no illict relationship with Rosy. Shivani feels good to know about sudhir's attitude for revealing that he has no extra marital affair where his mom always threatens shivani about it. Sunanadha even threatens shivani that sudhir will resign his job to stay with her.

Shivani does not loose her will power and decides to reconcile with sudhir for ameya's functional childhood and to obtain the dignity of a married woman without violence. Sudhir who never accomapined shivani to a therapist agrees to attend counselling to resolve the matter between both. Yet shivani knows that unless elders who arranged their marriage intervene his mom will not spare her and will create mishaps in the name of aged care. Shivani texts sudhir that he can easily manipulate her and would not attend counselling if she goes to him without elders intervention. She also knows that sudhir's mom needs a big lesson for creating violence and spreading rumours about shivani's cognitive ability wherein she proved by passing innovative online course –Mind, Thinking and Creativity at the World University Consortium.

DEPRESSION IS NOT A PERMANENT DISEASE-GOOD MEDICATION AND ADVICE HAS A CURE FOR IT.

Depression is neither endemic nor epidemic
But it can be chronic and can take toll on lives
It affects Quality of life and even mobility too
Good advice and right medication can cure it
Mental health is same as physical health
Once a patient with good medication and support from
    loved ones
Can make you win the battle without any more dangers
    from the illness.

Girish and Rajeshwari feel proud of their flaw less daughter shivani, but sad as the wheel of violence and enduring pain has pushed shivani into major depression.

Rajeshwari says that we sent our daughter like a flower and with your violent nehaviour you all have pushed her into depression and spread rumours that she has become incognitive inspite of which my our shivani has passed exams in major depression. They consult a good doctor for her therapy. Shivani who is sportive takes the mediction and slowly heals her emotional wounds with medication and by "Postive Thinking".

ELDERS DECIDE FAMILY GET TOGETHER COUNSELLING –

Elders who have arranged their wedding decide to arrange family counselling. Sunandha who is very adamant about her belief system that shivani should endure pain of violence in silence finally succumbs to a get together as per Sudhir who does not decide anything without his mom's knowledge.

Shivani tells her mom to be very firm and fair to face sunanadha who is very niave and cunning. Rajeshwari asks sunandha as why have they all troubled shivani so much and made her life each day struggle for existence.

Sunandha has no answer for every question they ask her. She tries to deviate the discussion with her illness and sudhir's dad becoming psychotic.

Elders who arranged the wedding ask suandha to look after her personal matters by herself and not to bother shiani anyfurther in the name of orthodox belief system that a daughter in law should endure any pain to save her marriage and become a pawn in the ugly game of violence and rumours.

Rajeshwari says to sunandha what if the same pain your daughter had to endure. How could you make my shivani suffer so much and threaten her each time with divorce threats. Sunandha doesn't speak a word as she is all guilt for spoiling shivani's career and quality family life by encouraging and provoking sudhir with violence over young shivani. Elders create boundaries for Sunandha and ask her not to create any more mishaps with vengeance.

For any of Rajeshwari's questions Sunandha doesn't answer even one question and she finds herself isolated for the very first time after shivani's maternity.

All elders even give shut up call to Sriinivas who supported his sister sunandha when she says that shivani has sent tons of messages to all family members to reveal the truth. They all say to Rajewshari that her upriasal is a good example to show that compassion and tolerance of pain is not weakness. These are the values hindu culture is embodied with. Girls should be educated well and violence and rumours on women should be nipped in bud.

Domestic violence makes women and kids vulnerable and weak. It entails many humiliations and mishaps. Marriage is all about companionship and not Control. There is no future for violence and every problem in marriages has a unique solution. Indian traditions and culture, festivals is all about gender equality. Holy books and Vedas have always symbolised women as a sign of "Shakthi". Life is like an encyclopedia and marriage is one very important chapter and not the entire book.

Maternity Suicide is never an answer, it entails grief, sorrow and irrevocable loss to the kids.

DREAMS OF KIDS ARE ALWAYS PIOUS – THE FESTIVAL OF LIGHTS UNITES SHIVANI SUDHIR AND AMEYA

Ameya always prays to god to unite her parents, her favourite God is "LORD GANESHA" – THE GOD WHO HINDUS WORSHIP AS OBSTACLE BREAKER.

Sudhir comes to India, elders counsel both shivani and sudhir together without each of their parents. Sunandha tries to intervene but inturn gets a shut up call. Sudhir understands methodically as how much potential loss has domestic violence created and made shivani fallen into depression. They both decide to forget the past and look in the future development of Ameya.

Sudhir learns his lessons, feels sad for shivani being affected by depression. He misses Ameya terribly and feels happy to see her grown taller. Girish invites him to his home and they spend quality time He shows empathy, and makes a promise that he would never cause any harm to shivani who is on antidepressants. Rajeshwari requests Sudhir to ensure her that he will send both ameya and shivani each year to India to spend quality family time with them. Ameya completes her family tree with her parents Shivani and Sudhir.

They return to Sydney a day before Diwali.

They clean their house and paint it in blue and White.

The walls are blue and the floorboard looks clean and neat.

The backyard is full of Oranges, which, are ripe and sweet.

They light the house with colourful lights and burn firecrackers.

Godess Lakshmi is worshipped with flowers and fruits.

Gone are the days of sadness and grief here are new chapters of life with happiness and peace.

SHIVANI OPENS A "WRITING SCHOOL" for Special kids with "Pyschological Disorders".

Ameya gets adjusted in her previous school "Hambeldon Public School "inspite of continuing her schooling in Daffodils School in India. Shivani opens a novel school at their home for the kids who are special. She names it as **SWAY** – in the fonding memory of SWAMY VIVEKANDA.

She tailors the school syallbus with Creative Writing and Drawing. All of her friends say it might be challenging, with these kids. But shivani who has a rough experience with Stress Disorders knows the challenges these kids have and how they face them each and every day.

She makes Sudhir understand that Creativity that there is an intelligent life force in each and every kid.

Creativity needs only visulaization and these kids can do as there is no strict time line for submitting the assignments. All the kids come Learn to Write, Play, and Draw with a free hand and no stringent rules.

Slowly **SWAY** becomes a popular school as she gives rewards to the kids who can put their mind and thinking in understanding the game "PLAYING WITH WORDS AND COLORS."By teaching the kids how to Rewrite and enjoy Writing Shivani wins her battle of Depression and her doctor says that she doesn't need any more medication.

SHIVANI THEN STARTS A FOUDATION – "HOPE AND FREEDOM".

On New years eve Shivani starts a online service by building her own website to start a Foundation "HOPE

AND FREEDOM".She knows the pain of Domestic Violence and how lives of women and kids are affected by Adversity.

She opens her website to empower the women with global higher education who are affected by such Adversity. She makes "FREE CREATIVE WRITING CLASSES" for kids coming from homes of Adversity.

NEW YEAR COMES WITH A NEW HOPE; FREEDOM BRINGS BLISS IN HER FAMILY.

They enjoy the Fire works on the "Harbour Bridge".

The colourful lights and the spectacular view makes ameya dance with bliss

She thanks her parents who have reconciled with each

She jumps like a bunny to the see the sparkles and lights. PERSERVANCE OF SHIVANI AND EMPATHY FROM SUDHIR AFTER A FAMILY COUNSELLING MAKES A BRIGHT FUTURE FOR AMEYA.

Shivani gives a big surprise to Ameya and Sudhir. She earns the best EDUCATOR AWARD AND PRICE MONEY OF $25, 000 DOLLARS. SHE PLANS AMEYA'S HOLIDAY TRIP TO "DISNEY LAND" on her 10th birthday with "TEJAS".

AUTHOR'S NOTE

The main purpose of writing this book is to prevent "MATERNITY SUICIDES" and create "HOPE OF HAPPINESS AND EMPOWERMENT". To make many people understand how EMPATHY soothes many wounds.

IF WE DRAW BOUNDARIES AND NOT WALLS, WE CAN HITCH OUR WAGON UP TO THE STARS.

IF WE COMMUNICATE WELL OUR KIDS DO THE SAME AND KNOW THE VALUE OF RELATIONSHIPS.

EMPATHY IS A UNIVERSAL SOLVENT AND EMPATHY CREATES HOPE AND PEACE IN HOMES OF ADVERSITY AND AVOIDS HUMILIATION AND DEPRESSION.

EVERY MOTHER DESERVES RESPECT AND EACH CHILD A FUNCTIONAL CHILDHOOD. A HOME WITHOUT VIOLENCE IS A HOME OF HAPPINESS.

---- Sarita Reddy